# SPIRITUAL LESSONS FROM LIVING

# Also by Harold Klemp

Animals Are Soul Too!
The Art of Spiritual Dreaming
Ask the Master, Books 1 and 2
Autobiography of a Modern Prophet
The Call of Soul
Child in the Wilderness
A Cosmic Sea of Words: The ECKANKAR Lexicon
ECKANKAR's Spiritual Experiences Guidebook
ECK Essentials
ECK Masters and You: An Illustrated Guide
ECK Wisdom Temples, Spiritual Cities, & Guides: A Brief History
Is Life a Random Walk?
The Living Word, Books 1, 2, 3, and 4
A Modern Prophet Answers Your Key Questions about Life, Books 1 and 2
Past Lives, Dreams, and Soul Travel
Soul Travelers of the Far Country
The Sound of Soul
Spiritual Exercises for the Shariyat, Book One
Spiritual Exercises for the Shariyat, Book Two
The Spiritual Exercises of ECK
The Spiritual Laws of Life
The Temple of ECK
Those Wonderful ECK Masters
Welcome to the Wonderful World of ECK! Your Membership Guidebook
The Wind of Change
Wisdom of the Heart, Books 1, 2, and 3
Your Road Map to the ECK Teachings: ECKANKAR Study Guide, Volumes 1 and 2
Youth Ask a Modern Prophet about Life, Love, and God

## The Mahanta Transcripts Series

Journey of Soul, Book 1
How to Find God, Book 2
The Secret Teachings, Book 3
The Golden Heart, Book 4
Cloak of Consciousness, Book 5
Unlocking Your Sacred Puzzle Box, Book 6
The Eternal Dreamer, Book 7
The Dream Master, Book 8
We Come as Eagles, Book 9
The Drumbeat of Time, Book 10
What Is Spiritual Freedom? Book 11
How the Inner Master Works, Book 12
The Slow Burning Love of God, Book 13
The Secret of Love, Book 14
Our Spiritual Wake-Up Calls, Book 15
How to Survive Spiritually in Our Times, Book 16
The Road to Spiritual Freedom, Book 17

## The Immortality of Soul Series

The Awakened Heart
The Awakening Soul
HU, the Most Beautiful Prayer
The Language of Soul
Love—The Keystone of Life
The Loving Heart
The Spiritual Life
Touching the Face of God
Truth Has No Secrets

## ECK Wisdom Series

ECK Wisdom on Conquering Fear
ECK Wisdom on Dreams
ECK Wisdom on Health and Healing
ECK Wisdom on Inner Guidance
ECK Wisdom on Karma and Reincarnation
ECK Wisdom on Life after Death
ECK Wisdom on Solving Problems
ECK Wisdom on Soul Travel
ECK Wisdom on Spiritual Freedom

## Spiritual Wisdom Series

Spiritual Wisdom on Prayer, Meditation, and Contemplation
Spiritual Wisdom on Relationships

## Stories to Help You See God in Your Life

The Book of ECK Parables, Volumes 1, 2, and 3
Stories to Help You See God in Your Life, ECK Parables, Book 4

# SPIRITUAL LESSONS FROM LIVING

## HAROLD KLEMP

MAHANTA TRANSCRIPTS

BOOK 18

ECKANKAR
Minneapolis
www.Eckankar.org

**Spiritual Lessons from Living,**
Mahanta Transcripts, Book 18

Copyright © 2020 ECKANKAR

Printed in USA

Text illustrations by Raoof Haghighi
Spine photo and text photo (page xii) by Art Galbraith

This book has been authored by and published under the supervision of the Mahanta, the Living ECK Master, Sri Harold Klemp. It is the Word of ECK.

Library of Congress Cataloging-in-Publication Data

Names: Klemp, Harold, author.
Title: Spiritual lessons from living / Harold Klemp.
Description: Minneapolis : Eckankar, [2020] | Series: Mahanta transcripts ; Book 18 | Includes index. | Summary: "We've come to solve the mystery of ourself, the mystery of Soul - who we are. And it's a wonderful journey." -- Provided by publisher.
Identifiers: LCCN 2020032277 | ISBN 9781570434358 (paperback)
Subjects: LCSH: Eckankar (Organization)--Doctrines. | Spiritual life--Eckankar (Organization) | Life--Religious aspects.
Classification: LCC BP605.E3 K56485 2020 | DDC 299/.93--dc23
LC record available at https://lccn.loc.gov/2020032277

∞ This paper meets the requirements of ANSI/NISO Z39.48-1992 (Permanence of Paper).

# CONTENTS

# FOREWORD

The teachings of ECK define the nature of Soul. You are Soul, a particle of God sent into the worlds (including earth) to gain spiritual experience.

The goal in ECK is spiritual freedom in this lifetime, after which you become a Co-worker with God, both here and in the next world. Karma and reincarnation are primary beliefs.

Key to the ECK teachings is the Mahanta, the Living ECK Master. He has the special ability to act as both the Inner and Outer Master for ECK students. The prophet of Eckankar, he is given respect but is not worshipped. He teaches the sacred name of God, HU. When sung just a few minutes each day, HU will lift you spiritually into the Light and Sound of God—the ECK (Holy Spirit). This easy spiritual exercise and others will purify you. You are then able to accept the full love of God in this lifetime.

Sri Harold Klemp is the Mahanta, the Living ECK Master today. Author of many books, discourses, and articles, he teaches the ins and outs of the spiritual life. Many of his talks are available to you on audio and video recordings. His teachings lift people and help them recognize and understand their own experiences in the Light and Sound of God.

*Spiritual Lessons from Living*, Mahanta Transcripts, Book 18, is a collection of his talks from 2006 to 2014. May they serve to uplift you on your journey home to God.

To find out more about Harold Klemp and Eckankar, please turn to page 313 in the back of this book.

Sri Harold Klemp, the Mahanta, the Living ECK Master can help us find spiritual treasure in our lives every day.

# 1
# LESSONS AND BLESSINGS

*L*essons and blessings. These come in various ways, and sometimes there's a lesson and a blessing packed in the same experience.

## A SKATEBOARDER'S INSTANT KARMA

My wife, Joan, and I were shopping at a grocery store and saw three skateboarders outside. They were dashing here and there in the traffic, not paying a whole lot of attention.

Management saw the skateboarders were putting the store's customers at risk and sent an employee to nicely ask them not to skateboard there. As the woman turned to go back into the store, the leader of the skateboarders looked around and, almost with a sneer, said, "So, what's she going to do to us?"

The very next instant, his hands flew up in the air and he fell flat on his brains—yes, on his seat. Unfortunately, the helmet was on his head.

Of course he jumped up quick as a whip and dusted himself off. Very embarrassed his buddies

*Sometimes there's a lesson and a blessing packed in the same experience.*

1

should see his downfall like that, he hopped on his skateboard and scooted off.

Well, the blessing is he didn't hurt his brains. And the lesson was, for us maybe, karma is of our own doing. So when he went flip-flopping all over like a fish out of water, he was just paying himself back real quick.

## KARMA DISHES BACK WHAT WE DISH OUT

You can call it the Law of Karma, or the Law of Cause and Effect, as if it's some great law that works rather arbitrarily. But it doesn't. For the most part, on the daily karma level it dishes back what we dish out. If you dish out ice cream, you get ice cream back. And if you dish out some bitter, bitter drink, well that's what you get back.

Karma may jump in there and balance the books for you right then. Or it may take its time because it sees you're wearing padding. So it'll wait a little while, until you're more exposed, and then get you.

Yes, there is good karma.

When we say about someone, "It's his karma," the understanding often is it's bad karma—that karma is always bad. But it isn't at all.

If we see someone who's enjoying the fruits of doing well in some arena of his life, the usual reaction is, "Some people are born with all the luck." Jealousy and envy creep right in. But if somebody is having a hard time, we say, "He got what he deserved. It's his karma."

So whether you're good or whether you're bad, you can't win if you've got a critic who doesn't have a good spiritual understanding of himself.

*If you dish out ice cream, you get ice cream back. And if you dish out some bitter, bitter drink, well that's what you get back.*

## PATCHY FACES CHANGE

Kathy is from Alabama, and she has a couple of finches at home. A finch is a nice songbird. Kathy was getting ready to present an ECK workshop on change, when the Master gave her a real good example of change right there in her own home.

Patchy, the male finch, spends most of his time trying to make the family nest more comfortable for his wife, Buffy. It's Patchy and Buffy, Mr. and Mrs. Finch. One particular day he was pulling at the netting around their cage. He was trying to take this netting and add to the softness of the nest, making it nicer.

You know how we do. We've got a nice home, a car, a couple of TVs, a couple of computers for the internet, and everything else, but somehow we want more. We want more netting. So Patchy pulled at this netting for awhile, but he couldn't break it off. Then he saw a piece of newspaper sticking up through the bars at the bottom of the cage. He tried pulling at it but didn't have any luck there either.

Kathy looked at him and thought, *I'm going to humor him.* So she got a paper napkin. With her scissors, she cut it into fine shreds and hung them over the bars atop the cage. As one or two of the shreds fell down into the cage, she thought, *Patchy's going to be over here right away, grab that stuff, slap it in the nest, and make everything really homey.* But there was a whole different reaction.

*Kathy thought, Patchy's going to grab that stuff, slap it in the nest, and make everything really homey. But there was a whole different reaction.*

What does Patchy do? He goes to the far corner of the cage, and he starts singing his "this is my territory" song.

He was afraid, but he was going to attack that strange thing that had just come into his well-ordered world. So he gets all set to charge and runs up to the side where the little strips of napkin are hanging in shreds. He gets within twelve inches, and there was a sort of line in the sand where his courage failed him. So he went back to the far end of the cage and sat there.

All of a sudden, he comes charging out again. And again, and again. He could get as close as eight to twelve inches, but that was it.

Well, all this activity made Patchy very thirsty. He'd look at those shreds, and then he'd go to his water dish to drink, drink, drink. Again he'd charge those shreds, but he couldn't get any closer than before. He'd turn around and go back to his water dish to drink and drink some more.

Finally, he got so exhausted he just couldn't do any more. So he climbed into the nest with Buffy and took a nap.

Later Patchy woke up all fresh. He probably had a good dream where he was an eagle. Again he takes up the charge, but he hits the invisible barrier at eight inches. He bounces off but keeps at it.

One of the shreds was hanging down a little bit farther than the others. Finally Patchy makes a dash, grabs ahold of that napkin shred, gives it a pull, and runs back to his corner. He studies the whole thing and determines, *Well, the thing didn't move! It didn't attack me. It's just sitting there. Maybe it's OK.*

So Patchy got all his courage up, resting in the fighter's corner like boxers do, and then his courage and his resolution pushed him out there once more.

He grabs that shred again, and now it comes floating down, just like a fluffy feather. In five

*Later Patchy woke up all fresh. He probably had a good dream where he was an eagle. Again he takes up the charge.*

minutes' time, he had cleaned up the shreds and plastered them into the nest. His world was back in order.

As Kathy watched Patchy going through his antics, she realized the Mahanta was giving her insight into the resistance some people have to change. And she took this into account as she prepared her workshop on change. She knew the Mahanta had allowed the whole experience to occur for her own enlightenment.

The Mahanta, the Inner Master, works in many, many different ways to bring people the understanding or the enlightenment that is necessary for them at a certain time and in a certain place.

*Kathy realized the Mahanta was giving her insight into the resistance some people have to change.*

## GOD IN OUR OWN IMAGE?

The topic here is, what sort of god do people make for themselves? Maybe Patchy had made his own god in the corner, a thing too fearful to be faced or to be reckoned with. We make gods out of the most foolish things. We make God in our own image.

During the early Middle Ages, the tallest, biggest, strongest, most magnificent buildings were the castles. This is where the lords lived, and they had life-and-death power over their serfs. The castles were the largest, most well-appointed buildings in those times.

Then a little later, the power of the church arose, because the clergy in the Middle Ages were even acting as advisers to emperors. Emperors stood on top, then the clergy, then the nobles came under them, and then on down through the hierarchy. The cathedrals were testimony to the power of the church.

## THE LOVE OF MONEY

You wonder what people have made as their god today. The biggest and tallest buildings are commercial buildings. Have people made money their god? I wonder, how much do people worship money and the things that it can buy?

It's not money that's evil, it's the desire for it—the kind that's overwhelming. It makes beasts of all those who are of that nature.

This is a commercial time, and business is good. I like business. I was always very much intrigued by it. Way back when I lived in Houston, on Sunday mornings when I'd go out to put up ECK posters, I'd always drive through the downtown area where the skyscrapers and business places were. That was at the time of the gas shortage. Oil was booming, and so Houston was booming too. It was thriving. As I drove around the streets on Sunday mornings, it was as if I could feel the heartbeat of the downtown area. And I liked it a whole lot.

So it's not money that's the root of all evil, but it's the love of money. Lessons and blessings.

## BILL LEARNS ABOUT HU, PAST LIVES, DREAMS, AND SOUL TRAVEL

*"Bill" and his eleven-year-old daughter had sleep disorders. So Deborah told him about singing HU.*

Deborah, from New York, tells of meeting "Bill," a bioengineering professor, and "Liz," his eleven-year-old daughter. Both had sleep disorders. Bill had trouble getting to sleep at night, and when he did sleep, he slept poorly. He was always on edge. Liz, his daughter, was a sleepwalker. Here you've got a dad and daughter, both having problems with sleep.

So Deborah told him about singing *HU*. And when he got home, he told his daughter how to sing *HU* to calm things down.

Now, Bill's belief system had been that when you die, that's the end of it. You're gone like a puff of smoke. Poof! The life you lived here has no more significance than a puff of smoke. And this had always scared him. He thought, *There's got to be more than this.* But worse, he felt he was passing on this legacy of fear to his daughter, and that's why she was sleepwalking.

One day, Bill mentioned his sore neck to Deborah. She asked him, "Has it ever occurred to you that it could be from a past life?"

A lot of us have had some problems with the powers that be in the past. And then in this lifetime, we suffer neck pains and the like and wonder, *Where is that from?* Well, it could be from hanging around the wrong places, like trees and scaffolds. Or sometimes, from the executioner's blade—all those cheery things. Somehow we crossed the powers that be, and then in this lifetime we say, "Oh, my neck hurts."

Bill went home and told Liz, even though he thought, *Boy, this'll really scare her.*

Well, Liz seemed delighted. For some reason, "past life" rang a bell inside her like she knew it was true. There was something to this.

So they did what Deborah said: "Do the technique of singing *HU* when you're trying to go to sleep. Just imagine an open door, and walk through it."

It was a good beginning, because now Bill could at least fall asleep. Then in the middle of the night he'd wake up, wide awake as ever. That bothered him, except there was one benefit that hadn't been there before: If something had been puzzling him, he now saw the answer to it. This was something that hadn't happened before. So it was a good beginning, but he still has a ways to go.

*Liz seemed delighted. For some reason, "past life" rang a bell inside her like she knew it was true.*

His daughter did this HU technique too. As she sang *HU* and walked through the open door, she began having these wonderful dreams. She slept completely through the night sometimes. The first time this happened, Bill sent an email to Deborah saying, "It works. She's having really good dreams."

Then Liz had a dream where she was snowboarding. She was going down a hill on a board, and she said it was so real. It was more real than things out here, and it was just a lot of fun! Deborah said, "If you'd like to try to repeat the experience tonight, you can do that again, but this time, take my dog with you. Invite my dog to go along."

Next morning, Deborah got another email from Bill. He said, "Liz did just as you said. She invited your dog, and everything in that Soul Travel experience was exactly the same, except your dog was running down the hill with her."

Deborah had explained to Bill that Soul Travel is you living and being aware in full consciousness at a finer level of existence than you already are at. So this was quite an experience for both father and daughter, and the lessons were good too. They learned to play the *HU: A Love Song to God* CD. They said, "Hmm, that's worth it." And now they chant *HU* every night.

So, lessons and blessings.

## JIMMY AND THE CON MAN

From Nigeria comes the story of a con man cheating Jimmy. Jimmy was a new ECKist of only six months. He had been going to an ECK Satsang class, and there he was picking up the basic principles of Eckankar.

Jimmy worked with a firm that dealt with auto

*Liz had a dream where she was snowboarding. She said it was so real. It was more real than things out here, and it was just a lot of fun!*

parts. One day while he was working there, a very well-dressed gentleman walked in the door. He had driven up in a luxury car. Jimmy was a young boy trying to act grown up. The man wanted some auto parts. So Jimmy got the parts. And then the man said to Jimmy, "I want to take these down the street to the repair shop, and when they finish fixing my car, I'll come back and pay for the parts." Jimmy agreed. He was a boy; he didn't know better.

And so hours passed, and Jimmy called over to the repair shop. No, there was no such guy there with fancy clothes and a certain kind of car. No, they hadn't put any parts in the car either.

Now Jimmy was in trouble. He knew that tomorrow morning when management came in and looked over what happened the day before, they were not going to be very happy with what Jimmy had done.

So Jimmy had made a blunder; Jimmy had been gullible. And tomorrow they would hold his feet to the fire. So he was really worried. He went to the checkout clerk and begged and pleaded with her. He said, "Please, please, don't tell management. Let me see if I can find the man."

He called the number on the man's business card, but a recording said, "This number is out of order." So now where does Jimmy go? He didn't know where to go. He couldn't locate the stranger; the phone number didn't work.

So after work, Jimmy went home. And he remembered something he had been taught in the Satsang class: If he ever found himself in trouble, he was to sing *HU* and write to the Master for help.

So that's exactly what Jimmy did before bedtime that night. And the Mahanta, the Inner Master, appeared to him in a dream.

*Jimmy remembered something he had been taught in the Satsang class: If he ever found himself in trouble, he was to sing HU and write to the Master for help.*

In the dream, the Master took Jimmy into an office like the one at Jimmy's workplace. He went over to the wastebasket, reached in, and brought out a business card. He held it right in front of Jimmy and said, "See that blacked-out area there?"

Jimmy said, "Yes."

The Master said, "Clean it up very carefully."

Jimmy cleaned it up very carefully. Under the blacked-out area was a phone number. And the Master said, "Now call that number."

Well, Jimmy woke up right away, but he didn't remember the phone number he saw on the inner planes. Then he somehow got himself back to sleep again.

The next morning, as soon as he got to work, he found the wastebasket, dug around in it, and came up with the card. Yes, there was this blacked-out area on it. So he took some ink remover and worked on it very, very carefully. He didn't want to damage the card or anything that might be under there. He removed the black ink very carefully, and there was a phone number.

He called the number. A woman answered. She identified herself as a former colleague of this man. She said, "We used to be colleagues, but he's a very bad man, a very dangerous man. If you have any dealings with him, be very careful." She gave Jimmy the address of the man's residence. And then she said another time, "Now be very careful."

But when Jimmy hung up the phone, he had the understanding that the Mahanta had already taken an interest in this matter. And that no matter what happened, no harm could come to Jimmy. This was the boy's understanding.

So Jimmy got a motorbike and jumped on. The

*But Jimmy had the understanding that the Mahanta had an interest in this matter. And no matter what happened, no harm could come to Jimmy. This was the boy's understanding.*

address was for a housing estate. It had a whole bunch of houses in there, and the address was only for the front gate. So now he had to find the house of this con man. He asked the security guards, but they were afraid to say anything. That's how Jimmy saw it. So he didn't know what to do. He bumbled around for a little bit, and after a while a neighbor came out and said, "The man you're looking for lives right there. He is usually home by two o'clock, and he tries to leave as early as possible in the morning."

Jimmy talked to the neighbor and pleaded with him. He said, "Please, if you see this man coming back, let me know. Call me. I'll be right over."

So the neighbor promised. And that very afternoon at about two o'clock, Jimmy got a call from the neighbor. He went over to the house, and there was the con man. While in the sitting room, the con man made a whole bunch of excuses as to why he hadn't paid. And there were contradictions to what he said that didn't make any sense. Then the con man went into his inner office, and he stayed there for a long time.

In the meantime, Jimmy was out in the sitting room, chanting *HU* the whole time. Pretty soon the con man came out, and he seemed surprised to see Jimmy still there. He said, "Come along in my car. We'll go out and look for some money."

You and I would say, "We're not going with you." We speak from years of experience and know you don't do that sort of thing.

*You and I would say, "We're not going with you." But Jimmy obliged the con man.*

But Jimmy obliged him. So they went out to the car, and Jimmy got in.

Now we think we can say good-bye to Jimmy. *It's the last we're going to see of you, Jimmy. He's going to make you disappear. And nobody will be the wiser, Jimmy. Wake up, Jimmy, wake up!*

## CONFIDENCE IN THE MASTER

But Jimmy had this assurance that everything was OK and that no harm could come to him. So the man got in the car, put the key into the ignition, and tried to start it. The engine turned over and turned over and turned over. But it would not start. Jimmy was right on the spot. He said, "Here, let me try." And we're thinking, *Hey, Jimmy, have you got a death wish or something?*

The first time Jimmy turned the key, the car came right to life. And so did the con man.

He jumped out of the car, ran into the house, and came out holding some money. He paid Jimmy for the parts and said, "Whoever you are, whatever you are, here's the money." He told Jimmy he dealt with all classes of people, but he couldn't understand why the boy appeared so strange and mysterious.

It was because Jimmy had such confidence in the word of the Inner Master.

Now, I do not advocate to any of you to pull such a stunt and say, "The Mahanta will take care of me." Don't count on it. Sometimes there's a lesson there for us to learn, and the Master won't do for us what we refuse to do for ourselves.

## SILAS AND THE MAHANTA'S PROTECTION

This story also happened in Nigeria. There are many experiences from chelas there of the very strong sort.

Silas is a doctor in Nigeria. It was about eleven-thirty at night, and he was at his desk. He was

*The first time Jimmy turned the key, the car came right to life. And so did the con man.*

reading Paul Twitchell's *The Flute of God*. Suddenly the Blue Star of the Mahanta sparked on the page. This happened a lot when he was reading the ECK materials. Then he turned the page, and the Blue Light sparked again. This was very unusual, because usually it just sparked one time.

All of a sudden he got this very strong urge to go into his sitting room. So he left his office and went into the sitting room. When he got there, he heard this strange sound coming from the ceiling—at eleven-thirty at night.

Something was wrong, and he knew it. There was danger.

Right away he called an electrician who lived nearby. In a few minutes, the electrician was there. He went into the room and looked at the ceiling. When he heard the sound, he ran out right away and threw the master switch. Then he crawled up into the attic and poked around for a good fifteen minutes.

When he came down, the electrician said a rat had bitten through the electrical wires. This had electrocuted the rat. Two wires were touching together, and the insulation on the cord was slowly melting. More and more of this wire was being exposed and would soon come in contact with combustible material.

"Just fifteen more minutes," he said, "and there would have been a fire. And it probably would have had very serious consequences for you and your family."

Then the electrician said, "Doctor, go to church and give thanksgiving." But Silas said silently to himself, *The Mahanta's protection*. The Master's timely warning had spared him and his family from almost certain tragedy.

> *All of a sudden Silas got this very strong urge to go into his sitting room. There, he heard this strange sound coming from the ceiling—at eleven-thirty at night.*

So the lesson is this: Some people say, "I never hear the Mahanta." They may hear, but they ignore. Because they won't listen to the nudges and promptings that are from a true source.

## KATHLEEN GOES THE EXTRA MILE

Kathleen tells this story. Her Satsang Society had missed out on getting a booth and a speaker's slot at the annual Body Mind Spirit Expo. Kathleen felt awful because that event was where they reached the largest number of newcomers. But they had missed out.

She called the woman in charge of reservations and was told the odds of their getting either a booth or a speaker slot so they could have a workshop were slim to zero. The ECKists were far down on the waiting list, and there were hardly ever any cancellations.

Kathleen was very understanding. She said, "Sure, I know how it is. But we've got a fully-prepared display for a booth." This is the one Eckankar has made available to Satsang Societies and ECK Centers. She said, "We've got this display, and we've got a workshop presentation if an opening turns up." The woman said, "That's good to hear." And she jotted down a note.

There was only a week left, and no cancellations. But the ECKists were still ready to go at a moment's notice and set the whole thing in motion.

Kathleen was thinking about it too. She thought that if they did get accepted, she was somehow going to have to come up with the five-hundred-dollar registration fee. The coffers were empty in the local ECK Center, and the cupboard was bare in the Vahana (missionary) fund too.

*If they did get accepted, Kathleen was somehow going to have to come up with the five-hundred-dollar registration fee. The coffers were empty.*

So Kathleen said, well, she'll just do what she has to, because she knows the Mahanta's will will be done. So she went to her small savings account and transferred five hundred dollars into her checking account.

Two days later at work, something surprising happened. An executive of the company came into her office with some envelopes in hand. He said, "Thank you for going beyond the call of duty" and gave her an envelope with the note "For going the extra mile" written on it. This was for a recent company initiative.

And there was something else in the envelope. She pulled out a check for five hundred dollars.

She said, "Wow! The Mahanta *is* on the field. The Mahanta, or the ECK, the Holy Spirit, *is* making things happen. Something's going on behind the scenes. This could happen yet. The way it looks, it may happen, but heaven knows how. We're way down the list yet, and no cancellations."

So the day before the expo's opening, Kathleen called the registration woman again. She identified herself and said, "Remember, we've got this display all ready to go, and we've got a workshop ready to go."

The woman said, "I'm glad you called. We do have a speaker slot. And I'm going to let you have it since you're ready and I haven't heard from anyone else."

## BE READY WHEN THE MASTER SAYS, "GO!"

Before they had even finished making these arrangements, the woman said, "A booth just opened up. Would you like to have that as well?"

Kathleen was delighted to take it. She was looking at this later, and she said it was interesting. She

*He said, "Thank you for going beyond the call of duty" and gave her an envelope with the note "For going the extra mile" written on it.*

found it so very unusual how, at the last minute, they'd gone from way down on the waiting list to the full-participation list.

And on top of it, their workshop was scheduled an hour after the expo opened. That meant as soon as the doors opened, they had only one hour to publicize, to put up posters everywhere as fast as they could. Which they did, because the team was well organized and they were willing to wait to the last minute.

Well, it was the last minute. So they put up the posters.

They had a nice turnout for the workshop, even though they weren't on the preprinted brochure or on the schedule. They did very, very well. At the booth they gave away hundreds of booklets, books, and other ECK info. Lots of people came by to hear the HU song on the CD player.

And so a lot of people were touched by this particular ECK event that nearly didn't happen. It was a blessing, of course. Kathleen recognized that. But here too, they were ready.

The lesson here: Be ready to go the mile. Be ready to go the full distance. Do your training. Get ready. Because when the Master says, "Go!" you want to be on the starting block so you can go. And that's how it is.

May the blessings be.

*Be ready to go the full distance. Do your training. Get ready. Because when the Master says, "Go!" you want to be on the starting block so you can go.*

*ECK Worldwide Seminar, Minneapolis, Minnesota*
*Saturday, October 21, 2006*

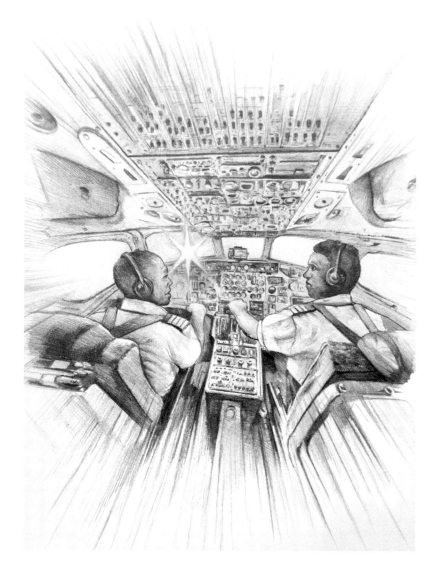

With the copilot flying, Deboee was very receptive to the Mahanta, to the Inner Master, and he listened for any guidance that might come.

Now followed a series of life-or-death decisions.

# 2
# IT'S A MIRACLE!

here are so many miracles that happen in our lives. Those of you who are in ECK just recognize the help of the Master and say, "Thank you" with a most grateful heart. You realize it's a blessing done for some purpose.

It's to help you on your way.

## WHY THE MASTER GOES AHEAD

There's a saying, which I'm just making up now: The Master goes ahead so that others may follow. And when people follow, they often say, "Gee, do you have to go over such rough stuff?"

The Master says, "Well, you should know what it's like before I kick the big ones out of the way."

And somewhere else it's said, Have compassion for everyone, because everyone carries a burden. And so it is. We look at our own selves and say, "My troubles are really the worst thing that could ever happen to anyone in this life." And at the same time, our neighbor or an associate is also carrying a burden that is equal to our measure.

Life gives us what we are able to bear, and sometimes we come to the point where we say, "Will there be any more? Will this have to go on?"

At times the answer is long in coming. We

*The Master goes ahead so that others may follow. And when people follow, they often say, "Gee, do you have to go over such rough stuff?"*

almost bend under the weight like an overloaded donkey and say, "Just one more stick on this pack, and it's all over. I'm going to crumble."

Such is life. And when we're through a particular experience, we look back and say, "Well, it's a miracle!"

> We almost bend under the weight like an overloaded donkey. And when we're through we look back and say, "Well, it's a miracle!"

## A LOOK AT GLOBAL CHANGE

There's a big controversy now about global change. If you get into this, you can find strong arguments on either side—why the globe is warming, why it's not. Why one is a long-term look and the other is a short-term look. And how, in the west side of the Antarctic, the glaciers are indeed calving off. When these big chunks of ice fall off, that's called calving. But on the eastern end, the opposite end of the Antarctic, the ice is actually thickening.

It depends on where you're going to put your observations and where your bias lies. There are many biases. There are some theories that now say solar flares can cause more damage or greenhouse effect than man and all his puny influence could ever do.

For instance, the theory is that a solar flare heats up the earth. The earth throws vapor back in the air, traps the moisture and the gases, and creates—in effect—a greenhouse. There have been studies done of these flares—what happened back in the 1700s and so on. Studies have gone both ways. You can take facts to prove anything you want. All you have to do is be very selective in choosing them.

## DEALING WITH PSYCHIC WAVES

The reason I'm bringing this up is that these fears are psychic waves. Whenever anyone can raise fears in the people, there's money to be had. And where there's money to be had, there's power.

So we find here that there are two forces always at play—the force of love and the force of power.

These are very potent, and each one of these forces is also in each individual. But their strengths vary from time to time, depending upon the psychic wave that sweeps through. And when it comes, then people gravitate toward the one that most fits them at that time.

The point is, when a psychic wave is occurring, it strikes the emotions. So people get very, very emotional about issues such as climate change. They get very emotional. And it's only the enlightened Soul that can see through the illusions and not be tipped off balance by them.

## GOD'S PLAN TO PURIFY SOUL

The balanced view, or the higher state of consciousness, sees the positive and the negative for what it is—neither good nor bad, just all part of God's plan to purify Soul. And Soul, that's you.

To purify Soul. That's what this whole conflict between the positive and negative powers is about.

The pushing and the pulling, and the tension between the two, catch people up in a psychic wave. It's like pulling taffy. Or like one of those stretching exercisers you pull to get really strong and muscular. It's that sort of tension. When you pull, there's a dynamic to it.

Way back, one of the bodybuilders, Charles Atlas, used to work with dynamic tension. Because with this dynamic tension—artfully, skillfully, and scientifically done—he promised he could turn a ninety-seven-pound weakling into a he-man. And

*When a psychic wave is occurring, it strikes the emotions. Only the enlightened Soul can see through the illusions and not be tipped off balance by them.*

nobody would ever kick sand in *his* face again.

Well, in a way, the same is true for Soul. Once Soul becomes strong, nobody can ever get close enough to kick sand in Its face spiritually. The sand, of course, is the illusion that's constantly being thrown up into the eyes of people.

## HU Opens the Heart to Healing

Katie is an acupuncturist. Patients who feel their condition isn't improving will sometimes ask her, "Isn't there something else, something more that I can do?" So Katie will check with the Mahanta, the Inner Master, to find out if this person is ready for a HU card or a *HU: A Love Song to God* CD. And if she gets the OK, she'll pass this along.

One of her patients was Jessica. And Katie had the nudge to give her both a HU card and HU CD. Jessica is now in her sixties. She had polio as a child, and most of her life she was under heavy medication. She'd sleep around twenty hours a day.

Jessica's doctor and Katie were both trying to get Jessica free from her medication. And when Jessica began to sing *HU* along with the treatments she was getting, suddenly her condition improved vastly.

Jessica said, "It's like a miracle!" And Katie observed, "That's how the ECK changes lives."

Jessica had a housemate named Linda. One day Jessica said, "Linda's always going a mile a minute." Katie, being ever alert to an opening, said, "Do you suppose Linda might be helped with meditation?"

Jessica said, "Oh, we sing *HU* together. In fact, Linda likes it so much she's inviting friends over so they can all sing *HU* together on Sunday." Katie studied this improbable scenario and mused, *So here*

*When Jessica began to sing HU along with the treatments she was getting, suddenly her condition improved vastly.*

*is a HU song led by non-ECKists for non-ECKists.
And they thought this up all by themselves!*

What's interesting is that Katie has seen such a correlation between the openness of Soul—especially one who embraces and uses the HU—and the patient's correspondent healing and upliftment in consciousness.

And it is so, because HU opens the heart to healing.

*HU opens the heart to healing.*

## THE ELEPHANT DREAM STORY

I'm going to call the person who told this story Carol. She says her favorite story is about her father, an atheist, and it's called "The Elephant Dream Story."

During a long-distance call to her parents, Carol happened to mention an insight she had gotten from some of her dreams. Her father is from Brooklyn, a very hard-nosed place. He's also an atheist. He said that dreams are nonsense. But Carol said he said it in a more colorful way.

A few days later, her parents called back. Her mother began to explain why they had called, then insisted that the father tell the story. But he didn't want to, and he was uncharacteristically quiet. The mother urged him on. She said, "Go ahead. It's your story. You tell it."

They sleep in a king-size bed. The mother wants everything neat, so she tucks the sheets in the bottom of the bed, and then tucks them in tight on both sides. If anyone gets in bed, they can hardly breathe, let alone turn; forget about tossing and turning.

Well at two a.m., in the dead of night, Carol's father suddenly leaped from the bed, pulling the top sheet, blanket, and bedspread clean off as he jumped in the air. He jumped right over a little marble night stand, rolled over on the other side, and landed inches from the edge of another table. This was all done in the dark.

It was an otherwise uneventful night. There were no sounds of breaking and entering. It was just quiet.

As the mother's sheets were torn away, she cried out, "What are you doing?" The father said, "Don't worry, dear. The elephant's chasing me, but I made it safely over the fence."

Then she scolded him. She said, "You didn't hit your head on the edge of the table. That's a miracle! So much for the nonsense of dreams."

Carol said that during this long-distance phone call, in a rare moment of silence, her father had no comeback. And he's never made any kind of derogatory remark about dreams again.

Just for general knowledge, do you know what the elephant is? It's the father's inflated opinion about the nonsense of dreams. He had finally escaped it. I thought that was so apropos.

*An atheist may feel there is no God. But that doesn't mean the hand of God won't reach down and lift him up and push him over the fence.*

An atheist may feel there is no God. But that doesn't mean the hand of God won't reach down and lift him up and push him over the fence.

## DIANE FINDS A KEY TO CHANGE

Diane lives in England. She and Alex were going to give an ECK workshop titled "How to Master Change in Your Life." And before that particular day of the workshop was over, they would both experience a lot of change.

Change is a curious thing. We like change for the good but not the change for ill. And when everything seems to go wrong, you finally reach the point where you throw your hands in the air and say, "I give up!" At this point, when the shields of resistance have been let down, the Master can come in and give some kind of assistance. Because until then, the lesson which is inherent in the experience is not learned.

So Diane and Alex were going to put on the ECK workshop "How to Master Change in Your Life." And the key word is *change*. Diane was to pick up the hall's key at a hospice reception desk. The hospice and the hall were alongside each other. But the receptionist said, "The key's been missing for several days."

The receptionist looked a little antsy. She had people coming in and asking questions. Diane let her handle them.

Then Diane said, "We booked the hall for a workshop, and it's to begin in forty-five minutes. We need that key."

Now, the receptionist's shift was going to end shortly, and the last thing she wanted to do was look through a box of keys. But she figured maybe there was some mistake; maybe the ECKists had gotten the wrong date. The receptionist was used to that. People did those things. So she checked her booking diary, and indeed this was the date. And the clock was ticking. The workshop was starting in less than forty-five minutes. So she had to look in that large box with a whole bunch of keys in it.

Well, the hall key wasn't in the box. So now the receptionist was clutching at straws. She said, "Go try the back and front doors of the hall. Maybe somebody didn't lock one. Maybe one of the doors is open." Diane checked. Both doors were locked.

And then Diane told Alex, "The hall key is

*When the shields of resistance have been let down, the Master can come in and give some kind of assistance.*

missing. It's looking more and more as if we're going to have to hold the workshop in the car park," the parking lot.

Diane had this vision going across her mind. She thought, *All the money spent on advertising the event is probably gone. All the effort spent in postering is probably gone. Four months of preparation wasted.* Well, it looked like that's what was going to happen unless they could do the workshop in the car park.

The clock had been ticking all this time. The first attendees were due to show up any moment. Yes, change is very uncomfortable. And it was very much so for Diane and Alex.

Then Diane came to the point where she threw up her hands. She said, "Mahanta, I need your help if you want this workshop to go ahead today. So please help me find the key in the next few minutes."

Almost that quickly, Diane saw in her inner vision the key in a letter box, a mailbox. She asked the receptionist to look. The receptionist said, "We don't have a letter box." Diane said, "Yes, you do."

She walked around behind the receptionist and pointed to the back of a letter box. The receptionist looked very startled. She took the letter box, reached in, and pulled out a basketful of mail. And in the bottom of it was a key.

Diane said, "That's it!" The receptionist said, "No, it's not. It's not the key."

But Diane was persistent. The receptionist thought, *Oh well, I'm going home for the day real soon. Why not humor her?* So she took the key out and looked on the other side.

It was neatly labeled Hall Key.

After the Mahanta's intervention, the workshop

*Diane came to the point where she threw up her hands. She said, "Mahanta, I need your help." Almost that quickly, Diane saw in her inner vision the key in a letter box, a mailbox.*

went on without any further hitches. Diane saw this as the Master's confirmation that he was always with her. And, of course, she was happier, because a change for the better is always welcome.

## ENGLISH HISTORY AND REINCARNATION

England. I have always had a personal interest in the history of England and also France. Those two countries, throughout history, have been sometimes walking hand in hand. Other times, one or the other will hit the other on the arm, and they go punching. Then they end up holding hands again. Nobility from one side or the other has migrated back and forth, back and forth.

*England and France have been sometimes walking hand in hand. Other times, they go punching. Then they end up holding hands again.*

I was thinking about English history and reincarnation. Queen Elizabeth I was the Virgin Queen and had no children. She was the daughter of Henry VIII.

The consciousness of people in those days was Don't let a woman do it, because she can't. In fact, in their recent history there had been a woman who had been in place for a short time, and everything was a fiasco. It didn't work out at all, and they said, "Well, what did you expect?"

Queen Mary, Bloody Mary, was in power. She was Catholic, and she killed so many Protestants. It was quite a mess.

During this time, Elizabeth learned to keep her head down because she was Protestant, just like her father, Henry VIII. She had no training in how to make decisions or perform royal duties, but she kept her nose clean till she took the throne.

Elizabeth I ruled forty-five years and died at the age of seventy. She didn't have any children, because she couldn't find a suitable husband. Her suitors didn't have the rank; they didn't have the class level that was required of a queen. There was one whom she was close to marrying, but he went off to a battle over in Ireland and came running home with his tail between his legs. He failed miserably. And she thought, *I can't marry this guy and share the throne with him. No way.*

England was in a very precarious position at this point. Henry VIII had squandered all the money that his father, Henry VII, had left. Henry VIII just used it up left and right. He didn't care. He would try to tax the people and get money any way he could. But by the time he died, there wasn't any money left.

And by the time Elizabeth became queen, England was looked down on by the European powers of Spain, the Habsburgs, France, and the others. They could have snuffed England out at any time. So she had to play a little game here. Sometimes she was coy, and then she would say she was looking for suitors.

*Spain, the Habsburgs, France, and the others could have snuffed England out at any time.*

She was biding her time so that her country could build up strength and get their navy going. During her reign the Spanish Armada came and was defeated by England. But it was more as a blessing of the gods. God's wind blew foul for the Spanish fleet, and then the English fleet went out and clobbered it. It didn't cripple Spain all that much, but it beat them back for the moment.

Well, that was Elizabeth I, the Virgin Queen.

Later came Victoria. Victoria lived to the age of eighty-two, and she ruled for sixty-four years.

A forty-five-year reign and a sixty-four-year reign are exceptionally long. Some people lived their whole life never knowing any ruler of England besides Elizabeth in her time or Victoria in her time. Victoria outlived many of her contemporaries.

Victoria had nine children. When she had her eighth and ninth, she wanted the use of anesthesia, because science offered it. She thought it was wonderful compared to the other way of bearing children.

## SPIRITUAL LESSON FOR SOUL

Now there's Queen Elizabeth II. She's already ruled for fifty-five years, and she's age eighty now. Very, very long reigns.

Well, this is the same Soul come back, doing what she had come to do as a Soul. As Elizabeth I she helped England become great. And then as Victoria, she helped England become greater. England saw supremacy over all nations. She ruled the waves with the Royal Navy. This was at the height of England's power.

*This is the same Soul come back, doing what she had come to do as a Soul.*

Now Elizabeth II sees England as no longer the most powerful country in Europe or in the world. And so it's kind of a Soul lesson—a spiritual lesson for that Soul to see this. And to oversee it—to see something being built, something at its peak, and then something that isn't quite in the ashes.

## A PILOT TRUSTS THE MAHANTA

The next story has to do with a DC-9 emergency over West Africa. Deboee was a pilot on a DC-9 passenger plane. One day the plane was flying out of Abidjan, Ivory Coast, with a full load of passengers, and they had an emergency during takeoff. They were headed for Monrovia, Liberia, which was to the west.

Suddenly there was a violent vibration. The copilot was flying, and Deboee said, "Go ahead with the takeoff." The other choice would have been to abort. This was how the guidelines read. With the copilot flying, Deboee was very receptive to the Mahanta, to the Inner Master, and he listened for any guidance that might come.

Now followed a series of life-or-death decisions. Deboee kept listening, and in some cases he did absolutely the wrong thing by the book. But it saved everybody's life.

First was the decision to continue with the takeoff or not, and aborting meant they would have ended up in the sea. And he said, "Lives were saved right there."

Deboee knew there was a tire problem, so he didn't retract the undercarriage, because that would have damaged the hydraulic system. Later, the Abidjan air traffic control center confirmed that they had left part of a tire on the runway.

Now came the decision to divert to Accra, in Ghana. This was well to the east. With the undercarriage down, the extra drag meant there would be too little fuel to reach the original destination of Monrovia. Fuel consumption would have been twice as much, and they would never have made it.

Then on the way to Accra, the engine on the same side as the burst tire developed an oil leak. The procedure said to shut down the engine. But the plane was overloaded. And with the undercarriage down, there was all this drag.

A DC-9 has two engines. And if he had shut the engine down, one engine alone couldn't keep the plane airborne. That would have been it. All lives lost.

Deboee brought the throttle back to idle just to see what would happen, and the plane lost altitude.

*Deboee kept listening, and in some cases he did absolutely the wrong thing by the book. But it saved everybody's life.*

So he had to choose here. He brought the throttle back up, pushed it forward, and they regained altitude. They kept flying in spite of the oil leak. And how did Deboee make these decisions? Well, the Mahanta had given him a nudge—had said to do exactly what he'd done.

So now came the question Should he announce to the passengers what kind of a stew they're in? And he realized, no, they'd panic, and they already have enough problems.

He just said, "We've got a tire problem, and we'll be landing at Accra." And the people were very calm. Once the DC-9 was over Accra, it had used up enough fuel to be well within a safe landing weight. They shut down the engine with the oil leak, and they made a perfect landing. Everyone was safe. Deboee credited this guidance 100 percent to the Mahanta. Deboee said that just a single wrong decision would have spelled disaster.

*How did Deboee make these decisions? Well, the Mahanta had given him a nudge—had said to do exactly what he'd done.*

## LISTENING TO THE INNER VOICE

Then he added something very interesting. Deboee drew a parallel to other people who listened to the inner voice. He said Bach, Beethoven, Mozart, Handel, and Tchaikovsky, to name a few, were all vehicles who listened to this inner guidance and acted. And we are all witness to the result of their listening. We can all hear the results through the music they wrote. Just a beautiful connection.

And the music certainly is gorgeous, except maybe for Schoenberg and his twelve-tone scale. The twelve-tone scale is atonal. Today it's the basis of much modern music. It's not like the eight-tone scale, which is tonal.

Someone once asked Schoenberg, "Why did you

bring out the twelve-tone scale?" "Well," he said, "because nobody else would." I thought, *There is a humble man, and a man with a mission. He knew he had a calling.*

## The Attorney Was a Seeker

Don sits on his local city council, and as a council member he helped draft a smoking resolution. Later it passed on a six-to-one vote. Because of the work he'd done on this smoking ordinance, he received an invitation to attend a workshop for a similar ordinance downstate. John, the city attorney, had also helped draft a lot of the ordinance; they had worked on it together. And John was also invited to the workshop.

So the two men decided they'd make the two-hour drive together. It was late January, and the weather was cold. Snow was beginning to come down, and it looked to be a long drive.

But they got to talking, and about an hour later the talk had turned to things like international and national politics. And then the topic turned to national karma. John, the attorney, wanted some understanding about national karma.

*John, the attorney, wanted some understanding about national karma. Now, Don was very surprised that the attorney would be interested in something like this.*

Now, Don was very surprised that the attorney would be interested in something like this. They had worked together all this time, but Don had never had the opportunity to talk about religion because it hadn't ever come up in the line of work.

So they talked about the influence of the religious right. And then John mentioned, "I'm a Methodist." And he said to Don, "What's your religion?"

This is where the conversation got a little funny. It went back and forth like a badminton match. Don said his religion was farther out than Methodist. And so John asked, "Unitarian?"

"Farther."

"Agnostic?"

"Farther."

"Atheist?"

Then Don said, "Farther yet. I'm a member of Eckankar."

And to his surprise, John had heard about Eckankar, just in merest passing. John asked more and more about it, and Don explained about the Light and the Sound that Soul perceives in Its natural state. And then they also talked about the levels of heaven, Soul Travel, and past lives. And not once did the fifty-six-year-old attorney flinch. So he's been around. He's been weathered.

And Don explained that when one has the viewpoint of Soul, it's like seeing a situation with an expanded, huge state of awareness. And John seemed to understand. He said, "Yes, I know. I had such an experience at the age of nine." Don was quite amazed at this. And then they talked more about things.

Don offered John the new *Eckankar Journal*, which gave many stories of people who had experienced the Light and Sound of God. It was eleven-thirty at night when they got to the convention hotel. The next day they were in the symposium, talking about the smoking ordinance, each one of them contributing according to his measure.

They came back late at night on Thursday, and they talked more about all these different subjects—about Eckankar and the ECK teachings.

John revealed that when he was nine he had read Genesis and asked his mother, "If Cain killed

*When one has the viewpoint of Soul, it's like seeing a situation with an expanded, huge state of awareness.*

Abel, and then there were only three people on earth, who did Cain marry?" His mother probably wished he would just keep this stuff to himself. John also asked her a lot of other awkward questions about the nature of God and other points about the Christian religion.

Of course, he was quickly becoming persona non grata, not welcome in his own household. And so from age nine, John had been a seeker.

When they got back, Don went into the house and brought out a *HU: A Love Song to God* CD and the booklet *Is Life a Random Walk?* John accepted both. Don would never have thought of John as a seeker, because he was a smart, able lawyer. Don had come to respect him because of how well John handled the city affairs. He had to draw up ordinances, give advice to the council, and other things. He was always astute—a very, very capable man.

The very next day, at two o'clock in the afternoon, Don got an email from the city administrator saying that John had tendered his resignation to the mayor earlier that day. Everybody was stunned.

Don marveled at how precise the Master's timing was. He said, "Here's this guy who gets the ECK teaching right now. We really get to talk on Wednesday, and then Thursday we drive back. This guy is ready for ECK!"

Well, to the ECK there is no time. It's always on time. Everything is in its rightful place at the right moment.

So there is no hurry. There is no racing to break the magical wire and win the horse race—none of that. It all happens according to the divine scheme.

*To the ECK there is no time. It's always on time. Everything is in its rightful place at the right moment.*

## Finding Your Calling

Back when they had still been driving home, the conversation had turned to being of service—a calling—something you need to do in this lifetime. That's why you've all come. You've come here to do something.

Find out what it is. Otherwise, if you go before you've served your calling, you've wasted the whole lifetime.

Rumi, the thirteenth-century Persian poet, speaks very eloquently about this and many other things. If you ever read Rumi, I would strongly recommend the version by Coleman Barks. There is a book, *A Year with Rumi*, with a little Rumi snippet for every day of the year. You're not overwhelmed by poetry, and it's a good thing to use sometimes in addition to your ECK contemplations.

What's an ECKist's calling?

Well, it's simply to tell others about the Mahanta and the Light and Sound of God. So simple. That's why you're here. To tell them about love, because it's in contrast to and—as the higher side—balances off against power.

*What's an ECKist's calling? It's simply to tell others about the Mahanta and the Light and Sound of God.*

*ECK Springtime Seminar, Minneapolis, Minnesota*
*Saturday, April 7, 2007*

Something was changing here too: Mark. Just like that—
a change in consciousness.

# 3
# CHANGE IS CHANGE

his noon I was thinking about you and all the miles you had come to be here. And I could feel the weight you carried as you came. So as I was making lunch, I turned on the radio to National Public Radio, NPR.

Weekend radio generally has Click and Clack, the Tappet Brothers. These are two very funny guys on the *Car Talk* show. They are very knowledgeable about automobiles, and they make it fun.

## A PROFESSOR'S WISH FOR WISDOM

Click and Clack opened this show with some jokes that listeners had sent in. I caught one that went like this: Three professors of philosophy were sitting around talking about—what else—philosophy. And suddenly an angel appeared unto them and said, "I shall give you one of three wishes. You can have wisdom, beauty, or money."

The first professor jumped right up and said, "I'll take the wisdom." And the angel said, "So it shall be given unto you as you have wished."

There was a flash of light, and then this professor had wisdom. His head sank to his chest, his

*An angel appeared unto three professors of philosophy and said, "I shall give you one of three wishes. You can have wisdom, beauty, or money."*

eyes were shut, and he sat there for the longest time. The other two professors were just sitting there listening, watching, wondering. But the first one seemed to be sitting there in some kind of contemplation. One of the other two said very quietly to his colleague, "He must be thinking great thoughts. Just think of all that wisdom this man has now."

Then they sat quietly a little longer, while they waited for this man to speak. He didn't. Finally one of the professors said, "Excuse me, would you share some of your wisdom with us? We would be so grateful." The first professor raised his head and opened his eyes. Sadly he said, "I should have taken the money."

Well, right away I felt better. I felt all your weights falling off.

## THE LITTLE HU SONG

*Years ago in the very early ECK seminars, Helen Baird introduced a song I call "The Little HU Song." Over the years it nearly got lost.*

Years ago in the very early ECK seminars, Helen Baird introduced a song I call "The Little HU Song." Over the years it nearly got lost. I asked my wife, Joan, and then she asked the Eckankar staff, "Has anyone ever heard this little song before?" One of the staff mentioned a longtime ECKist in the South, on the East Coast, who would probably know it.

And of course, Sherwood did know it. He had sheet music and words from way back, and he sent those over. But they were copyrighted in 1972, and they were not scored the way the song was originally sung in some of the early seminars.

By 1971 and 1972, the song was changing already. Everybody adapted it and put touches on it, because those were very unformed times. People just used this, that, and the other thing. They adapted freely. And the spiritual power that was in it originally was sometimes lost in the translation.

So this little song nearly got lost. We had looked around, and we found all these different versions of it out there. I said, "But they slipped off the original. It's time to bring it back." So I sang it to Joan. I told her how it goes, and she sang it back to me.

I'd like to ask Joan to come out here now and sing it and then lead you in singing it.

## The Little HU Song

The Light is HU
The Sound is HU
We open, open wide the door
To let the Light H . . . U . . .

The Light is HU
The Sound is HU
We open, open wide the door
To let the Sound H . . . U . . .

The Light is HU
The Sound is HU
We open, open wide the door
H . . . U . . . , H . . . U . . . , H . . . U . . .

"The Little HU Song" is to be used as you would any other song in *The ECK Songbook*, Volumes 1 and 2. It doesn't take the place of the rolling HU, which is what we sing to introduce a major session like this. It's to be used anytime that another song from *The ECK Songbook* would be used, apart from the rolling HU. I use the term "the rolling HU" because everyone comes in at a different time in his or her own voice. It makes such a wonderful, wonderful blending of all the human instruments that on this earth compose part of the orchestra—

*The rolling HU makes such a wonderful, wonderful blending of all the human instruments.*

the earthly orchestra—which is trying to echo the great Sound Current, the Holy Spirit, the Voice of God. And that's what it is.

## CHANGE AT THE BOOKSTORE

Joan and I went to a bookstore. Unfortunately, I keep buying books. Some of you may be afflicted in the same way. You buy the things five or ten times faster than you can ever hope to read them. But you've got a good selection when you're ready for the next one.

We've got this whole coffee table full of books just for our evening reading. Joan reads for us in the evening. Sometimes I get a little time in to read my own book apart from that. But we'll never catch up.

So here we were in the bookstore. We went to the checkout counter, where Joan and I paid for our purchase with a whole bunch of coins and dollar bills.

With inflation continuing to march along ever so swiftly, all these coins are becoming worth less and less—which is what inflation is all about. It's when the money gets worth less, and it takes more of it to buy what you used to get before. So we gave all this money to the cashier, and I said, "OK, now you're set with enough change for the rest of the day."

As she sorted it into her cash register, she said, "Change is change."

Now, the people in this particular bookstore happen to like books. And I thought, *Well, maybe she's philosophical. Maybe there's some wisdom here.* I said, "Do you mean change as in coins, or change as in *change*?"

*As the cashier sorted it into her cash register, she said, "Change is change." I said, "Do you mean change as in coins, or change as in change?"*

It was very near lunchtime. She looked at me and said, "Oh, no. I'm not going there!" She wasn't going to have some fool customer load her mind down with all kinds of unsolvable problems right before lunch. I thought she was a very wise woman to back out of that so nicely. She also had a good sense of humor.

Yes, change is change.

## A WHITE-HAIRED LADY'S
## CHANGE IN CONSCIOUSNESS

Another time, Joan and I went to the grocery store. We filled up the basket. We'd been away from home on other errands before the shopping trip, and it was going to be a little bit before we got home. So we decided to use the restrooms.

Joan went first while I was left to guard—no, not the stagecoach—the shopping cart. But I'm standing there thinking, *Hey, I could collapse a few minutes here. While Joan is using the restroom, I could go over there and use the restroom too.*

Later Joan told me that when she had gone over to the restroom, a little white-haired woman was standing in front of the ladies' room, waiting. Somebody was inside; the door was locked. So Joan took a couple more steps to the men's room and tried the door handle. It was open.

Joan and I have this motto that we follow assiduously: Any port in a storm. And any port when there's no storm, for that matter. Who cares? Nobody cares on airplanes, and everybody seems to do OK.

So the little woman sputtered and said, "But that's for the men!" And Joan just smiled and went in. And that was it.

In the meantime, I'm back at the "stagecoach,"

*Any port in a storm. And any port when there's no storm. Who cares? Nobody cares on airplanes, and everybody seems to do OK.*

and I decide to collapse a few minutes. I come walking along and try the men's room. Locked. So I take a few steps and try the door to the women's restroom. It's *un*locked.

So I say, "Great!" I push open the door, I go in, and there's this little white-haired lady standing at the sink. And she's looking at me.

Very much like the western gentleman, I say, "Excuse me, ma'am. The door was unlocked, and I thought this room was vacant." She's sputtering away, and she says, "But this is for the *women*!"

I said, "When there's a need, this is a unisex." Then I smiled as gentlemanly as I could, backed out, and was glad she hadn't started screaming. It would have taken Joan and all our friends at this store to get me out of it.

I go back toward the men's room, and just then Joan comes out with a big smile. I shake my head and go inside. Later I told her what had happened after she left the scene.

*I come walking along and try the men's room. Locked. So I take a few steps and try the door to the women's restroom. It's unlocked.*

## CHANNELS FOR THE ECK

Well, I got to thinking. Joan and I went in there minding our own business, shopping, just like you and your wife or you and your husband. And then the ECK, the Holy Spirit, decides, Hey, there's a little white-haired woman in there that needs a change of consciousness. And the ECK doesn't bother to tell *us* about it. Especially *me*. Lets me walk right into it.

Well, those are just some of the enjoyable little things that happen as we're channels for the ECK, for the Holy Spirit. And we get along as well as we can.

## JIM AND THE OUT-OF-BODY GOOD-BYE

Public acceptance of out-of-body experiences has grown so much over the last two or three decades. People just accept it now.

There was a time when anybody who spoke about out-of-the-body experiences would get a funny look. It was just something that wasn't said in public any more than you would talk about sex. Dirty word, brush your teeth, gargle. It fell into that category.

Anyway, Joan was listening to the radio and heard this little story that was an illustration of how things have changed.

A little girl asked her father, "Were you ever in a war?" He said, "Yeah, I was in Vietnam." He told her about boot camp and what it was like there. He spoke about how his drill sergeant had taken a particular dislike to both him and his buddy, Jim.

Drill sergeants will do that. They can look at someone, and they can see that they're happy, they look smart, or they have some other look. But they don't look as if they belong to a unit of sixty other soldiers. The drill sergeant is going to break down the individual personality so when it's time to operate as a unit, all these individuals can give up their individuality and become part of a unit and act for the greater good of the unit.

I don't know if it's gentler and kinder in the service today. But I went in around the time of Vietnam, and it wasn't kind then. And I doubt if it's very kind now.

Well, this sergeant was down on the girl's father. The sergeant would come up to him and say, "Don't get in my face!" This really wore on the father and his buddy, Jim.

*Public acceptance of out-of-body experiences has grown so much over the last two or three decades. People just accept it now.*

So as soon as they got out of earshot of the sergeant, they'd look at each other. One would turn to the other and say, "Don't get in my face!" The other would laugh, look his buddy in the eye, and shout the same thing back.

Then they went into combat in Vietnam. But they came home in one piece and went their separate ways. Jim went to work as a forklift operator, and he was killed in an industrial accident. The girl's father felt very bad about this. He missed Jim a lot.

*One night the father had a dream. He was just floating around somewhere. And who should come floating by in the sky out there? It was Jim!*

One night the father had a dream. It was a very special dream. He was just floating around somewhere. And who should come floating by in the sky out there? It was Jim! As they floated near each other, Jim shouted, "Don't get in my face!" So the girl's father called back, "Don't get in *my* face!" And then they laughed and laughed and laughed like two maniacs just having a good time.

They got to share some of the old times they had had. Jim was glad to hear his buddy was doing well. The girl's father was likewise assured Jim was happy where he was and that everything was going well. Pretty soon they said their good-byes and floated away from each other. Then the girl's father woke up.

Later he said to his daughter, "I think this dream was given so that Jim and I would have a chance to say good-bye to each other."

I thought this was one of those beautiful dreams that shows how the consciousness of people today has risen or changed so much that it can accept concepts like this.

## DYLAN HEARS THE SOUND

The names I'm using tonight are changed to protect people's privacy.

"Myra" and "Dylan," her grown son, were sitting on the porch, talking with each other. Myra looked at her son and thought, *Oh, you've caused me so many worries by the bad choices you've made.* But then Myra was honest. She said to herself, *I wasn't a good mother. I made a lot of bad choices myself, and they hurt Dylan. He's been angry with me all these years. So there's been this wall between us.*

Myra figured maybe it was too late for this wall to go away. She was an ECKist, and so she didn't worry about it. She just thought, *Hmm, what do you do?*

Lately she had noticed a change in Dylan. He was different. He was better somehow. That night he said to her, "You know, at night after you've gone to bed, I sometimes stay up and read your ECK books." He mentioned hearing birds singing. Myra said, "That's one of the sounds of God."

He went on, "One night while I was reading, everything turned a bluish-green." Myra said, "That's one of the lights or the colors of God."

There are many different sounds. The sound of birds is one. Blue lights, green lights, pink lights, yellow lights, white lights—these are all different colors of God.

Myra understands that she and her son are working through karma, but she's grateful to the Mahanta for helping her work through it.

*Dylan mentioned hearing birds singing. Myra said, "That's one of the sounds of God."*

## Myra's Doubting Grandson Sees the Light

Myra also has two grandsons. One Saturday morning, they came over to visit. "Mark" is the older; he's thirteen. "Jimmy" is eleven.

Myra greeted them with a lot of joy. She loves

them dearly. Then she said to them, "It's just about time for my spiritual exercises. You're free to stay out here or go to the den and watch cartoons on TV." They said, "No. No. We want to do a spiritual exercise with you." So Myra said, "OK." They went into her bedroom and sat on her bed.

She said, "All right. Look for the Light, and listen for the Sound. Look into your Spiritual Eye."

It wasn't five minutes later that she heard this snickering. Myra opened one eye. She's been around. She peeks. She saw the younger grandson, Jimmy, sitting with his hand covering his mouth, laughing. Over his hand, she saw these two laughing eyes. At the same time, Mark, the older boy, was whispering in one of those stage whispers intended for Grandma's ears, no doubt. He said, "She's making it up! She's making it up."

Well, this aggravated Grandma. She said, "You all get out of here, and let me do my spiritual exercises." She's from the South. She doesn't mess around.

So, laughing and snickering, the boys went out of the room. Myra likes her special HU session because of the love that comes through from the Mahanta. She feels all this love. So she settled in and began the spiritual exercise.

She's just getting into it, when she hears this very gentle knocking on the door. She opens her eyes, rolls them to the ceiling, and says, "What is it?" Mark, the older of the two boys, creeps in. He knows he shouldn't be doing this. He asks, "Can I do your spiritual exercise with you? Can I sing the HU with you? It calms me down and makes me feel better." "OK," said Myra. And now Myra laid down the ground rules. She said, "But this time I'll walk you through it. You can take it from there."

> Mark, the older boy, was whispering in one of those stage whispers, "She's making it up! She's making it up."

## MARK'S STEP-BY-STEP SPIRITUAL EXERCISE

So Mark sat down. And, as Myra tells it, "Like an old hen with one chick, I put my wing around his shoulders, and we started to sing *HU*."

After a while Myra became quiet. Then she described aloud the scene they were to visualize. She said, "We're walking on a beach. Feel the sun's warmth on your body." She took him through this spiritual exercise very nicely, step-by-step. "Notice the wind blowing a breeze that plays with our hair. The silky sand is squishing between our toes."

Very poetic, Myra is. I could feel that when I read this. I said, "Oh, yeah. Boy, I remember those days."

Then she said, "Notice the smell and sound of ocean waves rolling in to shore to kiss the sand at our feet." Very much the poet. She went on, "And look. There's a sailboat appearing on the horizon. Look, it's coming to shore, and there's the Mahanta at the tiller."

She described climbing into the boat. "The Mahanta is sailing the boat to an island. The island has a beautiful crystal castle on it." Myra stopped talking, and they sat quietly. They were listening, listening, still on the edge of the bed.

Then Mark said to her in a soft voice, "Uh, Grandma, what color is that light?" She's very down-to-earth. "What color do you see?" "White." "That's the best," said Myra. "Hush," he said, "it's still there." But Myra knew her moment to strike, and she replied softly, "Now, am I making it up?"

Mark was trying to keep what he'd got going on the inner. He said, "No." No, she wasn't making it up. It was true.

So something was changing here too: Mark. Just like that—a change in consciousness.

*Myra said, "There's a sailboat coming to shore, and there's the Mahanta at the tiller."*

## A FIREFIGHTER IS ASKED
## THE MEANING OF LIFE

Now, this story is about "Lou." He was a firefighter for many years in Nevada. One day a call came in about an attempted suicide. So he and his team of paramedics rushed to the scene.

When they got there, they found a woman in her late thirties. She was sitting on her couch. Her arms were folded, and she was very defiant, glaring at them.

This case was unusual, Lou said, because she confessed that she had tried to take her life. People who attempt suicide will usually say, "Oh, no, it was an accident. I wasn't trying to do that." But this woman fessed right up.

The clock was ticking. She had taken an overdose of pills, and they had to get her to the hospital real quick if they hoped to save her life. One of Lou's firefighters was on his knees in front of her, trying to coax her to get onto the gurney. They didn't want to have to put her there.

She wouldn't go. She said, "I've tried for thirty-five years to find the meaning of life, and I failed. My life is without purpose. I'm miserable, and I want to end it all. I resent all of you people here trying to stop me."

Now Lou, as the captain, had the responsibility to take charge of the situation. So he joined the firefighter at the couch, kneeling in front of the woman, with his eyes below hers so that he wasn't like an imposing authority figure standing above her. He'd learned this in his years of experience and training—to keep his eyes below the level of hers.

Then after a few minutes, she suddenly pinned

*A call came in about an attempted suicide. The clock was ticking.*

him with a challenging gaze. And in a very loud voice, with her finger pointed directly at his face, she said, "You! Can you tell me the meaning of life?"

Lou's mind went in all different directions. He was a little self-conscious, because a small crowd of paramedics and police officers were standing behind him as he was facing the woman on the couch.

Lou was an ECKist. He didn't know what to do, so he released it to the Holy Spirit. And then, just like that, the Holy Spirit, the ECK, blew this fog away and used him to reach this distraught woman.

## HERE TO LEARN HOW TO GIVE AND RECEIVE DIVINE LOVE

As he was wondering what to say, just as clearly as could be a sentence came to mind. He looked into her eyes with love, and he said, "We're here to learn how to give and receive divine love." And the room was very still.

She kept looking into his eyes. Then her face softened, and her eyes filled with tears. Finally, in a soft, quivering voice, she asked, "Are you God?" He shook his head and softly replied, "No, I'm just one of His kids, like you."

At that point her toy poodle came running from across the room and jumped into her lap. Now Lou, being an ECKist, knew that these events were all connected and meant something. And he said, "See, even your little dog wants to give you love." Then, half-turning to the audience behind him, he said, "All of these people care for you too. They want to make sure you don't hurt yourself."

*Lou looked into her eyes with love, and he said, "We're here to learn how to give and receive divine love."*

Then the woman leaned over with tears flowing from her eyes. She gave Lou a big hug. They stood up, he led her to the gurney, and she got on willingly. I'm happy to say, they reached the hospital in time.

A news item I read while preparing for this talk said job satisfaction among firefighters was 83 percent—very, very high. It was among the highest of all the different positions, except for clergy, which was up at 88 percent. A high, high 83 percent for the firefighters' job satisfaction. It's easy to see why.

## MINNOU'S REMINDER TO MEET THE MAHANTA

This is the story of "Alita." She's the mom of Minnou, a cat she's owned for ten years. I have to say, the only name that I haven't changed in these stories is Minnou's. I don't think she'll mind.

During the ten years that Minnou has lived in Alita's home, the Spiritual Exercises of ECK have become very important for Minnou. This is the HU session with the Mahanta, the Inner Master.

Well, Alita had just taken up knitting. She became so engrossed in knitting one day, she knitted clean through the time set aside for the HU session. OK, Minnou forgave her that day, but this HU session is for Minnou too.

You have to understand that animals have a state of consciousness sometimes that is much greater than that of the humans you find around yourself. They have an understanding of human nature—something that is far and away above that of many people. Except animals don't know how to speak; their vocal cords don't lend themselves to it. And they don't write because their paws don't lend

*Animals have a state of consciousness sometimes that is much greater than that of the humans you find around yourself.*

themselves to bending around pencils very well.

So, the next day, Alita was knitting away, totally lost, trying to keep track of the stitches. All of a sudden, Minnou made a meowing sound such as Alita had never heard before. She looked at her cat and asked, "Minnou, what are you saying?" But Alita couldn't break through.

Whenever she and Minnou run into this stalemate, they have a little "show me" exercise they do.

So Alita said, "Show me." And Minnou walked into the bedroom, stopped by the chair, which is Alita's special spiritual-exercise chair, and then looked up into Alita's face very expectantly, waiting for something. Alita thought, *Well, it must be an hour yet before the HU session with the Mahanta. I just can't figure out what Minnou is doing. She must have gotten her time schedule off.*

But then Alita looked at a clock, and she said, "Oh, it's nearly at the end of our session!" Then she realized that Minnou had waited through the whole session. She had let yesterday's slip by, but today she was saying, "No, Mom." Alita realized that Minnou's meows were simply saying, "Hey, it's time. This is the time we meet the Mahanta."

The interesting thing is that around this time Alita had been focusing on a contemplation quote which was dealing with the expression "God is love." And she realized then that Minnou had proved the point.

Well, that too showed a change in consciousness, where change is change, because Alita had to be more aware. She had to reach a higher state of consciousness if she was going to keep knitting and continue the HU sessions. At the same time, Minnou was showing that she understood things about

*Minnou's meows were simply saying, "Hey, it's time. This is the time we meet the Mahanta."*

the spiritual life in a way that Alita had undoubtedly never realized before.

Change in consciousness. Expansion in consciousness.

## Spiritual Kinship with All Life

I mentioned a book in the Fall 1986 *Mystic World*. I took just one little part of it and didn't mention the main character in the book. The book is *Kinship with All Life* by J. Allen Boone. He addresses the kinship which is the spiritual bond that binds all life, all created beings.

We accept humans so easily and well. But there are other beings too, like dogs and cats, and more beyond that: snakes, ants, and even the humble fly. These are all manifestations of the Holy Spirit here on earth. And there are the higher forms of flies and snakes and other animals, and there's a way to communicate with them.

But more than just communicating with animals, essentially the book is about relationships. Now, if you have any trouble at all relating to another human being—and I'm sure one or two among you do—you will find this book very helpful.

*Dogs and cats, snakes, ants, and even the humble fly are all manifestations of the Holy Spirit here on earth.*

## Strongheart and Relationship Secrets

The main character in the book is Strongheart. He was a magnificent dog in Germany between the World Wars. His father had been an international champion police dog. And Strongheart, this German shepherd, was the only one to beat his father in open competition. Just a beautiful dog.

Meanwhile in America, there was a producer-director and a woman who was a screenwriter. Both of them were very well known. They got together and decided they would like to find a special German shepherd who could star in his own movies.

He wouldn't be just one of the bit players. Those were a dime a dozen at that time, in the early 1920s. There were a lot of movies with a smart dog running around doing great things. But they wanted a special dog.

And so they searched. They looked and looked, and they finally decided on Strongheart. But that was not his name yet. He had a German name at the time.

They brought the dog to the United States because he was handsome, very intelligent, capable, and trained in police and military work. They were bringing Strongheart to see if he would be able to learn how to become an actor. And so they undertook the further education of Strongheart.

Now, this beautiful animal was unknown in the United States. Only a few who were into dog shows knew he was special. When he traveled from New York to Los Angeles on his way to Hollywood, he was in a baggage car just like any other dog. But just a little more than a year later, Strongheart had his own special section on the train. He had his own valet, his own press agent, his own marketing agent, and a special representative of the railroad to make sure that he got the best of everything. Strongheart was the number-one attraction in movies for three years.

How did Strongheart and J. Allen Boone get together? How did this work out?

J. Allen Boone did not want his quiet life interrupted by a dog. And this dog was huge. He weighed anywhere from a hundred fifteen to a hundred twenty-five pounds. But he was fast and agile. And he could do things with ease that other dogs had

*J. Allen Boone did not want his quiet life interrupted by a dog. And this dog was huge.*

never done before.

Well, Boone learned to communicate with this dog. And he passes along the secret in this book. And as Joan has pointed out, not only is the secret in this book, but at the end of the book there is a second secret. So if you've got the curiosity, I invite you to look into this book, *Kinship with All Life*, by J. Allen Boone.

I would like to thank you for coming. I always enjoy being with you. And indeed I am always with you. May the blessings be.

*Boone learned to communicate with this dog. And he passes along the secret in this book.*

*ECK Worldwide Seminar, Minneapolis, Minnesota*
*Saturday, October 20, 2007*

The sound of HU came from this owl in his dream.
Ever since, Carlos has been tuned in to the Sound Current.

# 4

# THE TENSIONS OF LIVING

*O*ne of the things I got together for this talk on the tensions of living was a *Far Side* cartoon. I don't know if you're familiar with Gary Larson, but some of his cartoons are really from the far side.

## PARLIAMENT OF HORSES

This cartoon shows a parliament, as in England. There are four rows of seats, four tiers. This is a parliament where the members are all horses, about forty different horses.

There's a look of consternation on all of the faces. Down front is where the speaker is standing. Somebody's bringing in the vote tallies and telling the speaker how the votes came out this time.

Now, again, this is a parliament of horses. The caption reads, "The entire parliament fell dead silent. For the first time since anyone could remember, one of the members voted 'aye.'"

Gary Larson works on several layers of meaning at once sometimes. His cartoons can be treacherous.

But what's even funnier, I happened to look at the eyes of all the horses. The ones sitting in the back row are looking down at somebody. In the third row, the ones on one side of this certain horse are looking to the right. Others in that row are looking to the left. The ones in the front two rows have got their heads back, and they're rolling their eyes upward.

Then it finally dawned on me who they are looking at. Way back in the third row, off-center a little bit, there's a horse with a silly smile on his face. The tensions of living—you can believe there was a little bit of tension there. Gary Larson is such a funny man. I've got all of his books.

Joan reads for us in the evening—our hour of pleasure. Right before we go to bed, when we've finished our reading, sometimes I select one, two, or three of Larson's cartoons that I think are really funny. And that often makes us late for bed, because either Joan can understand a cartoon, or I can understand it. Sometimes we can both understand it, but there are times neither of us can.

It makes for tension. We're trying to get to bed and sleep, but there's a tension of living: trying to go to sleep wondering, *What did that cartoon mean?*

## THE ZEN MASTER SAID, "WE'LL SEE"

There was a Zen master. He had a small band of followers who looked to him for guidance. One of them had a small son. This son wanted a horse very badly. So, after some time, the parents were able to get the money together, and they got him a horse.

His friends said, "That's good!" But the Zen master said, "We'll see."

*The parents got this son a horse. His friends said, "That's good!" But the Zen master said, "We'll see."*

Some years later, when he was fifteen years old, the young man was riding his horse. As he was riding, he fell off and broke his leg. It mended poorly so that he always walked with a limp.

His friends said, "That's bad." The Zen master said, "We'll see."

Then war broke out. Anybody who was eligible to be drafted was drafted. Young men from the neighborhood all had to go, except for this young man who had injured himself during the fall from his horse.

So when the neighbors and friends heard that the young man was exempt because of his leg, they said, "That's wonderful!" The Zen master said, "We'll see."

Tension. What did this Zen master mean? It didn't seem to bode well. But that's life.

The other day on the radio, I heard someone talking about a writer. He said the tensions of life are very real because no one knows what's going to happen in the next three hours. That's how it is when you don't know what's going to happen, what's to come. Life is a delicious morsel, because you never know really what's going to happen.

At certain times in your life, things are more up in the air than at other times. When they are, you're living on the edge. Your nerves are frayed, or sometimes you're being pushed too fast for what you can do. If you don't get it done, you wonder, then what? Because you don't know.

These are the tensions of living.

This is what the world is for. It's a place filled with such tensions. Why? Because it's the nature of karma. This is a schoolroom. It's a garden, really. It's a garden where everyone can grow spiritually according to his own lights.

*Life is a delicious morsel, because you never know really what's going to happen.*

Each of us here is growing—*unfolding* is more proper—at our own spiritual pace. I'll even go so far as to say that the Holy Spirit is directing each of our lives. It will lead you, and has led you, into the very life and circumstances that you need—the circumstances which are very good for you. You may not think so, but they're very good for you. Maybe not materially or emotionally or mentally, but spiritually they're very good for you.

Sometimes these tensions of living are most strong when people first hear about Eckankar and consider becoming a member. It seems that whenever you've got the decision to make, so many things are standing in the way that make it very hard for you to say "aye" to Eckankar.

## A MINISTER'S HARD DECISION

There's an evangelical minister in the Philippines. I'll call him "Carlos." (All the names here are pseudonyms.) He served his congregation for eighteen years, and he recently came into Eckankar. But now he's got a very hard decision to make. So far, nobody knows that he's an ECKist. So the question he faces is, should he quit his congregation, or his church, or should he continue to serve it? In other words, should he continue to serve it as an ECKist?

*Four years before coming into Eckankar, Carlos had a prophetic dream about his future in the ministry.*

About four years before coming into Eckankar, Carlos had a prophetic dream about his future in the ministry. He was down in a ravine with a few others. There was no way to get up, no way to get down.

Suddenly, a giant brown hand came over the top of the ravine. It was holding a golden chain. It let the chain down in front of Carlos. He grasped hold of it, and this hand pulled him up to the top of the ravine. He found himself on top of an enormous plateau. It was like a big pastureland, and Carlos was the only one up there.

Later, he thought about it, and he said, "Well, this dream is pointing me to a very hard decision to come." But that decision was still pending.

In the meantime, he had another dream. This time he was working in his grain field. An owl flew up, landed on a fence post right in front of him, and began to sing *HU*. "HU-U-U-U."

We have a couple of owls at home, and they come by every few weeks to see what they can catch at night. We hear the owls quite often. Maybe some of you do too. I always feel a kinship with the owl.

I also feel compassion for the object of his being there, because he's looking for his prey, of course. But such is the nature of life. The big and the strong eat the little. Or sometimes the little eat the big. Everybody's here in this world of karma, eating or devouring something. Because that's the nature of life.

## How the Holy Spirit Speaks

Carlos was overwhelmed by the sound of HU. And it came from this owl in his dream. Ever since, he's been tuned in to the Sound Current. Before that, he was tuned in to the Light. He could always see the Light. But since the dream with the owl in the grain field, now he can also hear the Sound of God.

We in Eckankar know that the Holy Spirit manifests Itself in the form of Light and Sound. This is how It speaks. And sometimes It compels someone to appear to the seeker in human form. It can be an angel. It can be an ECK Master. It

*Everybody's here in this world of karma, eating or devouring something. Because that's the nature of life.*

can be another master or holy man—anybody.

But this will be one level or one power of the Holy Spirit coming through. The degree of power that comes through will exactly fit the state of consciousness of the seeker to whom this individual appears. The Mahanta, the Living ECK Master, or the Inner Master in Eckankar, embodies the Light and Sound of God at the highest levels. This is a great blessing when he comes into your life.

Sometimes you'll see the Light of God in many colors, many forms. I've mentioned these before, but colors range all the way from pink to orange to lavender to blues. And then they go on into the yellows and the high yellows, into the pure white. The yellows and the whites are the pure spiritual God planes. Below that are the colors in the mental worlds. Below that, the emotional worlds. Those are the colors.

The Sound also varies. It can be anything from the sound of an orchestra to a violin, a bird, or people singing. It can be the sound of rain, a storm, or wind. It can be anything of this nature coming to you in your quiet moments.

So now Carlos faces a very hard decision. In the meantime, he continues to preach to his congregation. He's doing it now from the expanded point of view. His sermons have more depth, more breadth. His congregation is definitely benefiting from the kind of help that he is able to give them spiritually in his sermons.

The tensions of life. What should he do? Well, that's up to Carlos. A hard, hard decision. I don't think any of us who are in Eckankar envy him, because for many of you it was just that difficult too.

*Sometimes you'll see the Light of God in many colors, many forms.*

## CLAIRE'S TRUST AND THE BIG WHITE VAN

This is something that happened at an ECK Springtime Seminar a couple of years ago. It's an example of how the Mahanta, the Inner Master, can make things work out even though something seems impossible. If it's to be, and if the individual has absolute faith and trust in this divine power to do what needs to be done, well, then it will be done. And it's as simple as that.

"Melody" flew in from Canada, and at the end of that seminar she met "Claire." Claire was from the Ivory Coast, where there would soon be an ECK regional seminar. Since books take anywhere from six to eight months to arrive there by ship, Claire thought she'd do well to buy a stock of books at the ECK seminar. Then she'd pack them in her luggage and take them back so they'd be available for the ECK regional seminar. Just in case the ones coming by boat got delayed or lost.

So she made the purchase, picked up the boxes of books, and went back to the motel. Melody and a friend of hers helped Claire by unpacking the boxes filled with all these ECK books.

At the same time, Claire was packing the books in between her clothes so they wouldn't get damaged. She had already made arrangements with the airline to transport all her luggage. There turned out to be seven large, heavy bags.

Melody was a little bit concerned about this. She said, "How are you going to get those to the airport?" A regular taxi was far too small. And the airport shuttle wasn't going to work either, because there would be so many people on it they wouldn't be able to load all her luggage. So they weren't quite sure how to arrange this.

*If it's to be, and if the individual has absolute faith and trust in this divine power to do what needs to be done, well, then it will be done.*

But Claire and Melody went ahead and volunteered at the ECK seminar in one capacity or another. Claire didn't worry about it at all. She said, "The Mahanta will take care of it. When the time comes, he will provide a way for us to get there." And that was it.

After the seminar, on Monday morning, Melody, Claire, and a couple of friends were in the restaurant at the motel. They were having breakfast, and they were there for a good hour.

All of a sudden, Melody looked out the restaurant window, and she happened to notice a white van sitting there. On the side it said Airport Taxi. Melody said, "Look at that!"

So they jumped up right away and ran out to the van. Melody explained the whole situation to the driver. She said, "This is Claire. She's from the Ivory Coast. She's got to leave here at nine o'clock in the morning, with seven large bags. She needs to get to the airport on time and make her flight. Can you do it?" The driver said, "My name is Abraham. I happen to be director of the company. I will be here at nine o'clock, and we'll get her and her luggage to the airport on time." And so it was.

*Melody realized it's all about surrender. This incident showed her the Mahanta was there. It increased her love for the Inner Master.*

## IT'S ALL ABOUT SURRENDER

Later, Melody was thinking about these coincidences that the Mahanta had put together. The main coincidence was the van appearing after they had wondered and wondered how to get past this problem of transportation. How were they going to get to the airport with all that luggage? Well, this was all handled for them.

Melody realized it's all about surrender. This incident showed her the Mahanta was there. It increased her love for the Inner Master.

This is one of the realities that occur in Eckankar all the time. But you have to notice them. A lot of times we don't notice these things. They're happening, but our eyes are shut to them.

When they happen, we sometimes shut our eyes to them because we think something bad is happening to us. When actually it's very good for us spiritually. Just as the Zen master was pointing out. When we think something's wrong, there's tension. It may be actually very right.

*When we think something's wrong, there's tension. It may be actually very right.*

## Choosing Names

This is the story of "Haruni." I have fun making up these names to protect people's privacy. I try different names, and then usually I'll take a name that is very spiritual. I have a book that gives character names for people who are writing novels and the like. It has cross-indexes and gives names for people of every culture, and for Africans in general. It doesn't get into specific countries. It has some names from the English-speaking countries, and then it has some Indian ones, some for black Americans, American Indians, and even Eskimos. It's just fantastic.

I'll go through the book, and I'll look for a name that matches where the person is from. Then I'll try to find a name that is very spiritual for the individual, or one that matches the spirit of his story. So I have a lot of fun picking names like Haruni.

## Haruni's Mechanic Has a Dream

Haruni is Nigerian. He was having a lot of car troubles. Nearly every day, he went to his mechanic with one problem or another. The main problem with the car was that whenever Haruni would try to drive up even a very low hill, the car would sputter and barely make it to the top. Sometimes it would jerk. The whole ride was not very smooth.

Haruni used to like his car, but when this mysterious problem came along, he was having second thoughts, getting tired of the nearly daily visits to his mechanic. Yet his mechanic and his whole team were doing the very best they could, trying to figure out this problem. They set and reset the valves, and then they serviced the carburetor several times. They did this very thoroughly. And then they replaced the rings.

During all this time, Haruni had surrendered this problem to the Mahanta in a general way during his contemplation exercises. He didn't think it was necessary to be really specific. But finally he said to the Inner Master, "Show me exactly what's wrong with this car so that I can go over to my mechanic and tell him what's wrong, and then he can get the right parts and fix it, instead of doing all this fishing about."

So with this in mind, he went to sleep that night, having asked the Mahanta for the whole business: to show him everything.

The next morning, he woke up. He hadn't had a dream, and he knew the car would be acting up as usual. So he got in the car and took the same tired route over to his mechanic. He didn't have any dream to report; he had no wise words for the mechanic. He just figured the Mahanta would give him the information he needed in good time.

When the mechanic saw Haruni drive into the lot, he came up with a very confident look on his face. He said, "I know exactly what's wrong with

*The mechanic said, "A white man came to me in a dream last night, and he showed me everything that needs to be done to fix your car."*

your car." Now remember, this is Nigeria. The mechanic said, "A white man came to me in a dream last night, and he showed me everything that needs to be done to fix your car."

When Haruni heard that, he said, "Everything will be fine now." He knew the man in the mechanic's dream was the Inner Master.

Then the mechanic gave all kinds of orders to the other mechanics in the shop. He said to get such-and-such parts, and to get such-and-such tools. They brought all these things, and then the master mechanic set to work on the car.

Sure enough, the car worked, as Haruni knew it would. It had happened in good time, when the Master was ready, and when Haruni looked at his problem more specifically and asked for help more specifically. This then ended Haruni's many daily trips to his mechanic. And after that, he again loved his little car.

The tensions of living. There was certainly a lot of tension for the mechanic, trying to fix something that was more than he could figure out.

*The car worked. It happened when the Master was ready, and when Haruni looked at his problem more specifically.*

## CAR TALK AND OTHER TENSIONS

I've mentioned a radio program that airs here in Minnesota and across the nation. It's *Car Talk*, featuring Click and Clack, the Tappet Brothers. They are car mechanics who do an hour-long call-in show every week, and they are both very funny men. They've got a good screener who finds callers who often have a great sense of humor. It's a good show, and my wife and I try to catch it every weekend, because it works right in with our schedule at home.

They come up with so many situations where

there is tension—tension of the caller, trying to figure something out. And then Click and Clack work their way toward the solution, sometimes disagreeing with each other, sometimes agreeing. One brother will make a good point. Then the other brother will say, "Oh, yeah, I see what you mean. Yeah, it could be that." And on they go.

It's very interesting because these tensions of living are all around everywhere, all the time. From visiting a car mechanic, or a dentist, or a doctor, to a child going to school and wondering, *What's going to happen in the school yard today?* Or sometimes worrying, *Will my pet be OK?*

There are all these things that are constantly causing tensions to living. And these tensions gradually shape us, and make us, and bake us until we're done.

*These tensions gradually shape us, and make us, and bake us until we're done.*

## An Ecotour Guide's Lessons

This story is about "Ginger." She's from Florida, and she recently retired. Since then, she's been working as an ecotour guide.

One of these tours is designed so that the tourists will leave as small an imprint on the environment as possible. In other words, they may go in and look at the land or parks, but they'll try to leave no trace of themselves. They don't want to damage the ecology. They even try to improve it.

Anyway, Ginger joined a group of ten other guides. It was the start of a new school session, and a class of handicapped children wanted to go on one of the tours. Now, these kids were physically, emotionally, and mentally handicapped in one way or another. The tour boss said to these tour guides, "Would anyone like to volunteer for this tour?"

No hands went up, because none of them felt really sure that they were capable of doing a thorough job. How do you work with so many kids who are not just physically handicapped, but also emotionally and mentally handicapped, all together in one group? How do you work with such a broad range of consciousness? The tour guides weren't thinking in those words, of course. They were just wondering, Are we up to it? They didn't think so.

So the tour boss said, "Well, Ginger, I'm going to assign them to you. Would you do it?" Ginger said, "I'd be happy to." Except that wasn't quite so. Ginger had the same doubts that the others had. Besides that, she was the newest one there. She had just led a couple of tours so far, and they'd gone OK, but this was a big step. So she wasn't real sure.

This tour was to take place Monday morning, and Ginger had a lot of time to get ready for it. She got prepared and went to the rendezvous area very early on Monday morning. She had set everything up. Now she was ready.

The phone rang. It was the teacher at the school. She said, "The school board has canceled this tour because they feel it would be too dangerous for these children to be near the water." The location was somewhere near the Gulf of Mexico. And Ginger said, "But we're not going to be anywhere near the water." The teacher said, "It's too late to reschedule this tour because there are just too many board members to get hold of, and then we'll need time to see if we can reach a consensus. It's too late for today. But I'll get back to you if something turns up."

Later that very same day, the teacher called the tour boss and said, "Once the school board

*The tour boss said, "Ginger, I'm going to assign them to you. Would you do it?" Ginger said, "I'd be happy to." Except that wasn't quite so.*

heard the tour wasn't near water, they said everything was OK, and you can go ahead with the tour.
So, when's a good time for you? We can be there
on Thursday morning." The tour boss asked Ginger,
"Are you up to it?" Ginger said, "Sure, I'll do it."

## Ginger's Inner Preparation

Ginger had done her spiritual exercises in the
meantime. She wondered, *What did I miss? Why
was this tour canceled on Monday?* And then she
realized she had prepared everything except herself—spiritually. She hadn't asked the Inner Master, the Mahanta, what she should do to prepare.

During her spiritual exercise, the Master now
said to her, "Open your heart. Invite these kids on
the inner planes." And Ginger did. Then, all the
way to the rendezvous point on Thursday morning,
she also sang *HU*. She sang *HU* the whole way.

A little bit later, the bus came and dropped the
kids off. Ginger and the kids got along fine. They
were completely comfortable with each other. The
tour turned out to be a smashing success.

The teacher was so happy that she wrote an
email to Ginger's boss and said how grateful she
was for the care and consideration that Ginger had
shown for the children. And the children had loved
it. They would like to do it again.

Such commendations didn't come in often, so the
boss forwarded the email to all the other tour guides.
One of the other tour guides came up to Ginger and
asked, "What did you do to make that work?"

Ginger didn't have much time to tell her right
at that moment, but she said, "I did a spiritual
exercise. This is how I did it. Then I sang *HU*."
She mentioned things like open your heart, in-

*The tour turned
out to be a
smashing
success.*

wardly invite the kids during the spiritual exercise, and sing *HU* all the way to the rendezvous point.

Then Ginger gave the tour guide a *HU: A Love Song to God* CD. She said, "Here's a CD. You can listen to it yourself so you know how it goes." Now another teacher had been touched by this.

So Ginger's lessons included such things as open your heart, listen to the Inner Master, and above all, be grateful for the blessings the Master gives you.

Later, Ginger had another tour. This was with a group of children who had no handicaps at all. Ginger did the same thing as she had before, with the same results. And this group's teacher, too, wrote a note to the tour boss and said, "The kids had a wonderful time. We'd like to do this again. We'd like to commend Ginger because she was so open."

This technique worked for Ginger whether it was used for one category of children or another category. I'm sure she found that it would work even when there were adults in the tours. It will always work—if she keeps her heart open, invites people to come during her spiritual exercise, and sings *HU* all the way there.

*This technique will always work—if Ginger keeps her heart open, invites people to come during her spiritual exercise, and sings HU all the way there.*

## DINA HELPS A BATTERED WOMAN

This story is about "Dina." She is a financial planner who also volunteers as a life-skills teacher at a shelter for battered women. Once in a while the staff at the shelter ask her to help prepare a woman who is just about ready to go out and be on her own. Would Dina help this woman become financially savvy?

This is how Dina met "Sally." Sally said she was having terrible anxiety attacks. The tensions of living. She had gone through an awful experience with her previous mate. Sally wondered if Dina could help her with her anxiety attacks.

Then the voice of the Inner Master came to Dina very clearly. He said, "Share the HU with her." And Dina did. She shared the word. But Dina felt her voice wasn't very good, and she was hesitant to just sing *HU*, because she thought her voice would break and go off-key.

## A DEMONSTRATION OF HU

But when she sang *HU*, her voice came out strong and clear and on key. Everything was just right. Dina was surprised, but it was the very best demonstration of HU for Sally.

Then, Dina saw a wave of Sound and Light moving through Sally from her head to her toes. Sally said, "Wow, that was amazing!" She wondered what had happened.

Dina explained to her what had happened—that the Holy Spirit of ECK, Divine Spirit, had come into her.

Dina learned, observing Sally's life over the next few months, that Sally did very, very well. She was doing just fine, and she was making her way on her own.

*Dina realized that when the Master has need of you, he will give you all the tools you need.*

Dina realized then that when the Master has need of you, he will give you all the tools that you need. He will give you all the tools you need.

## DINA'S HORSE SAYS "NAY" TO LOVE

Dina also has a horse. She calls her horse Babe. Dina got an insight into divine love through an experience with Babe.

One day, Dina was feeling really down-and-out, feeling really sorry for herself. So she went out into the paddock where Babe was.

Dina came up to Babe and whispered in her ear, "Do you love me?" The horse looked at her and vigorously shook its head as if to say, "Nay." Well, I don't know if Babe *said* "nay" exactly, but anyway she was *thinking* "nay."

And then Babe turned and walked away from Dina. Dina, of course, was crushed. She needed love. She thought if she asked Babe—her horse, the one she takes care of all the time—if she just talked to Babe, certainly Babe would affirm this love and maybe say, "Aye." If a horse dare say that.

## NO STRINGS ATTACHED

Dina was feeling even more sorry for herself than she had before. But then she threw back her shoulders and quietly called after Babe. She said, "That's OK. I love you anyway with all my heart and being." Babe stopped in her tracks, turned around, came back, and stood by Dina's side.

*Dina quietly called after Babe, "That's OK. I love you anyway with all my heart and being." Babe stopped in her tracks.*

I think we all know the kind of love that has strings attached. Sometimes we have done it, or we do it. Then other people, if they're sensitive at all, will shy away. They don't want to be near such a person, because it's suffocating. In a way, it's almost a form of black magic because it takes life away from someone else.

Dina realized that the love she had expressed, when she said to Babe, "I love you with all my heart and being" was divine love. Divine love means no strings attached, no need to have love given back—just pure divine love.

This is the nature of real love. No strings attached.

*Above all,
be grateful for
the blessings
the Master
gives you.*

I'd like to again go through the different things we touched on tonight in "The Tensions of Living." The Zen master said, "We'll see." Then, an evangelical minister's very hard decision; and that decision is still to come. Then the big white van that, through circumstances and coincidences, was available right at the time it was needed. Also, Haruni's car mechanic has a special dream. Then an ecotour guide's lessons, which included such things as open your heart, listen to the Inner Master, and above all, be grateful for the blessings the Master gives you. Then Dina helps a battered woman gain self-sufficiency and be able to stand on her own. Also, Dina's horse says "nay" to love.

And so we come to the end of the talk this evening. May the blessings be.

*ECK Springtime Seminar, Minneapolis, Minnesota
Saturday, March 22, 2008*

The two- and three-year-old children saw immediately what was happening. They said, "It's a gift from God to you."

# 5
# SHIFTING GEARS

hen you're ready for the ECK
teachings, they'll make sense. And if
you're not ready for them, they just won't
click. So don't worry about it. If you feel
comfortable with them, OK. And if you don't, OK.
It's perfectly fine.

I like people, and I enjoy being around them,
whether they're ECKists or not. Often we have
good conversations.

## GROCERY-STORE CONVERSATIONS

I was in the grocery store, minding my own
business, and all of a sudden I heard this person
talking. I looked, and there was a woman beside
me. She was talking away, but she was looking at
the vegetables.

This was interesting. So I looked at her and
said, "Did you say something?"

She realized she had been talking to herself,
and she got very apologetic. She said, "Excuse me.
I just forgot myself."

I said, "That's OK, we all do that." If we're
honest, most of us will fess up. Sometimes our lips
move, sometimes they don't, but we're talking in
there.

Then, to put her at ease, I said, "In fact, some of the most interesting conversations have been with myself."

Another time, I was looking through the apples, going through them very carefully. Someone standing very quietly, two apple bins over, suddenly said, "I've never seen crab apples that you could eat."

When I looked, I recognized a woman I hadn't seen in a very long time. She's Irish with a French name—a very nice person—quiet inside. It was good to see her and chat with her.

I enjoy people. I realize that when I'm talking with them, the ECK, the Holy Spirit, is touching them in some way. Whatever way that is is fine. I don't stand there and say, "Hey, it's time for you to be in Eckankar."

People are of all kinds. This is a world where God has put a bunch of Souls together, just casually strewn them about and said, Let's see if they can walk with each other, bump into each other, fight each other, whatever they want to do.

You'll find these kinds of friendly, indifferent, or antagonistic relations between people and nations. They change from time to time.

We're always shifting gears.

## THE GOOD TIMES, THE BAD TIMES

For those of you who have come into Eckankar, you'll find you're shifting gears a lot, all the time. It can be for small things; it can be for large things. Even people not in Eckankar are always shifting gears. They're healthy, then not so healthy; able to run, then not able to run. All different kinds of things: they're young, then they're old—shifting gears. They're happy, then they're sad—they're shifting gears.

*People are always shifting gears. They're healthy, then not so healthy; able to run, then not able to run. They're young, then they're old—shifting gears. Happy, then sad—shifting gears.*

It's always shifting gears, going from one state to the other. That's how it is.

I would like to mention that for your privacy, all the names I'm going to use tonight are fictitious. Sometimes I go to a little character book for writers that I have, with names that are country specific. Or I just settle on easy names I make up myself.

The economic crisis that's going on now is certainly a shifting of gears from just a couple of weeks ago. The market's been diving, diving, diving. It's interesting. Before the market crash on October 29, 1929—Black Tuesday—it was the Roaring Twenties. The whiskey, the good times, and the money were flowing freely. And then all of a sudden the market crashed.

The first "black day" in the stock market was all the way back in 1869. September 24, 1869, was called Black Friday. That was the first one, and ever since they've been called black days whenever the market takes such a dip.

Between the Roaring Twenties and the Great Depression—shifting gears, very much so.

And what overcame the Great Depression? Was it the New Deal? Roosevelt's New Deal helped a little. But what helped most was when the United States went to a wartime economy in the early 1940s. Suddenly there were jobs.

Shifting gears, shifting gears.

*What overcame the Great Depression? What helped most was when the United States went to a wartime economy. Shifting gears.*

I was just a little kid then, at the end of the war. I can remember when the war was over, our family went to get a radio—just an ordinary table-model radio. A lot of things had not been available during the war—things like radios, refrigerators, cars, and tractors. Everything went for wartime production.

People had saved their money because there was nothing to buy. When the war was over, and America began to produce the regular things again—like radios, refrigerators, and cars—then people bought and bought and bought.

It was a relief after the war years of having to do without. Shifting gears.

All these different things are going on, all the time. And we find ourselves shifting gears. We may be doing it as a group, as a group of nations, as is happening during this economic downturn now. Everyone's worried about a recession.

The leaders, some of whom got us into this mess, are now saying they're going to get us out of it. And you say, "Oh, yeah. Right. Good luck." You sit there and shake your head.

## SPIRITUAL PURIFICATION

These things don't just happen. They are caused by people acting as unconscious agents of the negative power, the Kal. People don't understand.

So often they ask, why does God let Kal, or Satan, go on like this?

Well, the reason is because when all these things are set into motion—the good times, the bad times— it's in the shifting of gears from one state to another that spiritual purification occurs.

I find, too, in looking at the leaders of a country—whether it's a democracy or some kind of totalitarian regime or whatever—the people under the rule of leaders like that are there because there are certain lessons to learn right then. There are things to learn.

So sometimes they go through years and years of hardship. Like the people in the Soviet Union

*It's in the shifting of gears from one state to another that spiritual purification occurs.*

under Stalin, who went through years of it, and then they came out. Maybe they get a breather for a short time, and sometimes it's all too short a breather.

## THE YEAR OF THANKSGIVING

This spiritual year is The Year of Thanksgiving.

We're just about ready to go into November. In America, we celebrate Thanksgiving. It's one of the most enjoyable holidays for me, simply because it's not weighed down by all the gift giving.

There's nothing wrong with gifts. But when people overextend themselves—especially in a year like this, when they don't know where they're going to find the money to buy the presents to make everybody happy—well, it's hard.

Thanksgiving. It's a time to give thanks. A time to be glad to be alive, to be grateful for the blessings that we have while we're here.

Some people celebrate with turkey dinners and so on. That's fine; that's good. It's people being with people. And what do they do when they're with each other? Well, they have food; they eat and drink, and everyone has a good time being with friends.

It's a good time. It's a shift, certainly, from the rest of the year, when everybody is spread out from here to there and everywhere. And finally at Thanksgiving, they all come together.

*Thanksgiving. It's a time to be glad to be alive, to be grateful for the blessings we have while we're here.*

## HOW THE ECK FINDS DAVID

I'd like to mention to people who are new to ECK how some of the ECKists found Eckankar.

This first story is about "David." He's from South Africa, and he made his first contact, unknowingly, with Eckankar when he happened to work at the same hospital where a High Initiate of Eckankar worked. He used to see her sometimes at the subway station, right outside the hospital.

At the time, David was a born-again Christian. He was working in the hospital's maintenance department. As a born-again Christian, he would fast. But on his fast days he'd say inwardly, "God doesn't talk to us. We cannot see His light. It was only shown to His prophets, and only during biblical times."

So David felt lost, wondering whether he could himself ever see the Light. What struck him then was seeing this woman from work at the subway station. It seemed as if a light was shining upon her. He looked, and every day the light got brighter. One day, he talked to one of his coworkers. He said, "Do you see that bright light around that woman?" But his colleague couldn't see it.

*It seemed as if a light was shining upon her. And every day the light got brighter.*

Well, David wondered about that. In the meantime, he changed jobs and went to some other place. Then at some point, he came across an ECK book that gave a phone number to call to contact someone from Eckankar.

For some reason, the ECK teachings just seemed right to him. He called the number, and a woman answered the phone. She said, "Sure, come on over to the ECK Center." So he went over. He was looking forward very much to learning more about Eckankar. And guess who he saw at the ECK Center? It was the Higher Initiate from the hospital.

Then he remembered. He said to himself, "Oh, yeah, this is the woman at the subway station with the light shining upon her." So this is how David found Eckankar. But in a very real sense, the ECK found David.

Now, his life didn't go easy after that. He went through all kinds of things. His marriage didn't make it. But one time his former wife got in touch with him and said every time she dreams, she sees him. And of course, he saw her too. Where this goes, nobody knows.

So this was how David found ECK.

## PUTTING THE PIECES TOGETHER

Past lives can leave one with all kinds of hidden memories that are harmful to one spiritually. After many lifetimes, these things get buried so very deeply that the individual doesn't realize they're there. It may be a feeling of hostility toward authority or some figure in authority. And the individual doesn't understand why he has this feeling of antipathy.

I like the word *antipathy*. It has a certain sound to it. At home I sit in my workplace—which is my rocking chair, by the way. I work there, I eat there, I do everything there, because it's just handy. The radio is at arm's length if I want. I've got all kinds of books around, especially a dictionary and an encyclopedia.

I'm always going into the dictionary. Somebody will pronounce a word on the radio, and it sounds off to me. I'll say, "How is that word pronounced?" So I'll check it and find that the word has two or maybe three different pronunciations. Sometimes the person used the first one, sometimes the second one; sometimes even a third pronunciation.

Then I just decide, Which one am I going to use?

The one I'm comfortable with. Why not? Because it seems to be intelligible; otherwise it wouldn't be in the dictionary.

Other times I'll be checking the encyclopedia for a condition of some sort I want to look up. I

*Past lives can leave one with all kinds of hidden memories that are harmful to one spiritually.*

have a one-volume encyclopedia where I sit and a full set in another room. I'm not online, so I don't have the advantage of Googling something and getting all kinds of information.

I do things mostly the old-fashioned way, simply because of my sensitivity to electromagnetic radiation. I've got devices to help. Many of you have sent ideas and things over the years. Some worked well, some didn't work at all.

Joan and I are similar in that if there is high electromagnetic radiation, we get sick very quickly. But we've been building up stamina to where we can withstand more. So that's heartening. Because for a number of years, it was very rough going— very, very, very rough going.

Now we're slowly putting the pieces back together, and there are a lot of pieces to put back together. I feel like Humpty Dumpty sometimes.

When you get about our age, you find that you're always shifting gears. All of a sudden something comes up. You've never seen that symptom before. And sometimes they can be frightening. You say, "Oh, no. What's this now?" Or you go to the doctor, and he says you've got this or that.

Then you realize time is marching on, and as the years pass, you have to shift gears. Conditions change. And so you have to learn to change with them.

There was an article about Paul Newman, the actor, in the *Economist* when he translated (died) a while ago. He absolutely did not care how he looked when he aged. He just figured, *If somebody wants me to be in another one of their movies, they're going to have to take me as I am*. And that was it.

He donated all the proceeds from his popular Newman's Own line of salad dressing and other food products. He kept nothing. He was one of those

*I do things mostly the old-fashioned way, simply because of my sensitivity to electromagnetic radiation.*

very honest people, and he had these incredible blue eyes. Often he'd wear sunglasses so people couldn't see his eyes, because they were dazzling, like sapphires I suppose. And people would then make something of him that he didn't want to be. He was very much down-to-earth.

An excellent actor, a lot of fun. He shifted gears nicely. He accepted aging. He didn't fight it. He took it in stride. He took everything in stride.

## A PAST LIFE WITH WILLIAM THE CONQUEROR

Sometimes past lives can leave people with all kinds of deeply buried hostilities. If they'll let the Mahanta, the Living ECK Master help them release these things so they can move on spiritually in their lives, then the Master will set up some situation where this can come about.

Some years ago, "Tom" went to an ECK regional seminar, and its theme was past lives. While there, he had this strong feeling he had been a poor peasant in old England, and that a king had come through and taken his cow.

*Tom had this strong feeling he had been a poor peasant in old England, and that a king had come through and taken his cow.*

This was a death sentence in those days, because the cow was a source of food for a peasant and his family. This had happened during the time that William the Conqueror came up from Normandy, which is in the northwest part of France. He came into England and laid waste to the land. The king's men killed cattle and burned fields.

So Tom wondered about this. He said, "I wonder who that king was."

Some friends came over to visit him. These people were from England, and that's when Tom had a strong urge to look into the history of England to find out who that king was. He got nine books. He went crazy; he just bought history books on old England. Then he bought one called *Domesday: A Search for the Roots of England.*

*Domesday*, or sometimes *Doomsday*, was actually the record of a census William the Conqueror carried out. After he conquered England, he wanted to see how much land he had, what use was being made of it, and what other economic resources were there. This was about twenty years after the Battle of Hastings in 1066, when he beat the Anglo-Saxons in England. But when the Anglo-Saxons were being beaten and the Normans came in, William the Conqueror had waged total warfare. He had his men burn the wheat, kill the cattle and any beasts of burden—total warfare.

It was pretty much the same thing General Sherman did, centuries later, in his march through Georgia during the American Civil War. They laid waste to everything they couldn't use. Because this would break the back of the enemy. This was how it was.

And of course, people hated Sherman for it. Even years later they hated him for it, just as our friend Tom was hating this king who had caused all this trouble.

So Tom read this book, looking for the answer. Who was this king? He wasn't sure yet if it was William the Conqueror. But then his eye fell on the deathbed confession of the king. This is where the king confessed all and told what happened when he first came to England, right after the Battle of Hastings.

Tom read, "I fell on the English of the northern shires like a ravening lion. I commanded their houses and corn [meaning wheat], with all their

> Who was this king? Then Tom's eye fell on the deathbed confession.

implements and chattels, to be burnt without distinction, and great herds of cattle and beasts of burden to be butchered wherever they are found."

And right away, this flood of hostility came out of Tom. This must have been the king. But then Tom wondered, *Did I really live there?*

A few days later, he happened to look at the cover of this book about the census. The illustration on the front was of a peasant farmer milking his cow. That rang a bell, and Tom said, "Oh, yes. This was me, and that was William the Conqueror."

As soon as he recognized this flood of hostility coming out through him, then the Master was able to start working with him so he could let go of it and move on with his spiritual life.

*The Master was able to start working with him so he could let go and move on with his spiritual life.*

This is how it goes all the time. There are all these considerations. The spiritual life, always the spiritual life. This is the concern of the Mahanta, the Living ECK Master. How can you reach people so that they can shift gears and go into a higher state of consciousness? He does the best he can. He reaches out.

But a person can only receive the gift if his consciousness is as great as the gift. Usually he has to grow into it, because his consciousness is far, far short of the gift that's being offered to him.

## ANDY'S UPS AND DOWNS WITH SELF-ESTEEM

"Andy" is from West Africa. He was a shy, retiring person. When there was a meeting, he would always keep away from the limelight. He would never speak at all.

Then he remembered having a series of dreams with the ECK Master Rebazar Tarzs. He couldn't

remember what the dreams were about, but he remembered that they were spiritual instruction of a
kind that was supposed to further his education.

A few days after the last of these inner experiences with Rebazar Tarzs, he had another dream.
He found himself walking down a dirt road. At the
end of it, there sat a woman. She was in front of
a terra-cotta jar. And in this jar was a liquid called
Esteem. He had this strong feeling and said, "Gee,
I should have some of that Esteem." He hadn't
even realized how little self-esteem he had. So he
was drinking this liquid Esteem even while he
woke up. He wondered about this.

After this dream, Andy suddenly became more
outgoing, more gregarious. He would talk with
people. He enjoyed their company, and people enjoyed
his company. Everybody was having a real fine time.

But then sometimes he overdid it. Once at an
ECK meeting, the leader said, "Andy talks too
much." Andy remembered this man saying it twice
during the meeting.

But Andy couldn't bring himself to be quiet. So
the Master set up a situation to help him come a
little more into balance. The Master will set up a
false situation or a false problem, so that if a person solves that, then he overcomes something.

Andy had shifted gears from being too shy, but
now he kept talking all the time. He found as he
was talking to people, being really gregarious and
outgoing, that when they didn't accept his ideas,
he became angry. That bothered him. He thought,
*I'm out of control, but how do I stop?*

One night when he was driving home from
work, Andy came to an intersection. The traffic
officer, who was directing cars, put a hand up for
his line of traffic to stop.

*In this jar was a liquid called Esteem.*

Andy was sitting in the front car, right next to the traffic officer. Wanting to be helpful, he leaned out his window to warn her to be careful. She was out in traffic. He said, "The brakes might fail."

Well, she took it wrong. Maybe she took it as a threat. Maybe she thought he wasn't giving proper respect to her office. She was a high-ranking police officer there in Nigeria. She arrested him, and his car was confiscated. Next thing he knew, he was headed down to the police station.

He went through quite an ordeal at the police station. He spent the night in jail. The next day, he had an appearance in court.

When he came through all this, Andy looked back at the whole thing and saw that an overly outgoing nature—like having too much self-esteem and letting it run wild—can work against one and cause all kinds of problems.

He realized that the Master was working with him, trying to help him strike a balance between his former very shy, retiring self and what he was now. He needed to come to a place somewhere in between, where he didn't make a nuisance of himself. He had to learn when to speak up and when to shut up.

And he realized that if he had just been quiet and just sat there in the line of traffic, he would have been just fine.

*He realized that the Master was working with him, trying to help him strike a balance where he didn't make a nuisance of himself.*

## Rose and the Golden Moth

"Rose" works in a day-care center. Every day when she drives to work, she likes to sing *HU*, which is a love song to God.

When she got to work one day, she found she was to be in charge of twelve children, ages two to three.

*While Rose was
singing HU,
along came a
beautiful,
golden moth,
and it landed
on her blouse,
right above
her heart.*

She gathered up her little flock and joined the other children and teachers outside. As the little kids began to play and enjoy themselves, Rose found a quiet spot where she could keep on singing *HU*.

While she was singing *HU*, along came a moth. It was a beautiful, golden moth, and it landed on her blouse, right above her heart. Rose put out her hand, and the moth made its way down her arm to her hand and sat there.

The two- and three-year-old children saw immediately what was happening. They said, "It's a gift from God to you."

It was a golden moth—a beautiful moth. Several of the kids ran off to get another teacher. When that teacher came, she said, "Aw, it's just an ugly moth." A second teacher said, "It's just a moth." But the kids knew better.

So when it was time to go in, Rose and the kids talked about the moth as being a gift from God. Just before they went back into the school, they said to the moth, "We're going to have to say good-bye now." And the moth took off. It flew away, but it came back and landed on Rose once again. And the kids said, "You'll always be with us, but you've got to go now." Because the kids had to go too.

Then the moth took off for good. But it definitely could feel the love that was coming from the sound of HU and from Rose.

When Rose and the kids went inside, these little two- and three-year-olds talked about God's love and the moth—how it had been time to let the moth go, but it would always be with them. The kids said, "We know that, Miss Rosie. God is always with us."

The other teachers couldn't shift gears, but the kids did just as naturally as a river follows its bed.

They knew. And the adults, who supposedly knew much better than the kids, didn't know at all.

## "Honey, Do You Hear That Sound?"

Rose sings *HU* a lot because she loves to. One morning, her husband, "Don," woke up with back pain. He wondered whether it was a kidney infection, so they went off to the emergency room. While Don went in to get his exam, Rose was out in the waiting room. As she sat there, she silently sang *HU* to herself.

A very hyperactive man came in and sat down opposite her. He was holding a cell phone up to his left ear, and with his right hand he was flipping through newspapers and magazines.

Then he suddenly stopped. And, as if talking to no one in particular, he said, "This sound is very comforting and relaxing. I've never heard this sound before."

He turned to Rose and asked, "Is that a Bible next to you?" She said, "It is." And he said, "The sound seems to be coming from there." Of course, it was coming from Rose, but he couldn't figure out what it would be except the most holy thing he could think of, which was a book sitting there.

Just about that time, the man's wife came into the room. He got up and asked her, "Honey, do you hear that sound?" She said, "No, I don't. Just a lot of wheelchairs moving back and forth in here."

He said, "No, no, not that. No, no. Sound. I've never heard *this sound* before, and it's very comforting and relaxing to me."

*He said, "I've never heard this sound before, and it's very comforting and relaxing to me."*

## Building Spiritual Stamina

This man was very much like David in the first story, because David could see the Light, and this man could hear the Sound.

When one comes into Eckankar, there are three things that are very important: the Mahanta, the Living ECK Master; the Sound Current (that means the Sound and the Light of God); and the initiation.

I mention this because initiation is a way to get up to speed, to get the stamina to get ready for the spiritual gift that the Master is offering you. And until you are ready for it, you can't accept it. The initiation gives you the strength to build up the stamina.

Well, back in the waiting room, after a bit the man said to his wife, "Let's just go home. I don't need an appointment today after all."

And Rose just kept on silently singing *HU*.

## A Vacationer Searches for the Sound of God

This final story is about Rose again. She and Don had been at a retreat, and they stopped off at the Appomattox Court House National Historical Park in Virginia. This is where the Confederate General Lee surrendered to General Grant of the Union army. This surrender virtually ended the Civil War.

Don went inside to view an exhibit. Rose stayed in the car with the windows open and enjoyed the wonderful breeze. And she silently sang *HU* to herself.

Just about that time, a family came back to the van beside Rose. The husband was red-faced and looked angry. The wife was crying, and their young daughter was crying too. So it looked like a typical family on vacation and having a hard time of it. Maybe they wanted to stay while he wanted to go,

*Initiation is a way to get up to speed, to get the stamina to get ready for the spiritual gift that the Master is offering you.*

or vice versa. It looked like he had his way, because they were crying, he wasn't.

Pretty soon the man said to his family, "Stop crying. I'm trying to hear this sound." There's this sound again.

Rose kept on silently singing *HU.* In the meantime, this man was digging around in the van, trying to find the source of this wonderful sound. He said to his family, "Stop crying. Stop, please. I'd rather hear this sound than both of you crying."

Well, they wondered if he had lost one of his wheels. So they stopped crying and probably studied him very carefully. He said, "Just listen to this wind. Maybe it's the wind. Very comforting. I hope we have this breeze for the rest of our vacation."

The HU sound, this Sound of God, can come in all different flavors. And It will come in the way that strikes the consciousness of the individual It's meant to reach. The man certainly heard It, but it's unlikely that his family did.

The Sound is very conscious, very selective. It's very choosy. And the consciousness of each one of you is unique.

Nobody else has a consciousness exactly like yours. Everyone is different. Not only that, but as you move on through life, your consciousness changes. In ordinary people, it changes just by a little bit. But in Eckankar it can—doesn't always, but it can—change very, very quickly.

## A Powerful Instrument

Well, when the van pulled away, Rose looked over, and she noticed it had a Minnesota license plate on it. And this, of course, reminded her of the Mahanta and the Mahanta's presence.

*The HU sound, this Sound of God, can come in all different flavors. And It will come in the way that strikes the consciousness of the individual It's meant to reach.*

It also reminded her of these words from *The Shariyat-Ki-Sugmad*, Book Two:

> To the ordinary man the mantra would appear to be nonsensical, a sound which is only the response of the brain to a certain range of vibration transmitted by the air that surrounds him. But, nevertheless, it is a powerful instrument of love and detachment for that ECK chela who practices it regularly. He reaches out to people whom he will never know and changes the course of their lives from the Kal forces which might be gripping them to the ECK which will lead them to God. Few, if any, will ever learn what has happened, but the mantra built up by the ECKist either individually or collectively will bring about a change in the worlds; first, that of man and then that of the spiritual heavens where necessary.

Now, Rose did not sing *HU* in order to change anybody's state of consciousness. I have to mention this because sometimes ECKists want to get together in a group and raise the consciousness of maybe a country or something.

I always say, "Don't do that. You're just hurting yourself." Because when people do this, they're directing the force of the Holy Spirit, the ECK. It's black magic, pure and simple; black magic. And there's a price to pay for that. I can't tell people what to do, but I suggest they don't do that. Don't go there. Do you want trouble?

Everyone, including you, is exactly where they belong.

Tonight we went through a number of things. We saw how David found ECK through the Light.

*Now, Rose did not sing HU in order to change anybody's state of consciousness. Everyone, including you, is exactly where they belong.*

Next, a past life with William the Conqueror—
someone getting rid of aggression from deep inside.
Then Andy and his ups and downs with self-esteem;
he's still trying to find the middle way.

And Rose sees what the HU can do in the school
yard. She also sees what it can do in the emergency-
room waiting area, and also at Appomattox Court
House in Virginia when on vacation. Always the
Sound of God.

*Always the
Sound of God.*

I know many of you have gained spiritually and
will continue to do so. May the blessings be.

*ECK Worldwide Seminar, Minneapolis, Minnesota
Saturday, October 25, 2008*

Tom looked at her, and very calmly he said, "What I and my friends believe is that we are Soul, and God loves us because we are Soul. We are eternal."

# 6

# THE SECRET PATH TO HEAVEN

e're very much like a family. We have a number of guests here tonight, and I'd like to welcome you.

And also a number of youth. I'd like to start with some questions from the youth, because they're always challenging.

## KEEPING THE INNER FIRE ALIVE

The first question is: When everything is going right, I begin to take my spiritual life and connection with the Mahanta, the Inner Master, for granted. How can I keep my inner fire alive?

Well, life has a wonderful way of nudging us back on track. The mind has a very natural tendency to want to go back to the track it came from. That's the mind. So the experiences in life will see us having a good time—easy going, easy rolling. Then suddenly things will turn around and go wrong.

All of a sudden an individual says, Help, Master, I want to get out of this.

The Master says, Pay your dues and stick around. Put your attention where it belongs again. Try to

*Life has a wonderful way of nudging us back on track.*

get those habits back on the right track, and all things shall be well with thee.

And so it goes. We get bumped off track. Then we have to go climbing back up. It's like a long, high grade to get back on the track.

Finally we get there, and everything is going well. We're dancing along, moving, and having quite a good time. And all of a sudden, we slip off. It's like slipping off a mountain road and landing, luckily, on a road beneath us. And the long, painful climb starts over again.

So, how can you keep your inner fire alive?

I would say, Don't worry about it. Life will take care of it. The Mahanta's working with you. Whenever you get too far off track, you'll get nudged right back on. It's just the way life is.

*How can you keep your inner fire alive? I would say, Don't worry about it. Life will take care of it. The Mahanta's working with you.*

## THE ROLE OF HUMOR IN SPIRITUALITY

Now here's a good one: What role does humor play in spirituality?

Humor. What is humor?

Well, humor is not wit necessarily. That's something else. That's sharp, and it bites. It's certainly not sarcasm, which is often a part of wit. And it's not comedy. Comedy can be a combination of all of the above. It can be sarcasm; it can be wit; it can even have humor in it. It has all of this.

Way back when, before electromagnetic radiation became such a problem for us at home, Joan and I used to watch TV for an hour in the evening. That was our recreation time when we'd have our dinner. Among the programs we really liked were two British comedies.

One was *Are You Being Served?* This takes place in a department store in London. It's a very proper store, and everything is done very properly. Yet the characters, the salespeople, are all funny. Each salesperson has his or her quirks. The humor is built out of this, and so is the comedy.

But I think our very favorite program was *Fawlty Towers*. This was priceless British comedy at its very best. Twelve episodes are all that were made.

In a sense, it starts low-key. Everything is very peaceful in this little hotel, which is run by Mr. Fawlty and his wife. They have a little restaurant there too, and everything's going well. Slowly, as the show moves on, the action begins to speed up. Things start to go all wrong—usually against Mr. Fawlty. Some of the situations are very, very funny.

Here is the difference between wit and comedy and spiritual humor. Spiritual humor may get one laughing, but when the laughter starts, there is some spiritual content behind it. So when the heart opens, something good and solid comes in. Whereas, in the other forms of humor—comedy and so on—the high element of spiritual insight and understanding doesn't come in.

So I hope that's somewhat of an answer to, What role does humor play in spirituality?

## BEING GRATEFUL WHEN LIFE IS HARD

Question three is: What can stimulate us to be grateful for what we have when life is hard?

I would say simply, the Spiritual Exercises of ECK. It goes back to that time and again: Do the spiritual exercises. Sing *HU*.

We get so many letters from people around the world who tell of how singing *HU* or one of the other spiritualized, sacred words has helped them

*Question three is: What can stimulate us to be grateful for what we have when life is hard? I would say simply, the Spiritual Exercises of ECK.*

through danger, misunderstandings, illness, and all kinds of things.

People say it's a wonderful thing, this word *HU*. And it is, very much so. So do your spiritual exercises. That'll stimulate you to be more grateful for what you have when life is hard.

## A SMOKER, A GOSSIP, AND AN ATHEIST

*The last question from one of our ECK youth: How do I enjoy the company of friends who do things which are against my personal code?*

Here's a good one, the fourth and last question from one of our ECK youth: How do I enjoy the company of friends who do things which are against my personal code?

Now, these friends include a smoker, a gossip, and an atheist. Just like many ECKists, he has a real wide variety of friends. The quick and easy thing is to just get rid of them all! He can do that.

If you see somebody who has to settle for friends like this, you say, My gosh! What's the matter with you?

No, I'm just joking. It shows that the ECK youth are out there and they're willing to engage others who do not think exactly as they do. And believe me, there are a lot of people in the world who don't think the way we do. It takes courage to go out there and find these people. But if you're young, life goes on and you find that some of these friends fall by the wayside.

I had a lot of so-called friends. They're years gone. I don't think of them, and I'm sure they don't think of me.

Well, the smoker. Smoking can have secondhand effects that are detrimental to health. Maybe you can ask, Hey, don't smoke when we're inside. Or if we're outside, stand downwind of me if you would, if you're a real friend. Then you find out.

So, the gossip. Gossip is poison. It's just pure out-and-out poison. This is actually like a skunk walking around spraying things. And that's like poison. I wouldn't listen to gossip. I just wouldn't listen to it, because it'll pull you down. What kind of friends do we want?

And the atheist—that's OK. Unless the atheist is going to argue all the time about Eckankar and how no God is better than your God. Things like this get old.

So when it comes to friends, you pay your nickel and take your chances. Do as you feel best. Listen to the Inner Master, and go from there.

*When it comes to friends, you pay your nickel and take your chances. Do as you feel best. Listen to the Inner Master, and go from there.*

## ARTHUR AND THE LONG WALK HOME

Our talk tonight is "The Secret Path to Heaven." To start out, go with me on a trip to Nigeria, in Africa. This is where "Arthur" lives. His name, as everyone else's in this talk, is made up. The names are changed for privacy reasons.

Arthur once took a bus to another town to look for work. That night, the bus ride home was going to cost a hundred naira, and all he had was forty. So he did the best he could do. He said, "I've got forty, so I'm going to ride the bus as far as the forty naira will take me."

There were delays, and he finally got off the bus at around eight o'clock. By then it had turned dark, and he still had an hour to walk.

Now, forty minutes of that walk was going to be through very dangerous territory. There was a little good stretch and a little bad stretch. There were robbers working this area. But Arthur didn't have any money, so he said, "Well, what am I going to do?" He started to sing *HU*, because he wanted the Master's protection to see him through. He had no idea how he was going to make it home.

So he began walking. And as he was walking, suddenly he saw someone coming toward him in the dark. He wondered, *Is this one of those robbers?*

As Arthur kept chanting *HU*, this man came closer. Emerging out of the dark, he said, "Can you help me push my car out of the mud?"

Arthur said, "Sure."

So the man led the way off into the darkness. Arthur trusted the Inner Master, who said it would be OK. And a little bit later, they came to a car that was stuck in the mud. Inside was the driver's wife. The man got in behind the steering wheel to drive. The man's wife got out, and she and Arthur pushed the car out of the mud.

Of course, the man and his wife were grateful, but Arthur didn't even stop for a thank-you. He had about half an hour of some very hard traveling to do yet, very risky and dangerous, and he wanted to get on with it. So he started down the road in the darkness.

The man came driving up behind him. He stopped and said, "Please accept some money for your help."

Arthur said, "No."

The man said again and again and again, "Please, please take something."

So Arthur accepted just enough so he could get home on the bus from there.

He took this man with his car stuck in the mud as one of the aids the Mahanta had sent to him to get him safely home. And indeed, he did reach home safely.

If you wonder what the secret path to heaven

*Suddenly he saw someone coming toward him in the dark. He wondered, Is this one of those robbers?*

is, the way to find out is to sing *HU*. Or you can call upon the Mahanta and ask for help for whatever situation or trouble comes up. Sometimes you want spiritual understanding, sometimes you just want some sort of help.

## A HUNDRED AND TWENTY BARKS

Some years ago, "Ellen" was tutoring two children in their family's living room. It was a beautiful, sunny, summer day, and the wind was blowing through the living room. Everything was going fine. She was tutoring the kids, and they were doing well.

And then suddenly a little dog across the street began to bark—and bark, and bark, bark, bark, bark, bark.

Well, Ellen did real well for about forty minutes. She was being very calm, careful not to lose her temper. And then the father came in, took one look at Ellen, and knew right away what was going on. He said, "I've lived in this neighborhood for many years. That dog has got a hundred and twenty barks in him, and until he gets to the last one, nothing you can do is going to stop him."

And, of course, Ellen thought, *Good advice. Let the dog finish the barking.*

The next day, she was at the Temple of ECK, offering her services as a volunteer tour guide. This was around the time the Temple of ECK had first opened, and there were still some people in the town where the Temple is who were upset. Things were not the way they used to be, and people had heard all kinds of stories about some groups without realizing that Eckankar was not one of those groups.

*The father said, "That dog has got a hundred and twenty barks in him, and until he gets to the last one, nothing you can do is going to stop him."*

So Ellen was at the Temple, serving as a tour guide. One of the people who came in was a woman who was very upset. She started to rant and rave and dumped everything that was boiling inside of her on Ellen. Every bit of anger came out.

But at that moment, Ellen remembered the dog with the hundred and twenty barks from the day before. She knew that until this woman had said her hundred and twenty words, there was no way to stop her. So Ellen listened with honest sincerity. She just listened to the woman. And the woman went on and on until she came to her hundred and twentieth word. Then she looked straight into Ellen's eyes and said, "Thank you for being so kind."

The two of them then went on a tour of the Temple. As Ellen said, "Just us two. Two children of God." By the end of the tour, they felt comfortable enough to give each other a hug.

Ellen says that ever since this experience, she has always remembered this technique, which is basically listening to another person without any opinions about You're right or You're wrong. None of that. Just accepting the person and listening to what that individual has to say. And when it's all out, the show is over.

## WALTER TWICE SAVED

"Walter" has been retired for a number of years. But way back when he was one year old, he was riding in his dad's car. His dad was at the wheel, his grandfather was in the passenger seat, and little Walter was propped up right in the middle between them. Of course in those days, there were no seat belts.

They were driving along, and suddenly, ahead

*So Ellen listened with honest sincerity. And the woman went on and on. Then she looked straight into Ellen's eyes and said, "Thank you for being so kind."*

of them a car came straight at them. The driver was slumped over the steering wheel. Walter's father just had time to think, *It's too bad Walter will never have a chance to grow up.*

But then suddenly the driver jerked awake and saw what was happening. He pulled to the right, trying to get back in his lane, and the two cars sideswiped. Walter's father later said all he heard was a soft ding as the two cars hit. The other car rolled over four or five times.

Walter didn't say what happened to the driver. But he was probably going ninety to a hundred miles an hour. He was whistling along. At that speed, without a seat belt, he was either very seriously injured or killed.

Years later, when he got into Eckankar, Walter realized that when one is supposed to come to the path of ECK, the protection of the ECK Masters is already there.

More recently, Walter was living in Las Vegas. He rented a car to visit relatives and friends in San Diego. In the car were Walter, his wife, and his grown daughter. She was in the backseat. As they were driving along the highway, Walter got up close behind one of the big rigs, one of the eighteen-wheelers. He got within fifty or sixty feet, because he was going to pass.

As he was lining up, getting ready to pass, a big sheet of steel was kicked up by one of the back tires of the semi, and it came straight for Walter's windshield. It came so fast. Things happened so quickly. The only thing Walter had time to think was, *It's going to take the heads off my wife and myself. I hope it doesn't get our daughter in the backseat.*

*Years later, when he got into Eckankar, Walter realized that when one is supposed to come to the path of ECK, the protection of the ECK Masters is already there.*

Even before he could finish thinking this, in the air in front of the car, Rebazar Tarzs, the ECK Master, appeared. When the sheet of metal came, Rebazar batted it down into the radiator of the car, where it made a very loud noise and left a big hole. The family was shaken, but they were also very grateful for the help.

Many people don't believe in the ECK Masters. They say, "Oh, those guys—Rebazar Tarzs, Fubbi Quantz, and all the others—are just a figment of your imagination. You guys have got a great imagination, but it's science fiction, fantasy fiction." But it's not so.

*Protection is one of the benefits for being on the secret path to heaven.*

The family was grateful for the protection they received. And this is one of the benefits—this benefit of protection—for being on the secret path to heaven.

## THE SECRET TO HEAVEN

I should mention here that it's secret only because the consciousness of people is either open, when it's not secret, or the consciousness is shut, and then it's a secret path to heaven.

As far as they're concerned, these people who cannot see or cannot hear, there is no path. It's all made up; it's make-believe. There is no Sound, there is no Light, there is no Master.

Those of you who are in ECK have to ask, Now, who is really living a dream? Really, when people don't know what's happening to them, in this unconscious state it's often living a nightmare.

Times are hard for ECKists too. I'm not saying you come into Eckankar and you're sailing on the smooth, easy highway. Because when you come into Eckankar, now you've got to start working off the karma so that you can work your way closer to heaven.

Open your heart more to love. This is what the whole secret to heaven is.

It's just simply love. It's all about God's love. That's all. Nothing more, but nothing less.

## CARRIE FOLLOWS AN INNER NUDGE

Our next story occurred during the holidays. A friend had asked if "Carrie" would come with her to a holiday party for her company.

Well, Carrie was tired. She was very tired, and she would rather not have gone. She had a lot of other plans too. But the Inner Master gave her a nudge and just said, "Go." So without another word, Carrie went to the party.

She looked around and saw that her friend was with a group, and they were having a good time. Carrie was drawn to a certain part of the room. A stranger was there. People were just standing around talking, and she had this nudge to go up to the man and say, "Hi, I'm Carrie." But she didn't have a reason to do that.

She wondered, *What am I going to say?*

The Inner Master just said to her, "Go over and introduce yourself, Carrie." So she went over and introduced herself. Then the man gave his name. When Carrie heard his name, she began to laugh. He said, "What are you laughing at?" And she said, "I think you and I have a friend in common."

His eyes narrowed, and he said, "We do? Who?" She named this person. He said, "How do you know him?" And she said, "We go to church together."

The man's eyes opened really wide, his jaw dropped, and in this big, nice, resonant voice, he

Open your heart more to love. This is what the whole secret to heaven is.

said, "Church? What church?"

She said, "Eckankar."

He said, "Eckankar!" real loud. His wife, "Ann," was just a few feet away, and she turned around quick.

The friend that Ann's husband and Carrie had in common was Ann's dad. Her dad is an ECKist, and he had often talked about Ann. Ann had been in Eckankar a long time ago, but she hadn't had contact with any ECKists for quite some time.

## "There's My Sign!"

So, Ann came right over, and she looked at Carrie. She wanted to know what was going on, and her husband told her. Carrie said, "You know, your dad and I are friends."

Ann hadn't talked to any ECKist apart from her father for five years. She said, "You wouldn't believe what I've been through these last days and weeks. Just today, I was so frantic to find a book about Eckankar. Anything. I looked through all my stuff. I couldn't find one book on Eckankar."

Then she went digging through her car, and there in the glove compartment, squirreled away back in the corner, she found one of the ECK books written by Paul Twitchell. She read it, and read it again, and read it all day long. Whenever she got a chance at work, she read this book.

She told her husband, who wasn't an ECKist, "I've asked God for a sign if I should become a member of Eckankar again and study the ECK discourses."

So when Ann finished her story, she said, "I can't believe it. I asked God for a sign. And what could be more in front of my face than this sign

*Ann told her husband, "I've asked God for a sign if I should become a member of Eckankar again and study the ECK discourses."*

right here? There's my sign!"

And, of course, it was Carrie.

Ann said, "God put this right in my face. How could I miss it?" So she had her answer. She and her husband both came into Eckankar. She rejoined, and he became a new member. Ann was really struck by how immediately the ECK, or the Mahanta, answered her question.

The Mahanta is just the ECK, which is the Holy Spirit. The ECK is not some unknown concept. It's the Holy Spirit. But it's a concept you probably are not used to if you are not in Eckankar.

The Mahanta is the personalized form of the Holy Spirit—something that people can relate to. This is the Mahanta, the Living ECK Master. It's a big mouthful. The Mahanta is the inner side of the Living ECK Master. And the Living ECK Master is the outer side, the one who sits up here on the stage and tries to remember where he was in the talk.

In case you came to be awed tonight, sorry. You can't have everything. You're getting more than you know.

## BACK TO THE PATH OF ECK

I've found that by the time people come to an ECK talk or respond in some positive way to the teachings of ECK, it's just a matter of time before they come back. And I mean come back to the path of ECK.

Because people who have come this way have walked many a weary, karmic mile in past lifetimes. By the time you come to Eckankar, you're usually well acquainted with the idea of past lives and reincarnation. You may not accept such concepts,

*People who have come this way have walked many a weary, karmic mile in past lifetimes.*

but at least you're familiar with them.

In time, things will change for you so that you will be more open to the teachings of ECK. When that time comes, well, at least you know where to go.

Sometimes it's not you who is the next one to come to ECK. You may be drawn or inspired to tell somebody who is facing a hard time. Tell them about HU.

Just say, "Hey, I've tried HU. You might try it. It works." And then it's up to that person to try it out. Does it really work or doesn't it? Sometimes nothing will happen, sometimes there's a great feeling of peace, sometimes they'll even see colors.

It can be any number of different colors. Just think of the old-time Christmas lights, plus many, many more colors. When you see something like this, it is part of one of the manifestations of the Holy Spirit.

This is part of the Light. Sometimes it's a blinding white light. Sometimes it's a blue light; this is when you are seeing for the moment at the Mental Plane. There's the Physical Plane, and then comes the Astral, and then the Causal. The Causal is a subplane of the Mental Plane. Then there's another plane that's a little higher—the Etheric Plane. It's violet, ultraviolet, that sort of color. And then you get into the white areas of light, which are the first of the true spiritual worlds.

I could go on into this, but it's in the ECK teachings elsewhere, and in my talks.

## TOM WAITS FOR THE RIGHT TABLE

In this next story, we're off on vacation to Florida. "Tom," his brother, his sister, and their spouses were in Florida on vacation. One night

Just say, "Hey, I've tried HU. You might try it. It works." And then it's up to that person to try it out. Does it really work or doesn't it?

they decided to go out for a seafood dinner.

It was a very busy restaurant. They got in line and waited a very long time. Lots of people were there. It was a big place, crowded and noisy. Finally they got to the head of the line, and they saw the restaurant staff clearing a table off to one side.

But Tom suddenly got this feeling not to take that table, not to sit there. So when the hostess came up to get them, Tom said, "Isn't there a table somewhere else?" And just then, off near the center of the room, a group of people was leaving.

Now some in Tom's group said, "Hey, we're hungry. We've waited long enough. Let's eat. Let's eat!"

Tom could understand, but he had this strong feeling: Don't sit there! The people left, and the hostess said, "Sure, but you're going to have to wait while we make it ready."

So she showed somebody else to the table off to the side. And finally Tom and friends were seated at this very nice table. He said, "Great table." It was pretty close to the center of the room.

They were studying the menus very carefully, when suddenly Tom heard a woman behind him say, "My daughter is in Eckankar, and I don't know anything about it."

## THE BEST MISSIONARIES OF ECK

Usually when Tom is with this group, he defers. He lets his sister or one of the others talk about Eckankar. But he felt really great. He turned around, he stood up, and he said, "I'm in Eckankar. And so are all these people at this table." The woman said, "Really?" He said, "Really."

The woman seated beside the ECKist's mother

*Tom heard a woman behind him say, "My daughter is in Eckankar, and I don't know anything about it."*

said, "What theology does Eckankar teach?"

This caught Tom off guard. He said, "Beg pardon?"

And she said, "What theology does Eckankar teach?"

Tom looked at her, and very calmly he said, "Well, I don't know what you mean by theology, but what I and my friends believe is that we are Soul, and God loves us because we are Soul. We are eternal."

This was his very brief explanation. After that, there was a lot of small talk, and they asked a bit more about Eckankar. Then they talked about this, that, and the other thing. After a while, they both returned their attention to their own tables and the people there. Life went on as usual.

Later, Tom couldn't help but wonder if maybe, in some way, the ECKist's mother felt more comfortable now, having met and talked with several ECKists. Of course, he didn't know. But at least another person had been introduced to Eckankar and to ECKists.

The best missionaries of Eckankar are you. You're the ones who take the message to the world.

*People measure the teachings of ECK by you. They look at you and begin to wonder— there's something special about you.*

People measure the teachings of ECK by you. You often don't even have to say a single word about Eckankar. But they look at you and begin to wonder about that something special—there's something special about you.

I'm glad that you are here this evening. I love you. And may the blessings be.

*ECK Springtime Seminar, Minneapolis, Minnesota*
*Saturday, April 11, 2009*

Love does not restrict itself to only those of a certain species or race, or any of that. Love is love. And this is what the ECK teachings are all about.

# 7
# SPIRITUAL LESSONS FROM LIVING

*O*ur talk for this evening is "Spiritual Lessons from Living."

I was reading about Mark Twain. Sometimes, especially in his later years, he would take to wearing a white suit and scarlet socks. He said, "This is my don't-give-a-damn suit."

He was that sort of man. He just didn't care. One time when he was in London, he went across the street from his hotel to the public bath dressed only in his bathrobe and slippers. This was during the Victorian age, and it caused a scandal—which he loved. He was such a shy man.

## WHAT YOU SEE IS WHAT YOU GET

We have a lot of visitors here tonight, so I'd like to welcome you. It's always hard to figure out what people will want from a spiritual leader. Can you live up to their expectations? I don't think so. Anyway, what you see is what you get.

When I look in the mirror, I'm not so happy either. It's as if the years get more unkind as time goes by. I've been debating about whether to have

> It's always hard to figure out what people will want from a spiritual leader. Can you live up to their expectations? I don't think so.

a new official photograph taken. When I sat for the current one, about fifteen years ago, I felt very fortunate that it was passable. But it looks really good to me now. It doesn't look like the guy in the mirror, but that's OK.

Another thing is wearing blue clothes all the time. I don't. And I'll tell you why not. One time I was at a seminar and saw this young man in a blue suit. It was very much like a suit I wore at the time. And he had his watch on with the face to the inside of the wrist, the way I wore my watch. That was too much.

I had a hard time taking that. I said I've got to break people of this habit of expecting an ECK Master to walk around in blue clothes all the time. So when I'm in public, I usually don't, except at a seminar.

When I meet people out and about, they're pretty much used to seeing me in casual clothes. And when I'm casual, I'm very casual.

## THE WATERMELON STRAW

I was in a food co-op a couple of weeks back. I had heard on a radio show that the way to tell a ripe watermelon was to take a straw from a corn broom. It has to be a corn broom. The speaker said, "Lay the straw on a watermelon, and if the straw moves, the watermelon is ripe."

I thought, *Oh, sure, magic.* But I really liked this idea and decided to try it.

So I've waited. I missed last year's watermelon season and had to wait all through the winter. I waited all through spring, and I waited until late summer.

Then I went to the food co-op with my little straw. As I was practicing with it, I tried to tell

*I had heard on a radio show the way to tell a ripe watermelon. I really liked this idea and decided to try it.*

the guy in produce how to do it, but he was above that sort of thing. He knows how to find a watermelon for display. He just keeps cutting them open until he finds a ripe one.

So here I am. I've got this idea from a radio show where several people from the Deep South had called in and said, "This works. Nothing else works. Tapping it or pounding it with the knuckles doesn't work. But try this; it works." So I was in the food store trying this to see if it worked, when several ECKists from the Eckankar Spiritual Center came in. They were curious about what I was doing.

Well, I was having pretty good luck. Unfortunately, watermelons aren't on my diet. I couldn't just take one home, cut it open, and say, "It works." So, I'm ashamed to say, I persuaded one of the staff.

Of course, I kind of let him work up to it himself. I asked, "Would you like to try this straw? I think this is a good one." He tried it, but it never moved as much for him on that one watermelon as it did for me.

And I wondered, *How does this stuff work?* But I never asked him, "Did it work?" So I hope everything went well.

Spiritual lessons from living—they're of all kinds.

*Spiritual lessons from living— they're of all kinds.*

## COMPUTER SMARTS, KARMA SMARTS

"Kathy" is the main character in our first story. And I'll mention here that all the names will be fictitious, for your privacy. But you'll know your own story.

Kathy's daughter got an offer from a computer company, and it said, "Special offer. If you're a student going to school, you can get a real deal on our computer." Well, Kathy's daughter, being a student, didn't have the money. But Mom did.

So Kathy bought this computer for her daughter. But Kathy also wanted one for her own use at home. Of course, she didn't think about being honest when she ordered the computers. A good deal is a good deal.

They both came on the same day. Her daughter's worked great. But Kathy's computer had problems from day one. Not only that, the computer got worse and worse, as they can do if you're not honest with them.

And that's not all. Kathy's other daughter came home, and apparently, she isn't in college. When she tried to use the computer, it wouldn't work for her either. Because the computer knew the contract. And everybody had to honor that contract; otherwise it wouldn't work for them.

But when the college student came home, the computer always worked for her.

Kathy said, "Oh, I get it. There was a contract. I wasn't true to the contract. I was trying to get something for nothing."

This was a strange thing. It kept on for several visits. Finally, Kathy got the message. She said, "Oh, I get it. There was a contract. I wasn't true to the contract. I was trying to get something for nothing." So she donated the computer and bought herself a brand-new one for full price.

Now, here's a very funny thing which I find going on in our society. There are so many people who are under the illusion they can get something for nothing—that they can somehow reach into someone else's pocket, take out the money, and have their neighbor's money for themselves. *This is fine*, they think, especially if the government says it's OK.

It's not OK. Stealing is stealing.

Someone who is a true ECKist will do everything in his or her power to take care of their own affairs, because that's how it is.

## THE VET, A CAT, AND PRAJAPATI

This is a story about a vet, a cat, and Prajapati, an ECK Master who takes a special interest in animals.

Our story begins with "Mike." He's a young man. He was riding his bike down on the beach, and there he saw a surfboard. Nobody was around, so he took it home, got on the internet, and went to a site that specializes in help wanted and lost items. He put a notice up—"Found: A surfboard."

A little bit later, he got a call from a veterinarian. He identified his surfboard, and they made arrangements. So Mike took the surfboard over to this veterinarian, whom we'll call "Doctor Ken." Doctor Ken said to Mike, "If your family ever has need of my services, I'll give you a discount."

Not long after this, the family cat became very ill. They remembered the offer from this vet. So they took the cat, Simba, to him. When the doctor came in, he looked at the cat and said, "This cat is very sick." He didn't need to do a whole lot of poking and prodding to see the cat was hurting here, there, and everywhere.

Doctor Ken said, "I'm one of the very few vets who practices energy medicine."

This sort of energy medicine is sometimes called remote treatment, which may be offered by a chiropractor or some other healer. It's very effective, but it takes a certain kind of patient. I think cats are very open to this sort of thing because it's

*Mike put a notice up—"Found: A surfboard." A little bit later, he got a call from a veterinarian.*

energy, and cats are very sensitive to energies.

While Simba was being treated, Mike's father told Dr. Ken all about the ECK Master Prajapati.

The next day, Mike's mother, "Ann," came to visit Simba. She saw that the cat was in terrible condition, and she began to cry.

When Doctor Ken came into the room, he started asking all kinds of questions about Prajapati. Then he went on to describe him. He said, "Prajapati came to me in a dream last night. Don't worry. He said everything is going to be OK."

Three days later, Ann went back to the veterinarian. The doctor said, "I've got the blood-test results. But before I call them up on the computer, I want to make sure Prajapati is here." He wanted to go into contemplation, shut his eyes, and be assured that the ECK Master was present. So Ann shut her eyes, and she began to sing *HU*, our love song to God. At the same time, Doctor Ken called on Prajapati.

After a bit, Dr. Ken opened his eyes and said, "He's here. My skin is tingling. I can feel him. Can you feel him?"

Ann said, "Yes, he's here."

Then the doctor turned around, faced the computer, booted it up, and got the results. Finally, he turned back around with a big smile on his face, and he said, "The blood tests are all OK. Everything's normal. You can take Simba home."

The spiritual lesson here is that love is so strong that it can reach out through the Divine Spirit, the ECK.

I mentioned an ECK Master. It means a Master who is well attuned to the Holy Spirit. This love had come from the Holy Spirit, through the

*Doctor Ken said, "Prajapati came to me in a dream last night. He said everything is going to be OK."*

ECK Master Prajapati, to take care of one of the least of Its own. And this is how life is.

## Animals in Heaven?

Will Rogers was a comedian during the early twentieth century. He once said, "If there are no dogs in Heaven, then when I die I want to go where they went."

That was his opinion, and it was interesting that he was so far ahead of his time. Because today, people are wondering, Are cats and dogs and goldfish and all kinds of pretty little birds going to be in heaven too?

Somehow the standard version of heaven is that all these won't be there. And people wonder, What kind of place is this going to be?

I don't know. But in the ECK heaven, all these are there too, so don't worry.

Love comes down from the Holy Spirit. The Holy Spirit is the Voice of God. It comes from the Divine Being, whatever you want to call the Creator. We call It Sugmad.

This love comes down, and It sustains all life. This love is the Voice of God, the Holy Spirit. And it is actually this Voice of God that maintains and sustains the lower worlds. It is pure love, and this love is not the domain of humans only, but also of animals.

*This Voice of God is pure love, and this love is not the domain of humans only, but also of animals.*

## Texas Longhorn Saves a Little Bull

This story is about "Carol." She lives in cattle country, in a small town near San Angelo, Texas.

One morning Carol went outside. Her neighbor was outside too, and on his lawn were three bulls.

One was a huge longhorn, and the other two were little black bulls.

Unfortunately, one of them was lying down. He had eaten too much of a big green bush, and he had become bloated. Now, those of you who work with cattle know that if an animal becomes bloated, if it can't get up, then it probably won't make it. It's going to die.

*Those of you who work with cattle know that if an animal becomes bloated, if it can't get up, then it probably won't make it.*

We knew that at home on the farm too. If there was such a case, the wives would get on the phone and call up the immediate neighbors right away, because maybe one farmer or another knew what to do.

A bloated cow looks really different, like a big balloon lying on the ground with legs sticking straight out. It's a strange-looking thing.

There's no way to get a cow like that up most of the time, because they're just too big. But there was something that sometimes worked. Farmers always carried a jackknife. They carried it everywhere for everything. So the farmer would take the jackknife and poke it in a certain place around one of the ribs. I was just a small kid when I saw them do it. The air went out of the cow just like a balloon, and then the men got her up. They would kick her, just enough to get her moving. Then there was hope.

But, apparently, they didn't know about this in Carol's town. So Carol and her neighbor, "Don," looked the situation over, and they didn't know what to do. Don got on his phone, and he called around trying to find the owner. He couldn't find the owner, so finally they decided they should call the sheriff. Maybe the sheriff would know something. About this time, the longhorn bull walked over to Don.

Now, these are huge animals. From my experience on the farm, all our bulls weighed well over a ton, and you did not want to be anywhere near them. But this bull came up to Don and looked very concerned. Don scratched the bull's head. And then this massive bull walked over to Carol and began to lick her arm.

Whenever Don walked over to look at the little black bull that was down on the ground, this huge longhorn would follow him. Don said to Carol, "Do you see that? Every time I go over there to check on the bull, the longhorn comes right along." This was quite unusual.

Well, the longhorn decided that Don and Carol weren't going to do anything. So he tried to get his horns underneath the downed bull and lift him up. But he could only get one horn at a time under the little bull, because longhorns' horns stick straight out to the side. And they don't curl much to speak of—at least not the ones I've seen.

Each time the little bull would get partway up, he would slip off. So the next time the longhorn got the little bull up a bit, Don used his foot to balance the little bull on the horn, until the longhorn got him up.

They got this bloated little thing up on his feet, but he was just standing there. It hurt to walk, I imagine. Then the longhorn stuck the little bull with his horn and kept sticking him, sticking him. Apparently that hurt worse than the bloating did, so finally the little bull began to move. Pretty soon the air passed through, and he was OK. It was the love of this huge longhorn for his little friend that ultimately saved his life.

Here again is an example of divine love showing itself, animal to animal. And of course, Carol

*It was the love of this huge longhorn for his little friend that ultimately saved his life.*

and Don did their part.

Love does not restrict itself to only those of a certain species or race, or any of that. Love is love. And this is what the ECK teachings are all about. Purely love, and just love—simply love.

## PETER'S MOTORBIKE MARVEL

This next story is about "Peter," a Nigerian. One day, he was riding along an expressway. He was in the fast lane on a little motorbike. A passenger was on the back, and they were moving right along.

Although Peter didn't know it, a speeding car was coming up behind him. If he didn't move right away, he was going to be run over. At that moment, Peter noticed a man—a white man in a long-sleeved blue shirt—sitting in front of him on the gas tank. So now this little motorbike, in the fast lane on an expressway, had *three* riders.

From my experience of years ago in Africa, anything's possible. You see some of the most marvelous things over there—things that would never be allowed here in the States. And you just sit there and look. And you say, Wow, this is wonderful!

The people are so very casual. And yet it's very often a hard life, and they're doing whatever it takes to get done whatever needs to get done.

So then this third rider, sitting in front of Peter, very gently and gradually moved the motorbike into the other lane. And at that moment, the car coming up from behind sped past. Its driver had never intended to slow down. The car would have run over Peter and his passenger.

Later, Peter learned that these were robbers, and there were security people hot on their trail. They were stopping for nothing.

Peter then realized that it was the Mahanta, the Living ECK Master who had appeared and actually steered him to safety. He was grateful for it, because, he said, unless he had had this help, he would no longer be here. He would be dead.

## YOUR UNIQUE PATH TO HEALTH

In the last two decades, I've seen a lot of health practitioners. They range all the way from medical doctors to chiropractors, homeopaths, and acupuncturists. About the only person I haven't gone to is a witch doctor, probably because there wasn't one available. But I do have limits.

I've learned over the years that no matter who you are, you are a unique being. There is no one else like you, spiritually or even physically. Oh, you may look like a lot of others. You may roughly have many of the same conditions other people do, but they will not be identical. Because your life is a reflection of your state of consciousness, it's unique.

*Your life is a reflection of your state of consciousness.*

Because of who you are and who you were spiritually in your past lives, you've had experiences unlike anyone else. And because of those experiences, you've reaped all different sorts of karma than anyone else.

Sometimes you go to somebody for help, and it doesn't work out. It can be the best practitioner in the field, and 95 percent of the recommendations may work, but 5 percent won't. It's that 5 percent, I've found, that is sometimes very troubling. And unfortunately, it sometimes even goes to more than 5, maybe to 10, 15, or 20 percent, until you say, Will this never end?

I went to a nutritionist, who is not a member of Eckankar but has a very good reputation. I went to her almost a month ago. And her recommendations went very, very wrong. So I've had a greater number of conditions I've had to work through. I'm grateful just to be here. I'm on the mend, though, so don't worry about it.

Over the years, as I was coming to grips with the electromagnetic radiation sensitivity that I have, I tried many, many things. Frankly, a lot of them didn't work, but a few did.

This is how life is. You do the best you can.

For many people, 90 percent of the conditions they have are due to poor nutrition. This is why it's such a good area to look into if you have any health conditions. I mention this, but let the patient beware. Keep your eyes open. Check it out.

I have ways and means at home to undo conditions. I also have the help of friends in the healing arts. I'm grateful to them, and I'm grateful for all we have learned from people about various techniques. I've met some very good people, both in Eckankar and outside of Eckankar.

*For many people, 90 percent of the conditions they have are due to poor nutrition. This is why it's such a good area to look into if you have any health conditions. But let the patient beware.*

## LYNN'S DARK NIGHT OF SOUL

"Lynn" was going through a very dark night of Soul some eighteen years ago, before she found Eckankar. This dragged on for a few years. At the time, she didn't realize it was her own karma coming back to haunt her. Karma has a way of doing that.

The things she was facing were four in number. First, she had left her marriage of twenty-three years. The second thing was that her son was in trouble with the law; he had had drugs in the house that Lynn had left just three weeks earlier.

The third thing was she was drinking too much because of a troubling situation she had gotten into. And fourth, all this stress made her not show up for work. She was a dental assistant, and now her job was in jeopardy.

All this was on her, and she sometimes just wanted to throw her hands up and give up living. She just didn't know where to go anymore.

Around this time, a friend let her stay in her mother's house. This house had recently been burglarized. The police had come in and used black ink powder to check for fingerprints, and it had gotten all over everything. Then a professional service came in and cleaned it up. But they missed some spots, and along came Lynn in her white dental uniform.

She was driving to work one day. She was late. And she noticed smudges on her white uniform. She was absolutely disgusted. She said, "Dear God. It can't get any worse than this." This was her prayer, of sorts.

Just about that time, she heard an unwelcome rumbling in her bowels, and—oh, no!—she had an accident right there. Not with the vehicle, but with her body. It left no question; she had to go back to the house and launder her clothes. She had no choice.

But she was strangely happy. God had heard her prayer. This put things in a new perspective. Now, it took a little bit to get everything cleaned up and put a new uniform on. Then she very bravely set off for work again. But she knew God had heard her.

Life was still hard. And one night, very soon after this, she had a dream.

In the dream, she was standing in the middle

*But Lynn was strangely happy. God had heard her prayer. This put things in a new perspective.*

of a wide road. A truck was barreling down the road right at her, and it looked as if it was all over for her. She was frozen with fear, she couldn't move. So she just shut her eyes. She surrendered. What else could she do?

Just at that moment, she felt a gentle hand on her arm. A man appeared, and he moved her very surely off to the side of the road and onto the sidewalk, out of harm's way. This was still in her dream. She looked at this man very carefully, memorizing his face. She said to herself as she was waking up, *I suppose somehow I'm going to be romantically involved with him sometime, but he's just not my type.*

What she didn't know was that she would be *spiritually* involved with him, and he would be very much her type. But that was still to come.

In the meantime, her life straightened out. She met a good man and married him. About a year after they were married, through her husband, she found out about Eckankar.

The two went to an ECK service together. They went into the room and sat down, and then she looked around the room. She noticed a picture on the wall. It was the picture of the man who had helped her in the dream, who had pushed her out of harm's way. Much later, she came to realize too—at least I hope she did—that her spiritual life was being taken care of.

She needed to work through all that karma so she could meet the Master. And because she had worked through that karma, she was now qualified to come to the path of ECK. And so she did.

Well, when Lynn saw the picture, she knew, and she began to cry and cry. I know; it happened

*What she didn't know was that she would be spiritually involved with this man, and he would be very much her type. But that was still to come.*

to me too. Because suddenly there's this joy in the heart when you come into the presence of the one who's going to help you home. And she knew. She knew she was in the right place.

## KATHY'S ATHEIST FRIEND GETS HIS ANSWER

We've mentioned Kathy earlier. She's the computer mom. Well, Kathy had been talking with an atheist friend of hers. We'll call him "Bob." She said, "Would you like to come along to an ECK seminar with me?"

He said, "Sure." Not a lot of enthusiasm, but friends are friends.

He had told Kathy the reason he no longer believed in God. He said when he was a boy, he used to have prayers. He'd pray to God for help with this and help with that. And God never answered him, never got him out of any of these troubles.

Kathy said, "Maybe you needed to go through those experiences to grow spiritually." But no, Bob wasn't having any of that.

Anyway, they went to the seminar. They made small talk while standing in line, waiting to go into the main hall. Looking around at all the activity, Bob said, "Why is this seminar in Minneapolis?" Kathy said, "This is where the Temple of ECK and the Eckankar Spiritual Center are."

"Why are they here?"

"I don't know why they're in Chanhassen. Eckankar used to be in Menlo Park, California."

Kathy didn't know. But she mentioned Menlo Park, California, because she knew her friend used

*Suddenly there's this joy in the heart when you come into the presence of the one who's going to help you home.*

to live in that area. His company was still located there, so she figured it was a good connection. It would be something familiar.

During my talk that evening, just out of the blue, I mentioned that the reason the Eckankar office moved from Menlo Park, California, to Minneapolis was that it was simply too expensive for our staff in California. I could foresee that things were going to get worse. So at that point, the ECK said, "Go to Minnesota." So we came to Minnesota.

When I explained this in my talk, Kathy nudged Bob and said, "Are you aware that he just answered your question?"

Bob's not sleeping. He's not slow or anything. He said, "Yeah, I know."

What struck Kathy was how seamlessly Bob's question was answered in the Master's talk. It just wove in very nicely, and then the talk went on into something else.

Now, I would like to take credit and say, "Yeah, I know a lot of stuff. It's nothing; I do this all the time. It's nothing at all." And then shuffle my feet, kick my toe against the back of one heel, and say, "Aw, shucks."

But it really doesn't work like that.

My job, basically, is to stay as clear as I can and keep out of the way of what the ECK wants to give forth as a message. Yes, I prepare a talk, but I say a lot of things that aren't in that.

Of course, the talk doesn't come out of thin air either. I work on it a long time before I get here. But then sometimes I get nudged left, right—not this story, not that story—this one, that one. And so eventually we end up with the talk I'm giving right here from this chair.

*My job, basically, is to stay as clear as I can and keep out of the way of what the ECK wants to give forth as a message.*

## CHANGED IN A POSITIVE WAY

Years ago, Kathy worked for an employer who was not a member of Eckankar. He was of another faith. In fact, he used to make fun of Eckankar.

But after one seminar, he called Kathy in, and he said, "Listen, I know you went to an Eckankar seminar, but I don't want to talk about Eckankar. I don't even want you to mention it. I just want to tell you this: Every time you come back from one of your seminars, you're changed in a positive way. That's all. You can go." And that was it.

I noticed this too, way back when I was getting into Eckankar. I'd come home from the seminar, and people would know there was a difference in me. They would ask me all kinds of questions: Did I have a good time? Where did I stay? What was the food like? And, by the way, what happened in the seminar itself? Well, I'd tell them what I could and let it go at that.

This is the sort of thing that happens. They're all spiritual blessings from living—living and learning. I'm learning every day.

When I got this position, some people thought, *Wow, he must have it made.* I knew different. I knew better. I knew that at this point, my learning was going to begin in earnest. And, boy, has it ever. It really has. It will get you where you aren't looking. It'll blindside you. Surprises will come up, changes in plans—everything.

What you learn is to be a very random individual. You're earth-based for sure—your feet are here—but Soul is in heaven.

We are Soul. We do not have a soul; we *are* Soul. We have a body. We have a human body. And our job is to take the best care of it we can and

*What you learn is to be a very random individual. You're earth-based for sure—your feet are here—but Soul is in heaven.*

make it go as far as possible, as well as possible.

So that's our talk for this evening. Whenever and wherever you go, I want to say to you, May the blessings be, and I love you.


*ECK Worldwide Seminar, Minneapolis, Minnesota*
*Saturday, October 24, 2009*

Then came the sound of bells. Beautiful sounds of all tones and all loudness from near and far. It was as if she and all the singing people were being called to service by the bells.

# 8

# A GOLDEN CONTRACT

*I*'d like to welcome all of you to the 2010 ECK Springtime Seminar here in Minneapolis, Minnesota. I know you've come many miles, and I'm grateful that you have shown an interest in the teachings of ECK.

I try to give you what I can, and sometimes I feel it's enough, sometimes not enough. But all in all, it really doesn't matter. If there are some two thousand of you here, there are two thousand different states of consciousness. Each of you is Soul; each of you is a unique individual. So no matter what I say, there are going to be at least two thousand viewpoints of what I said.

Time's going so fast right now, so very fast. I feel pretty much like the snail that was run over by a turtle. When somebody asked the snail, "What happened?" he said, "I don't know. It all happened so fast."

I think philosophical thoughts all the time. And I wonder about things, like one of the imponderables: If a man says something in a woods where no woman can hear, is he still wrong?

*Each of you is Soul; each of you is a unique individual.*

Well, the title of this evening's talk is "A Golden Contract." And all the people mentioned during this talk are going to be given a pseudonym for their privacy.

## WHAT IS THE GOLDEN CONTRACT?

This is the golden contract: that every encounter, without exception, is there to move Soul along spiritually on Its way back home to God. That's every encounter, every event, without exception.

Something's trying to nudge you back home to God. And that means if you're a real hard nut to crack, to soften you up with love. Because that's what all this is about. This is what *you* are about. God is love. And Soul, being a creation of God—from God—is at heart a unit of love too.

As Soul was sent into the lower worlds, It had to put on these different sheaths—the Mental body, the Causal body, the Astral body, and a Physical body.

These sheaths grow on the outside and begin shielding the love that is inside a person naturally at the Soul level. The love isn't able to get through into this world to where a person can behave, talk, and feel like a creation of God. Sometimes people feel they are created in their own image. They get so carried away with themselves that we generally, in spiritual terms, refer to them as being on a power trip.

Basically, there are two different kinds of people: the heart people, who are motivated by love, and the people who are more motivated by power. Their thing is to always get one over on everyone else. That doesn't mean heart people won't rise to high levels in leadership—here, there, anywhere, even in Congress. Yes, all things are possible.

Miracles are possible.

I'm joking, because in Congress there are many fine people on both sides of the aisle. And there are so many others who are purely on the side of power. That's basically what they want. They lie, they cheat; it doesn't matter—it's all truth to them. And you wonder. You say, "Hmm, truth goes a long way in their world. You don't need to give them much of it, and they're off and running, spinning and doing all kinds of fanciful things with it." And they're perfectly content.

Well, we were all there once too, if we are not still. Because it's a human condition. But at some point, spiritually, we grow out of this, and we become more filled with love. That's what it's all about.

## SHIRLEY REMEMBERS THE GOLDEN CONTRACT

"Shirley" recognized this golden contract she has with the Mahanta, the Inner Master. She'd say, "This is the golden contract I have with the Mahanta, and today is no exception." That means no matter what happens today, it's part of the golden contract.

So try to see if anything comes up for you as you're meeting people you haven't met before, or people you've met before and are having a reunion with. Ask yourself, *How is this event or person bringing me closer to divine love, or closer back home to God?*

*Ask yourself, How is this event or person bringing me closer to divine love, or closer back home to God?*

Anyway, Shirley had lost sight of the basics, and she gave an example. It was a few weeks before Christmas, and she went shopping. She went to one of the huge stores. She was looking for decorative tins filled with popcorn. These were large tins, and her friends always liked them. She would give one to her manicurist, to her hairdresser, to the people at the health practitioner's, and so on. People very much enjoyed this gift.

So she went to the usual store. But it had been renovated since last year, and it was now about two or three times larger than before. She had absolutely no idea where to look for these tins of popcorn, so she asked a number of employees where to find them. But none of the employees she met spoke English.

Now, Shirley is a senior citizen, and she was getting exasperated because she was getting tired, walking around asking all these people, "Where are the popcorn tins?" They didn't know what she was talking about.

Finally an employee seemed to understand, and she waved to urge Shirley to follow her. The woman didn't speak too much; she just said with her hand, Come on, I think I know where it is.

So Shirley went off after her, and they went up one aisle—but no, it wasn't there. And then down another aisle—no, it wasn't there. They went back and forth, back and forth, and they crisscrossed this huge store many times. By now, Shirley's good humor had gotten up and gone home.

She was getting really upset. She was thinking about all this: how she was so inconvenienced, how nobody spoke English, how nobody could find her popcorn tins, and how she was going to complain to management. Outrageous! Purely outrageous!

All of a sudden, she caught herself. "Wait a minute. This isn't how I think," she said. "This isn't how I behave. What's going on here?"

Then an answer came through to her very gently. It was a picture of her health practitioner

*By now, Shirley's good humor had gotten up and gone home. All of a sudden, she caught herself. "This isn't how I behave. What's going on here?"*

saying to her, "Shirley, you need to get on an exercise program. Considering everything, you ought to go on a walking program. You've got to walk."

When she saw this, she said, "While I'm standing here complaining, wondering *What's going on? What's this all about?* the Mahanta, the Inner Master, is getting me started on this walking program!" Then all her exhaustion just drained away. Her energy came back, and she felt great.

They also found the decorative tins of popcorn. But the employee had seen how very hard it had been on Shirley and kept saying, "I'm sorry. I'm sorry." Shirley put her arm around her and said, "It's OK, it's OK. It's just fine." The woman was so upset, she wouldn't calm down. So Shirley was there, with her arm around the woman, trying to get her to calm down and realize it was OK, that everything was going fine.

Just about this time, the store manager came walking by. He was used to seeing upset customers, and an employee would often be trying to calm them down. But he had never seen an upset employee with a customer calming her down.

He came up and asked, "What's going on?"

Shirley gave him a thumbnail sketch of what had been going on. And he said, "I wish I had a camera. This is a Kodak moment."

This was an example of a golden contract. Because as soon as Shirley caught herself and remembered that every person, every event is there for a reason, then she was on the right track. The manager, I'm sure, took something away from this. And the employee did. And certainly Shirley did.

The golden contract. It's a good principle to keep in mind and work with.

*As soon as Shirley remembered that every person, every event is there for a reason, then she was on the right track.*

## Keeping Lulu Bird Safe

Another example is of a frightened bird in a cage. This is a story about "Paula." Her husband gave her a little bird in a cage. She didn't say whether it was a canary, a budgie, or a hawk. But since there were three cats in the household, and all were looking at that cage where the little bird was, I would assume it wasn't the hawk.

Now, there was only one place to put the cage, and that was on the refrigerator, which stood next to the stove. They figured the bird would be safe there. They didn't stop to think that if the stove was not on, a cat could jump on the cupboard, walk across the cold stove, and take one short hop right up to the cage where the little bird was. They hadn't considered that.

About this time, Paula's mother came for a visit. The night before she came, Paula had a dream, and the next day she told her mother about it. She asked her mother to help her see what was going on.

In the dream, Paula had been in her own kitchen working, preparing food, and suddenly this feeling came over her in the dream that made her say, "What am I doing here? I don't belong here." She was very afraid. Then she had this notion to go over to the cage. She opened the door, and just at that moment, the bird pecked her on the head very, very hard. It hurt, and it woke her.

Paula asked her mom, "What does this mean?" And her mother had a pretty good handle on the whole thing. She said, "It wasn't about you. It was about Lulu, the little bird."

Then her mother said, "You weren't feeling what *you* were feeling; you were feeling what *Lulu* was feeling. That little bird is scared that the cats are

There were three cats in the household, and all were looking at that cage where the little bird was.

going to get her. So you've got to move that cage."

The couple acted right away. A few days later, they called the mother to report that they had moved the cage. They had put it on the living-room wall, up away from anything, so that the cats could not get to the little bird, Lulu.

Paula learned something here. She learned about the deep feelings that birds and animals have too. I would say our society is becoming ever more aware that there is such a thing as consciousness in pets. And because of that, there are more rights for pets.

## DIFFERENT STATES OF CONSCIOUSNESS

No, I don't advocate becoming a vegetarian. Some people—I'm one of them—do better with some meat. If you want to save all life, then you have to consider the feelings of plants too. There have been studies done which show that when a plant has a leaf plucked off, there is definitely a response— a reaction to the pain that it feels.

So it just depends upon where you stand in the food chain. Eventually, everything here needs food to live. And it's going to have to take from something that was living.

Now, I know some will agree, and some won't agree. We're not here to argue a case, because these things are indefensible. They're a matter of belief or knowledge. Everybody's beliefs, as far as they're concerned, are based on knowledge. And there's no way to argue beliefs. We let each other be.

This would be the purest example of a demonstration of divine love—when we can let other people be, just so they don't hurt us or hurt other beings.

We have to look at states of consciousness too—what's higher, what's lower. Then again, you've

*This would be the purest example of a demonstration of divine love—when we can let other people be, just so they don't hurt us or hurt other beings.*

got different states of consciousness in people viewing or considering a situation. Some are going to say, "That state's higher," while others will say, "That state's lower." Some may say, "The plant state is higher than the animal state," and others will disagree with that. Viewpoints are all different, and you can't argue those things.

## THE SCRUFFY ORANGE CAT

Now here's another example of a golden contract. This is about a scruffy, little orange cat.

"Julie" knows how to keep out of the way of Divine Spirit and let It work. But human emotions do sometimes want to forget that. The human emotions want to say, *Not Thy will, but mine be done.* That's how it is. They get it backward.

Julie and her husband went to visit her husband's brother and his wife. As they drove up and got out of the car, Julie saw that "Sandra," the sister-in-law, was feeding a cat. It was hungry and frightened, with matted fur. It was just an awful-looking sight. Then Sandra explained, "It's not a stray. It actually belongs to people that live down the street. But they just don't take care of it, and I can't do anything about it. I won't do anything about it."

Julie had the feeling that she should do something, that she should take things into her own hands and just grab the little cat and take it home. That would save it from a bad situation. But a little voice inside her said, *Don't do that. Just wait.*

So she waited. She and her husband went home. For the next several months, she often had the feeling that she shouldn't let this go so long. Then they went back for another visit.

Julie looked for the scrawny little cat. But in-

> *The human emotions want to say, Not Thy will, but mine be done. They get it backward.*

stead what she saw was this magnificent, well-cared-for, fat cat sitting on top of a post. All the children were running around it, laughing. And the cat was sitting up there like the king of the neighborhood.

Julie wondered about this, so she went to her sister-in-law. Sandra said, "A funny thing happened. A little while after you left, the neighbors suddenly began taking better care of the cat."

Here's what had happened: Julie had done a spiritual exercise where she envisioned Prajapati. He is an ECK Master whose special interest is in animals. She kept seeing Prajapati with this little neglected cat. Prajapati was petting it, taking care of it, and loving it—all the things the cat needed. Julie kept doing this exercise for several weeks.

It was during this time, apparently, that Sandra's neighbors suddenly began to take an interest in their cat. They began to take care of it, to pet it, comb it, and feed it. Mainly, they gave the cat love. And this is all the cat needed.

When Julie and her husband were driving away after their visit, Julie looked over, and there was the cat, sitting on the hood of a car. Kids were running around the car, laughing and just enjoying the company of this beautiful golden Soul, this orange cat.

Julie realized that if she had stepped in and just taken the cat because nobody cared for it back then, all these different interactions would never have happened. There would never have been this chance for people to show their love, to give their love to this cat, and for the cat to give it back to these people.

So this was again an example of the golden contract.

*Julie had done a spiritual exercise where she envisioned Prajapati, an ECK Master whose special interest is in animals, with this little neglected cat.*

## A Child's Rocker

This story is about a child's rocker.

"Irene" was driving to the store. As she was driving along, she saw a sign that read Garage Sale. She was curious and went to it, but there were mainly baby things. Irene is a senior citizen.

But then, over on one side, she saw a child's rocker. She just looked at it. It kind of struck her. And then a little voice came. Of course, this little voice was the Inner Master, the Mahanta. It said, "Buy this rocker, because it will give great comfort." So Irene bought it.

That night, her daughter came over. Her daughter is a teacher at a special-needs school. Irene happened to remember the rocker. It was still in her car. She asked her daughter, "Would you be able to use this?"

Her daughter said, "I'm sure there will be someone who will be able to use it."

At the school the next day, there was a little autistic child. After lunch, all the kids were supposed to take a nap. But this child never would. He would just roam around the room, around and around. He wouldn't rest, and so the teachers had to keep a very close eye on him. But that day his eye caught sight of this little rocker sitting on the far side of the room.

He went over to it, looked at the chair, and sat in it. It felt great. So he sat in the chair, and he just rocked and rocked.

When she heard about this, Irene realized the chair was bringing comfort to this autistic child. And what was interesting about the rocking chair— although she didn't say this—was that she hoped it would not only bring comfort to the child, but

*The Inner Master, the Mahanta, said, "Buy this child's rocker, because it will give great comfort." So Irene bought it.*

maybe even a breakthrough.

Breakthrough—this was the key word. Because as the child rocked and rocked like this, he was rocking himself, trying to get out of this fixed state of consciousness he was in. It's pretty much like a car caught in a snowbank. You can rock the car, rock the car, rock the car—and with a little bit of luck, the car will come free, and then you'll be ready to go on again.

Well, the same with this child. If the child could only rock himself free. Because after all, any kind of state or condition a person is in—that you're in, that I'm in, that anyone else is in—we put ourselves there. And it's up to us, ultimately, to get ourselves out of that position.

The ECK book *ECK Wisdom on Karma and Reincarnation* may be very helpful to you in understanding more about this.

*Any kind of state or condition a person is in, we put ourselves there. And it's up to us, ultimately, to get ourselves out of that position.*

## A NEW LOOK AT ATLANTIS

As a side note, I'd like to mention that a lot of people in the world today have quite a strong attraction to Atlantis. There are two good books on this subject written by a man by the name of Frank Joseph.* One is *The Destruction of Atlantis*, and a couple of years later, he wrote *The Survivors of Atlantis*. He puts together all the different information available from geologic surveys, people who study myths, historians, astronomers, and archeologists.

* Use discretion in considering this author's other titles. His works on Atlantis and Lemuria are well documented and support a compelling case. However, the author has been known for criminal behavior and extreme political views that Eckankar completely rejects.

He says that Plato got the date wrong for the final sinking of Atlantis. Plato put it at about eleven thousand to twelve thousand years ago. But what Plato didn't know when he got the story from Solon, who got it from one of the Egyptian priests, was that the Egyptians had four different ways of reckoning time.

Plato was thinking in terms of the way we think of a solar year—three hundred sixty-five days or so. But the Egyptian priests had another way of looking at it where a year was about a month, which was a lunar year. And when you apply this time calculation to twelve thousand years, you come up with a date as recent as about 1200 BC for the actual sinking of Atlantis.

This was during the Bronze Age. And it fits. Eleven thousand or twelve thousand years ago, there would still have been Stone Age people. To suddenly have a big, strong empire with all the enormous buildings Plato spoke of would have been totally out of time and place then. Things don't happen like that.

There's a good argument for the sinking of Atlantis having occurred in 1198 BC. In fact, by different evidence gathered from astronomy, myths, and elsewhere, the author even narrows it down to November of that year.

There were four cataclysms in Atlantis. Three of them had happened over the previous several thousand years, and then came the final one around 1200 BC. The final one was also accompanied by a comet that had been going around the earth and getting closer and closer, so that people were literally scared to death.

The Atlanteans were much bigger than the indigenous people of any other lands. To some, they

*The Egyptian priests had another way of looking at it where a year was about a month, which was a lunar year.*

were giants. The Bible mentions something to this effect: "There were giants in the earth in those days." That's in Genesis.

Frank Joseph also points out that Atlantis wasn't actually a continent. This land mass just west of the Pillars of Heracles, or Gibraltar as we know it today, was an island about the size of Portugal. It was a maritime nation, and the Atlanteans traveled widely. They went up by the British Isles (though the land masses were a little bit different then) and all the way to the Americas. They were widely traveled people. They went over toward the east also, and they came to Egypt. There's a record in Ramses III's victory temple of a battle that had been fought with the Sea People. The Egyptians had another name for them, but it equates to the Sea People.

It's just a fascinating history. The Egyptians were defeated at first, time and again, but Ramses III was a very wise and clever general. Eventually he arranged it so his forces overcame the invading Atlanteans. The Egyptians asked, "Why did you come here?" And the Atlanteans said, "Because our homeland sank. We had to go somewhere."

The Egyptians even drew pictures of what the Atlanteans looked like. You can't really tell what dress they would have worn, because when they were captured, they were put into chains. After that, they were executed, and that was the end of it.

In Frank Joseph's next book, *The Survivors of Atlantis*, the author makes a very compelling case as to why the Bronze Age had flourished during the time of Atlantis—how the Atlanteans were key players, and how there are mines in the Upper Peninsula of Michigan that were worked at that time and which were abandoned at the time of the

*It was a maritime nation, and the Atlanteans traveled widely, all the way to the Americas.*

sinking of Atlantis.

It's all a very intriguing story. And the reason people have such a strong affinity for Atlantis today is that so many of today's people were Atlanteans.

## THE WHITE FEATHER

The title of this next story is "The White Feather." I'm going to call this person "Mark." Mark is from the United Kingdom. He was on a plane to the United States last October on his way to Minneapolis for a business meeting. In the seat beside him, there happened to be an ECKist.

Mark didn't know anything about Eckankar. He was going to Minneapolis on a business trip. But he had just lost his mate of twenty-five years, and there were times the sorrow was about to crush him.

His seatmate soon went to sleep and left an ECK book lying on the tray table. The title was *Those Wonderful ECK Masters*. Mark was curious about this.

He picked up the book, and he read about the ECK Masters and about Eckankar. When the ECKist awoke, Mark asked him, "Please tell me more about the ECK Masters in Eckankar." The ECKist said, "Well, you're in luck, because there is a seminar in Minneapolis. It's open to the public."

Mark made a decision right on the spot. He was going to go straight from the airport, straight to the convention center where the seminar was, and he was going to learn more about Eckankar.

At the seminar, he had a strong nudge to go to a workshop, "Keys to Secret Worlds." As he listened to what the people were saying, he kept thinking, *Yeah, I understand that. I believe it. I agree.* Then he told the others who were there about the loss of his mate.

When she had died, he asked her for a sign. He said, "Show me that you are all right. I want a white feather. This will be a sign that I will understand to mean you're OK." And he said, "It's got to be tomorrow. Not the day after, not a week from now, not a year from now. But it's got to be tomorrow."

He went to bed that night. He was very restless. He got up the next morning, cleaned himself up, and he went out to the car. There on the hood was a white feather. And he said, "She's OK."

But then he began to wonder about the spiritual worlds. He began to wonder, *What are they?*

Soon he was on the plane, and he saw the ECK book. The ECKist then extended the golden contract and said, "Hey, there's a seminar open to the public." Mark took advantage.

A door was opened, but he had to go through it. And he did. He went through the door, and then he learned. He mentioned at the workshop that as soon as it was over, he was going to go to the bookroom and find books where he could learn more about these teachings and more about the spiritual worlds.

There are a lot of different spiritual worlds. I've mentioned them in my talks. They're in the books and other writings. But the golden contract here was signed, I would say, with a white feather.

## CHRISTINA FINDS THE TEACHINGS OF ECK

"Christina" was a Catholic woman from California. She said she was praying in bed, when this nudge—here again comes that mysterious nudge— told her to turn on the TV to a certain channel. A special spiritual seminar was being broadcast. The

*Christina was praying in bed, when this nudge—here again comes that mysterious nudge—told her to turn on the TV to a certain channel.*

speaker's topic was on "dream work," as she phrased it—how to use dreams to gain a higher perspective or an insight into a higher state of consciousness. At the end of the program, the name Eckankar came on the screen.

She was impressed by what the speaker had said, so she went to the public library to research what Eckankar was. She wondered about it. She had never heard of this before.

She found information, and she read several of the ECK books. She also learned about HU. This is the ancient name for God. And she ordered the *HU: A Love Song to God* CD.

We're now going to jump ahead about two weeks. It was a Sunday morning. Christina was in church. She got there a little early, to spend time meditating before the priest began his homily.

As she began her meditation, Rebazar Tarzs, the ECK Master, came to her. She described him in his long, deep-red robe. He took her by the hand, and he said, "I'm with you now, and you will soon be called to service."

When she opened her eyes, she looked directly at the priest, who was also looking at her. She wondered, *When did he begin his homily?* Because she had tuned out entirely. She had been gone—over there somewhere with Rebazar Tarzs.

The priest was just saying, "In ancient times, a person's cloak was a necessary, valuable, and highly respected article of clothing." Then it struck her: Rebazar's red cloak, and that the priest would choose such a moment to speak of a cloak. She thought, *Well, this is a happy coincidence.*

Now we jump two more days forward. Christina was playing the HU CD and doing her spiri-

*Rebazar Tarzs, the ECK Master, came to Christina. He took her by the hand, and said, "I'm with you now, and you will soon be called to service."*

tual exercise. In this twenty-minute session, something happened that she called breathtaking and humbling. Rebazar Tarzs joined her again. He pointed her to a path to the sun. And on the way there, she saw the love of her life and other family members. They greeted her, and they said, "Love is the answer."

And indeed, love *is* the answer. These members of her family who had gone on before had learned this. They knew it now, if they hadn't known it before as completely as they did now.

Rebazar then took her by the hand, and they went through the sun to a beautiful mountain community. Now, Christina says he took her through the sun. But the sun, in this case, is one of the Sun Worlds. This is one of the subplanes of the pure Astral Plane. There are the Sun Worlds, the Moon Worlds, and the Lightning Worlds. These are all mentioned in the ECK writings.

This was one of the Sun Worlds, and Rebazar Tarzs took her through the Sun World to a mountain community. But the odd thing about it was that they could still see the sun.

Things are different there. They're not the same as they are here, where things are three-dimensional. Things are four-dimensional there. It's different. It's hard to explain. In fact, it's impossible to explain. You'd have to be there.

Through the ECK teachings, Christina found herself there and experiencing this. She was with a number of people, and they were all singing the HU song. They were dressed in white. She was one of the throng singing this HU song. And the sun didn't burn them. It was warm, and it was comfortable. It was almost like a warm embrace.

*Christina found herself in one of the Sun Worlds. Things are four-dimensional there.*

It was as if the goodness and the love of God had encompassed her and all these people.

Then came the sound of bells. By this time, she was hearing the next plane up beyond the Astral Plane and its subplanes. She was hearing the bells from the Causal Plane. This is one of the Mental worlds—the lower Mental world. There's the Causal Plane, the Mental Plane, and then the Etheric Plane. These all come before the Soul Plane, which is the first of the true spiritual worlds.

Beautiful sounds. It was as if they were of all tones and all loudness from near and far. Bells. And then it was as if she and all the singing people were being called to service by the bells.

This is what Rebazar Tarz had told her two days ago—that she would soon be called to service. Well, it was service, but in a way she had never expected.

When the HU song came to a close, she awoke refreshed and at peace and, as she said, humbled by the experience. Within a short three weeks from beginning to this time, she said she'd had the most profound mind-transforming and Soul-inspiring events of her life.

"As of this day forward," she said, "I know that how I live life will never be the same."

I want to mention the golden contract again: Every encounter, without exception, is there to move Soul along spiritually on Its way back home to God. My love goes with you—*is* with you—on your way home.

*She said she'd had the most profound mind-transforming and Soul-inspiring events of her life.*

*ECK Springtime Seminar, Minneapolis, Minnesota*
*Saturday, April 3, 2010*

There's a lot of protection that the students of ECK get from the Inner Master. And they're also helped in other ways.

# 9

# TEACHER AND STUDENT

The talk this evening is "Teacher and Student." It's a fitting title in Year of the ECK Teacher.

I was out in the garden, picking green beans. There were so many of them. The sun was hot, and I was trying to hurry and get in before it got too warm. I happened to look up our driveway, and here was this red fox, sitting there, watching me. Then he lay down, resting on the pavement. I wanted to make sure he wasn't hydrophobic, so I whistled and called at him.

A fox is known for camouflage. Yet nothing I did seemed to bother him. He was just very relaxed. So I stopped making a fuss and went back to picking the green beans. He had likely been watching for weeks and knew I was harmless.

For the life of him, he probably couldn't understand. *What's he doing, working so hard? Look at me.* He was relaxed, easygoing—quite something that a person should try to emulate, because it's a good life.

Teachers come in all sizes and shapes. And ECK Masters, too, are such.

*Teachers come in all sizes and shapes.*

People sometimes look at an ECK Master and say, "Hmmm . . . he doesn't measure up to what I know a master ought to look like, act like, be like. So he's not an ECK Master." We build up our perceptions about what a teacher is, who a teacher is, and how he should act by looking at masters, teachers, and preachers from other paths. We say, "There should be a certain amount of dignity." Or maybe, "He should be wearing a robe." And certainly, "Take those glasses off, would you?"

I say, "Uh-uh, then I can't read my notes."

And they expect all kinds of aimless talk. I've got a lot of that. Then they say there's too much. So it's hard to please everyone. I have a hard enough time pleasing myself.

## CREATIVITY: GOD'S GIFT TO US

*Life becomes more challenging as each decade passes. It's a good thing, because it evokes the spirit of creativity we have when at our best.*

An interesting thing those of you past the age of fifty have likely noticed is that life becomes more challenging as each decade passes. It gets to be more fun. Oh, it's a lot of fun. You're scrambling every minute, trying to figure out what's next. And it's not because of forgetting; it's just because there are a lot more things to do. Those of you who are under fifty and don't believe it, just wait.

That's not to say it's a bad thing. It's a good thing, because it evokes the spirit of creativity we have when at our best. This is the gift God has given to you—and to me.

Whenever you run into a situation, you think, *OK, this is a brand-new one.* Sometimes the body plays tricks on you, and you don't know what's going on. You try to figure your way through it, and you wonder, *How am I going to make it this time?* Sometimes they're just little things, annoying things, easy to get irritated about.

But along comes the next bigger one. At that point, there's no irritation, just scrambling wide open, trying to accept what the ECK, or Holy Spirit, is trying to teach us, trying to show us.

Because there's a lesson in every single experience.

We like our lives to go easy. We want them to go smoothly. And when they do, it's interesting—our creativity often goes to sleep. But when things get hard, then we become awake. And the harder they get, if we're at all spiritual, the more creative we become.

What keeps people from being creative is the old bugaboo, attachment. That means having a real fondness for some way of doing things or perceiving a thing.

So we go to sleep. But then when things get really hard, we wake up. And we ask, *Now what? What do I do now? What's the lesson? Where's the open doorway?*

*There's a lesson in every single experience.*

## The Love That You Carry

There was a nice comment to a member of the ECK staff from a desk clerk working at the Hilton. The ECKist called to check a reservation and got this kind individual. He remembered that last year was A Year of Creativity, so he asked the ECKist, "Have you been creative this year?" She assured him she had, very much so.

As they were talking, she said, "By the way, this is Year of the ECK Teacher." The clerk then said he always liked being around the ECKists. He said it just feels good—that they're wonderful people. I thought this a wonderful endorsement.

Many of you are encountering people here in the convention center and in the hotels. And they can feel the love that you carry.

They can tell there's something special about you. And of course, that special factor is learning about divine love and how to put it into practice in your everyday life.

In this light I'll briefly mention the *Eckankar Journal*. This annual publication is full of stories that you, the ECKists, have shared so others can see how the Holy Spirit and the Inner Master have been working in your life. The miracles, the insights into the future—all the different things. I mention it in case any of our guests this evening want to have a look at what many ECKists are experiencing.

*People can feel the love that you carry. They can tell there's something special about you.*

## SOUND AND SILENCE

The ECK teachings are based on two elements— the Light and Sound of God. These together are known as the Voice of God. This is how God speaks to us.

I remember when I was in the service, my job in the air force was to eavesdrop on the communications of the Soviet Union. The transmissions were noisy with static and sometimes just very faint. We were the voice interceptors. We would just make quick notes by hand in Russian about what we heard. Then it would go to the scribes. They would transcribe it; they'd work it all out. And if there was a passage or a word they couldn't understand, they would replay it.

We had tapes on reels, where you could put your finger on the reel and roll it back again and again and again. There was a trick the old scribes had—the ones who had been there for a couple years and were very good at the job. If they couldn't hear something, instead of turning the sound up, they turned it down. And then it was easier to hear a word.

Now, as I was saying, the Sound and Light are the two elements of God in expression. And when it comes to the Sound, and even the Light, we can take only so much at a time.

We can only take so much sound. We need silence too, an equal amount of silence. Because otherwise we come into an imbalance. When people have too much of one or the other, they can't handle it.

I'm not just speaking of an actual audible sound, although in our spiritual exercises it will be that. You never get too much of that because the spiritual exercises last only twenty minutes to half an hour, depending on how much time you put in. Then when you come back, you're back in this world, and these sounds out here are at a much lower frequency than the ones you would hear inside yourself.

Not that they're high-pitched by any means. Some of the sounds are like singing *HU* here. And then others will be like the wind blowing, or a train rushing by, or a train whistle in the distance. Or like a passenger jet flying in, ready to land at the airport. It can be all kinds—birds singing and water running—just about any sound.

Each one of these sounds comes from a certain area of the spiritual worlds. And it's a tag, if you will, that simply says this is where you are. You may never figure it out exactly, but you can get a rough idea where you are.

If you hear the sound of a flute, then you can be assured—no matter what initiation level you

*Sounds out here are at a much lower frequency than the ones you would hear inside yourself. Some of the sounds are like singing HU here. Others will be like the wind blowing, or a train whistle—just about any sound.*

are—that at that very moment the Master, the Inner Master, has taken you up to the Soul Plane for a brief experience to get you used to what it's like to live in that higher state of consciousness.

## ASSIM'S PROTECTION ON THE ROAD

All the names I'm using in the talk tonight are fictitious for reasons of privacy. "Assim" lives in Barbados, and he tells us how singing *HU* helped him. At one point, it probably kept him from serious injury.

Heavy rain was falling, and he had been with friends. It was late at night. They said, "It's raining so much, why don't you just stay with us?" But Assim knew a family member had dropped in unexpectedly, and the house was full. So he excused himself politely. He said, "Well, thank you very much. I'll be on my way. I want to get home."

So he set out. And whenever he drives alone, he likes to sing *HU* because it's soothing and makes him feel calm.

The road he was on wasn't exactly a highway, but people use it like a highway because it's fairly straight. He was going along at a pretty good clip—not real fast, because of the rain, but moving right along. He wasn't seeing any cars coming from in front, and there were no cars behind him. It was just an empty road.

As he went along, suddenly his car began to slow down. It was going slower and slower, and he was getting worried. This was not a good place to get stalled. He would be stranded out here in the rain, spending the night, hoping someone would come along and do something to help him. Finally his car just died right there.

*Suddenly Assim's car began to slow down. He was getting worried. This was not a good place to get stalled.*

Then, as the windshield wipers were still going, he saw something on the road ahead of him, just a car length ahead. It was long and grayish-white, and it covered both lanes of the road. It was a light pole. Here was this metal light pole, just lying right there. It didn't look like anyone had knocked it over. It was just lying there.

He wondered, *What's this?* He got his car started, drove around the light pole very carefully, and went on his way.

Again he began to sing *HU* as he continued on home. And he was thinking how fortunate he was that there was no one behind him. Because if there had been, and he had hit this pole—if his car hadn't slowed—then there would have been a terrible wreck. Even with no one behind him, if his car hadn't slowed, Assim would have been in a lot of trouble.

So, going on home, he wondered at the help of the Master, the help of the Teacher, to protect him from harm. There are stories like this in the *Eckankar Journal.*

*Going on home, Assim wondered at the help of the Master, the help of the Teacher, to protect him from harm.*

## THE ECK'S SCHEDULE

Often when I go shopping, I see a lot of people. They're good people; we have a lot of respect for each other. They're fun to joke with and ask questions of, such as, "When's the rutabaga coming in?" "Let me go check. I'll see. California's having a warm spell, and they don't dig them before the first hard freeze. Makes them sweeter." "Oh, OK. Great."

Then I wander off to the meat counter and exchange pleasantries there. "How's everything going?" "Fine, good." Then they ask, "Well, what do you want today?" I give my order, and I say, "Well, I'll be shopping yet a little while. Take your time packaging it." They say, "OK."

Most times they remember to have it all wrapped up by the time I get back. Once in a while they forget, because it seems the second I walk up to the meat counter, everybody in the world runs up to it too and wants something. They're so busy, they don't have time to turn around.

But I figure it's the way the ECK is putting everything on schedule. Whether we like it or not, everything is exactly as it's supposed to be, and everything is where it belongs.

## BAHARI HEARS THE MASTER'S KNOCK

This next story is from someone I'll call "Bahari." He's from Gabon, in West Africa. Even before he came to Eckankar, he had heard the HU sound. He'd be about ready to go to sleep, and here would come this sound. He often wondered about it: *Where does this come from? What's it for? Does it have any meaning?*

Well, he didn't know, and he didn't really worry about it too much. He just knew it wasn't a sound from down here, and that was enough. It was just a very pleasant sound. Later, when he began to study the ECK materials, he found out this was the sound of HU. This was the Voice of God speaking. Sometimes it sounds like a beautiful choir of hundreds singing this sound, and other times it will be just a single sound, like a solo voice.

But it was during this earlier time that Bahari first experienced the protection of the Master. He had come home one evening at eight-thirty. He

*Even before Bahari came to Eckankar, he had heard the HU sound. He often wondered Where does this come from? What's it for? Does it have any meaning?*

was exhausted, really exhausted. He came into the house, and the first thing he did was to put his food on to cook. He had prepared it the day before. He just put it on the gas stove, and then he went into his bedroom.

He went in there to get his work clothes off, so he sat on the bed to remove his shoes. He was so tired, he fell asleep taking his shoes off. While he was sleeping so peacefully, he forgot about his meal cooking on the stove.

*Suddenly this very loud knock jarred him awake. He sat up and looked wildly around.*

Suddenly there was this very loud knock. It jarred him awake. He sat up and looked wildly around. Then he jumped up and ran into the kitchen.

It was midnight. He had been sleeping three and a half hours. The pot was glowing red on the bottom. Everything inside was burned to a crisp, and smoke was coming from it. In no time at all, there would have been a fire. This fire would have trapped him, because the kitchen was between his bedroom and the exit.

Later, when he came into ECK, he realized that this loud knocking came from the Inner Master, also known as the Mahanta. The Mahanta is the inner form of the Master; the Living ECK Master is the outer form. Now, the two can't be separated as such. I'm just doing it because we live in a world of duality. It's easier for people to understand.

The Mahanta carries out the functions of the Inner Master, and the Living ECK Master carries out the functions that need to be done out here. Like making sure you get the ECK discourses, if you're a member. And being up here, talking to you at seminars. That's me, right here, doing my part. But the two elements are one and the same.

## A NUDGE SAVES A NEIGHBOR

Some time later, Bahari was leaving work. This is when he ran into the second life-saving experience. This one happened fairly recently. It was quite a while after his life had been saved by the Master's knock.

This time he had left work at 10:00 p.m. And on his way home, he was supposed to deliver a package to a certain address. But he got this strong, strong feeling that he should stop at home first, even though it would have been more convenient and quicker to go drop off the package. So he went out of his way to go home first.

When he got there, everything was fine. His home was in order. He quickly picked up some money in case he wanted to buy something while he was out. Then he picked up the package that he was to deliver—his final errand of the day.

As he was going past the neighbor lady's home, right next door, he smelled smoke. It was very warm out, and the windows were open. He looked around. It was so late at night that people were inside, many of them asleep. He went to his neighbor's door, and he began pounding on it.

She didn't answer. He realized she was sleeping soundly. So he grabbed the door and began shaking it, pulling at it, and making one big commotion.

Suddenly he saw the light go on inside. The neighbor lady woke up and quickly put out the fire. Then she opened the door and thanked him.

She said she had come home exhausted, very much as Bahari had done before. She had put something on the stove, and she just meant to rest for a moment. The next thing she knew, Bahari was pounding on the door. Her kitchen was also

*Bahari was supposed to deliver a package. But he got this strong, strong feeling he should stop at home first.*

between the exit and the bedroom. And very likely she wouldn't have made it out either. She probably would have been overcome by the smoke.

But Bahari had answered this nudge, this very strong nudge. He knew now that it came from the Mahanta, the Inner Master. So, as he continued on his way, he was very grateful. And he thought how the ECK works is a wonder.

Student and teacher. There's a lot of protection that the students of ECK get from the Inner Master. And they're also helped in other ways.

## ALLOW OTHERS FREEDOM TO BE

"Joyce" wrote to me about her daughter. She called her daughter retarded. Some people may recoil and say, "Oh, *retarded*. What an offensive word!" But I figure if the mother wants to use *retarded*, and that's what she's comfortable with, having dealt with the condition for many years, I'll respect her choice. And if she had used the word *handicapped*, I'd respect that.

Some people feel the only proper way to speak of a condition where someone is not able to get around and function as freely as others in society is to use the term *developmentally disabled*. Others go for *challenged*, such as physically challenged, emotionally challenged, or mentally challenged. The point here is not which is the proper way to speak of it today. But because it's very interesting, I looked it up.

*Handicapped* was used first in 1891; *retarded*, four years later, in 1895; and then came *developmentally disabled* in 1975—quite a jump in time. Then, in 1983, *challenged* was the buzzword.

Rather than become fixed on which term or

*There's a lot of protection the students of ECK get from the Inner Master. And they're also helped in other ways.*

expression is the right one, we ought to respect the people who use whatever word they want, if they are the ones who are dealing with a condition like this—either for themselves, a friend, or a family member. The greater stance, if you will, is to allow freedom to others to be, to think, and to act as they will, so long as it doesn't encroach on our own space.

*The greater stance is to allow freedom to others to be, to think, and to act as they will, so long as it doesn't encroach on our own space.*

## JOYCE'S DAUGHTER AND THE BEAUTIFUL SMILE

Well, Joyce's daughter had become very ill. Doctors gave a diagnosis of pneumonia and poison in the blood. In the hospital the daughter was throwing herself around so violently that the people there strapped her down so she wouldn't hurt herself. She was having transfusions for two days. They were trying to get that poisoned blood out of her, and they couldn't have her moving about, because it would have taken the needles out of her arm.

So, the daughter was in a fevered condition, and they had secured her to her bed. Then when the mother, Joyce, walked into the room, she saw Rebazar Tarzs, an ECK Master. He was seated there beside her daughter. He had his right hand on her head, and he was just holding it there. The mother knew who he was, and she just began to cry in relief and gratitude.

The daughter was soon released from the hospital. Her health had improved, and she went back to the place where she lived. It wasn't home, but it was *her* home.

After this, the daughter was changed. She was changed entirely. Before, she had been resistant to Joyce's love. When her mother tried to kiss her, she would back away, as if to say, *So what's this?* But now when her mother came, the daughter just wanted continually to be kissed. And then she would give back to her mother a most beautiful smile.

There are those of you who have had to deal with someone in a condition where it seems life has served them badly. It's not badly at all; it's for the spiritual benefit of all involved. It's there for learning. It's there to learn love, to give love.

## LOVE, RELATIONSHIPS, AND WISDOM

Someone wrote to me about having a very hard time finding love. The secret of love is To get love, you must give love. You've really got to open yourself and give freely of yourself. You can't fake it. It's got to be so. And when you do this, you become a magnet for love. Then the right person will come along, because you're no longer repelling. You're attracting, because of your open heart.

*The secret of love is To get love, you must give love. Open yourself and give freely of yourself. And when you do, you become a magnet for love.*

Even when you're in a relationship, it takes a long time to get engaged in it, if you will. It takes time because there are past hurts—all kinds of things that are in the past that need to be overcome.

A relationship needs to build too. It needs to grow more deeply than the first physical attraction, which is strong. But then it will grow into something that is very deep, if you let it.

Probably the hardest thing for people to remember during an argument is Only one of us should be talking at a time, and one of us should be right at a time. Let the other be right. And this is hard. It's wisdom—a lot of wisdom. Because when you're in the heat of battle, you're not thinking wise thoughts. The emotions have taken the field.

You've got to get apart from that. You've got to stand above it like an astronaut in space. Look down, and catch yourself. Look down as you would upon a Shakespearean stage: just players in the physical body, having a bad day.

*But if you can get through such things, the love will grow deeper over time. Open your heart completely.*

There are such things in many relationships— many things. But if you can get through them, the love will grow deeper over time. And the time will come when you simply cannot think of yourself as apart from your mate. You're one. Your mate's pain is your pain. Your mate's joy is your joy. Those of you who have stayed the course, you know what I mean.

If I can leave you with one thing this evening, it's this: to get love, you've got to give it. You've got to open your heart. Open it completely.

The longer we spend getting experience in this life, the more we learn about love.

May the blessings be.

*ECK Worldwide Seminar, Minneapolis, Minnesota*
*Saturday, October 23, 2010*

Eppie knew this was the Mahanta's way to heal her broken heart. Her heart was wide open now, and she felt such gratitude.

# 10
# ALL IN GOOD TIME

*O*ur talk title is "All in Good Time." It could almost have been called "Coincidences," because several of the stories have strong coincidences in them which, of course, are anything but that.

## THE CONDO SITUATION

"Tom," "Maria," and their adult son, "Jerry," made a sudden decision to move from Florida because of the large oil spill there. Maria was very sensitive to the fumes of oil on the water, and she was choking. So the family decided to sell their condos. The couple had a condo, and the son, Jerry, also had a condo. And they moved straight up to Minneapolis.

They hired a real estate agent, an eighty-five-year-old woman, who was supposed to work on their behalf. They had asked the Inner Master to guide them to the right person.

Their condos were all in good shape because they had planned to stay there for many years. They had new carpets, new furnishings, new tiles, new appliances—both places were in really good condition. They thought, *Even in a down market, if you price it right, the condo will sell.*

> Several of the stories have strong coincidences in them which, of course, are anything but that.

But there were multiple listings, and the eighty-five-year-old real estate agent figured she had done her share of work in this life, and she would just coast along. She wasn't too worried or too interested. And people weren't interested, so there were no showings.

In the meantime, these ECKists were up here in Minneapolis. They were paying rent up here, and they were also paying mortgages down there. They were paying for electricity, upkeep, maintenance fees, and so on.

Time went on, and there was still no action in Florida. The real estate agent simply would not act, even when the couple and their son dropped the prices on the condos. They figured the agent would post this so people would know. She didn't post it, so people didn't know, and people didn't come.

By now, the ECKists were getting desperate. They called some of their friends and said, "If you find buyers, then we'll give you a finder's fee." But nothing happened. They were real concerned. They called down to Florida several times, trying to get things moving.

About this time, the ECKists were saying to each other, "Wait a minute. Let's go back to square one. Let's see if we did everything right. We asked the Master to find us a real estate agent. Uh-huh, that worked out."

They were sitting there, scratching their heads. Then Maria remembered something she thought she had heard me say in a talk: "At some time we have to repay karmic debts either in body or in coin."

As Maria thought back, she saw how a lot of times in the past, they had paid in coin instead of in body and health. She and her husband were in frail health, and they really didn't need another

*Then Maria remembered something she had heard me say in a talk: "At some time we have to repay karmic debts either in body or in coin."*

beating in the health area.

She said, "In the past, when our car needed repairs, we would joke about it. We would say the car took the hit for us." That was fine. And then, within a week's time, both their refrigerator and dishwasher broke down. The grins and the laughter were a little thinner by then, but they thought, *Well, better to pay in coin than to take it in body.*

Maria made a connection here. She said, "Wait a minute. Is it possible that the condos are playing the same role as the car and the appliances did? Maybe the condos are giving us a chance to work off karma and some negative thoughts—maybe something we did to somebody else in another lifetime." And then she had a daunting thought— *maybe in this lifetime, before we found Eckankar.* She wasn't sure.

As she passed this information on to her husband and son, they said, "Oh, yeah! That makes a lot of sense." Then they said, "This is really great! Let's go out to a restaurant." So they went out to a restaurant to celebrate.

Only in Eckankar.

But the point is, in that moment, their attitude had changed entirely. They were full of joy, full of happiness, and they said, "Hey, everything's going to work out now."

And it began to work out rather quickly. Within the next week or so, both the couple and their son got calls that somebody wanted to buy their condos. Then the closing dates of the two separate condos were within two weeks of each other. And they got their checks within a day of each other.

Maria and her family were looking at all these coincidences, and they said, "The Mahanta's hand was in all this." This was so their karma could be

*"Maybe the condos are giving us a chance to work off karma." In that moment, their attitude changed entirely. They were full of joy.*

balanced in a less taxing way than taking it out of their health.

Maria summed up the lesson of the experience: "I have learned a secret, and that is to maintain a state of gratitude, no matter what life hands you."

## RIDDLE OF THE SPHINX

In Eckankar, our teachings are about learning through experience. You get a lot of ideas in your head, and you say, "Oh yeah, I understand that." But you don't really understand until experience teaches you. Parents know what I'm talking about when they try to explain something to a teenager.

Usually every decade an individual lives adds more wisdom. If you're in your forties, you know a lot more than you did when you were in your thirties. It's the same when you're in your fifties; you know a lot more than you did in your forties. And when you get into your fifties, you realize that those in their sixties probably know more than you do. But you don't care to know. You suspect it is so. And it is. But you don't worry about it, because life is that way.

The ancient riddle of the Sphinx goes sort of like this: What walks on four legs, then walks on two legs, and then again walks on three legs? The answer to the riddle of the Sphinx is man. Why?

Because man as a baby crawls on all fours. And in the strength of youth and middle age you walk on two legs. Then when you get to old age, you use a cane, so you have three legs.

## AN ADVENTURE OF COINCIDENCE

"Lisa" and "Dave" were spending their first anniversary on Tobago. That's the tiny sister isle of

*Maria summed up the lesson of the experience: "I have learned a secret, and that is to maintain a state of gratitude, no matter what life hands you."*

Trinidad just north of Venezuela, in South America.

Lisa and Dave were in their car, with Lisa driving and Dave as navigator. He had the map. Now, Tobago is mountainous and forested, as I understand. They planned to go to a sleepy little fishing village, but to get there they had to go along certain roads. They needed to stop for gas, so they said, "OK, at that first turnoff, we'll stop and fill up, just so we're sure we can make the whole round trip." They also had two other places where they could stop for gas, if necessary.

Well, they missed the turnoff, and it wasn't easy to turn around, considering the terrain. So they said, "Well, we'd better just go on until we get to the second spot on our map where there's going to be a gas station." And there was a gas station—with a sign that said "Closed until two p.m."

They thought, *Great. We'll wait until two o'clock.* But some of the locals said, "No, it isn't going to open today. By tomorrow morning, surely." Lisa and Dave said, "We're in trouble now." And they got in the car. They couldn't go back, so the only way they could go was forward.

Lisa drove very carefully and didn't accelerate unless she had to. And they turned off the air conditioner. They did everything they could to squeeze more miles out of the fuel in the gas tank. They wanted to make sure they would get to where they were going, because it wasn't the sort of road to get stranded on at night.

As they were driving along to their intended destination, they got to the third gas station marked on their map. And the sign said "Closed." But the local people said it would open at two. So they were very happy that something was finally going right.

They were right down by the seashore, and it

*Lisa and Dave said, "We're in trouble now." They couldn't go back, so the only way they could go was forward.*

was only noon. They said, "OK, we've got time. We'll have a little lunch." So they had a nice fish dinner right by the sea, and everything went well. When they finished lunch, there was still time left, so they decided to go for a walk. The road ran a ways outside of town, and they started heading down it.

A little bit later, the road ended in a single track. They decided to sit down and rest, since they had just eaten.

So they sat on a bench alongside the road. Nearby, a fisherman was working on his gear. As he was working away, Dave struck up a conversation with him.

Then the fisherman looked at Dave and said, "You know, twenty-five years ago or so, we were on a project together in Trinidad." And Dave remembered. He said, "Oh yeah; it's you, is it?" The fisherman said, "Yeah."

So they exchanged pleasantries, and Dave asked how everything was going with him. The fisherman said, "Oh, pretty good. I'm repairing my fishing boat. I need a certain part. But the problem I've got is that the supplier who could get me the part I need is over in Trinidad, and I don't have a way to reach him. I don't have his phone number, and I can't get there."

It just happened that Dave knew this supplier. And he said, "Hey, I know the guy. I'll get in touch with him, and he can get the part to you for your boat, and everything will turn out fine."

Lisa was looking at this whole thing, and she saw a lot of coincidences here. First of all, they just happened to miss the first turnoff. And then the second gas stop was closed. OK, coincidence. They ended up in this town, where they had to wait after lunch. So they took a nice walk, and

*Lisa saw a lot of coincidences here.*

they happened to sit down on this bench. And there happened to be this fisherman, who happened to be an old acquaintance, and on and on.

She said, "Wait a minute. I see the Mahanta's hand in all of this." She could see the Inner Master, who is just the inner form of the ECK, Holy Spirit. She made the connection and saw that all these apparent coincidences were brought about simply to help the fisherman. And also to make a connection that, in time, might be very good for all the principals concerned.

But she was most struck because she knew then of the love, caring, and compassion that the Holy Spirit, the ECK, has for those in need.

## MIKE AND HUCKLEBERRY MEET AGAIN

In *The Slow Burning Love of God*, Mahanta Transcripts, Book 13, I tell the story of a man, Mike, and his dog, Huckleberry. There were a whole series of coincidences that had brought them together then. After that, they were together for fourteen years, then Huckleberry died.

Now three more years had passed, and Mike still missed his dog. He hadn't told anyone that he missed Huckleberry all this time.

But one day in contemplation, he happened to see Huckleberry there. And he said, "Huckleberry, you're always welcome in my home. May the blessings be." That was all he did, and he just let it be.

The next day, he went to work at the courthouse. This is one of those coincidences beginning to unfold here—it was the same courthouse where he had met Huckleberry those many years ago. While he was there, a private attorney called him and, just out of the blue, she said a certain person in

*She knew then of the love, caring, and compassion that the Holy Spirit, the ECK, has for those in need.*

the courthouse was giving away a beagle puppy. That was what Huckleberry had been—a beagle. And for some reason, this woman felt Mike was supposed to know about the puppy.

The man with the puppy turned out to be a deputy sheriff Mike knew. But Mike hadn't known the deputy had a puppy he wanted to give away. He and his wife were expecting, so they decided it would be a good thing if the puppy wasn't in their home. Therefore, here was a puppy for the taking.

Mike said, "I'll take him." So that weekend he went to the deputy's house, and the pup jumped right into his car. And when Mike got home, the puppy seemed to know exactly where everything was. Because this was Huckleberry—same dog, new body.

This is how reincarnation works. This is the business of four legs in infancy, two in the strength of life, then three legs with a cane, and then we start all over again on all fours. Well, we're looking to break that cycle at some point so that reincarnation here on earth isn't necessary.

Now, everything happens in good time, in its own good time. Huckleberry didn't come back until it was the right time. And the people in Tobago got to where they were supposed to—to the fisherman—in good time, at the right time.

## BIRDS OF A FEATHER OPEN EPPIE'S HEART

"Eppie" and her adult son hadn't seen eye-to-eye since his youth. But after years of ECK study, Eppie realized that it was her anger and her temper that had caused this rift between her son and herself. There was more, but her anger played a big role. They had this karmic relationship, and Eppie explained it very nicely when she said, "We write our

*When Mike got home, the puppy seemed to know exactly where everything was. Because this was Huckleberry— same dog, new body.*

own script, and then we direct and star in our own play." In other words, we make our own trouble.

She was referring back to ten years before, when she had worked a night job. She would get off in the morning at six o'clock, jump in the car, go home, pick up her son (because there was only one car between them), and take him to work.

Well, on this particular day on their drive to work, they got into words. Tempers became heated, so that by the time they got there, he jumped out of the car, slammed the door, and walked off without even looking back.

Eppie said it felt as if she had been stabbed in the heart. She was deeply hurt. As she drove along, she was looking for a place where she could pull over, because she couldn't breathe. Her chest was so tight, and her arm was hurting her. These weren't good signs, and she was very concerned.

Off in a strip mall down the road, there was a pink neon light of some kind. She decided that would be a good place to stop, and she pulled in.

Now, as she had been driving by herself, she got this nudge that she ought to have a puppy or a kitten so she could have companionship and heal her broken heart.

When she pulled into the driveway of this strip mall, she saw that the pink neon sign was for a pet shop. It was a nice coincidence. She looked and said, "Whoa, a pet shop. OK!"

She expected it to be closed, because it was before seven. Nobody opens at seven. But she went up to the door, and the little sign said "Open." She opened the door and walked in, and the little bells on the door tinkled to let the owner know somebody was coming in.

*Eppie got this nudge she ought to have a puppy or a kitten so she could have companionship and heal her broken heart.*

Eppie called out, just to let anybody there know that it was nothing to worry about; it was just a customer come early. Then a very nice woman came out of the back. She said this was the first day of business. She opened early because she hadn't been able to sleep the night before. She would be in the back room, and if Eppie needed any help, she could just call. Eppie said, "Fine."

She looked around for kittens. No kittens. So she looked around for a puppy. One puppy, but the puppy was sleeping. Eppie has a kind heart, so she didn't want to wake the poor little thing; it was too early. So she looked around, and she saw a big table in the room. It was the size of a large door, and in the middle of it there was a piece of driftwood. On this table were twenty-five to thirty little birds, just hopping around.

On top of the piece of driftwood were a cockatiel—a small parrot—and his mate. The male looked at Eppie, studied her very carefully, and then started walking along this piece of driftwood. He kept his eye on her. He was taking her measure: *Yes indeed, uh-huh. Got some kind of psychological problem here, I believe.*

He came close, and then he stopped and picked up a twig. It was about the length of a little finger. And he did a cute little somersault. Birds are cute like that. Then, while upside-down, he took the twig out of his beak and held it up to her. Eppie saw it as a gift of peace, a gift of love.

Eppie very carefully took this little twig of peace because she needed peace. When she took the twig, the male cockatiel jumped on her hand and began walking up her arm, and his mate also walked up. There were other birds on the table, and some of those came over—birds of a feather and those not

> *While upside-down, the male cockatiel took the twig out of his beak and held it up to her. Eppie saw it as a gift of peace, a gift of love.*

of a feather. They all got in line and started walking up Eppie's arm. The male cockatiel came up right underneath her throat. He was making room for all the others, so they could hop up and get aboard.

Some of the birds migrated over to Eppie's other side. So she was standing there, looking like a bird stand, she said. All of a sudden she heard a gasp behind her—just after she had noticed a sign on the table that said "Please do not take birds off the table."

She had been standing there, trying to shake the birds off gently onto the table before she heard this gasp, but they wouldn't go. They just hung on. Birds of a feather and not of a feather, all together. They all hung on. Then the shop owner said, "My God! How did you do that?"

And Eppie said something to the effect of, "'Tweren't me, Sheriff. They did it." The owner said, "Well, how are you going to get them off?" Some had never been handled, she said. But they handled Eppie very nicely.

In answer, Eppie leaned down. She put her left hand on the table. The leader stepped off, and all the little birds of a feather on the left side—and those not of the same feather—got off onto the table. All the birds on the right side also got off when she put her right hand down on the table.

Eppie knew that this was the Mahanta's way to heal her broken heart. Her heart was wide open now, and she felt such gratitude. So Eppie thanked the shop owner very much for letting her look at all the little animals there.

Then Eppie went home. As soon as she walked in, the phone began ringing. She picked it up. It was her son, apologizing. Eppie said, "You have already been forgiven." Because she knew that when her

*Twenty-five to thirty little birds all got in line and started walking up Eppie's arm.*

heart was broken there was no room for love. And now there was no room in her heart for sadness, for hurt. There was just love—a heart full of love.

## INGRID USES HER SECRET WORD

This story is about "Ingrid," a member of Eckankar from Sweden. She had just taken her Second Initiation. This is offered to an individual after two years of study. And with it comes a secret word.

When she became a member of Eckankar two years ago, she said, "Boy, I'm really going to rip through these initiations because I want to learn all about God Consciousness as quick as I can."

*Each initiation opens your consciousness more so you can understand the miracles of life that happen around you every day.*

And that's what each initiation does. It opens your consciousness just a little bit more so you can understand more of the miracles of life that happen around you every day. This life is a miracle, and it's a blessing to be here. And the blessing in ECK is to be aware of what's happening.

Her whole life, Ingrid had had negative thoughts and feelings of anger and hatred. She knew they had been such trouble; they hurt inside. What really bothered her was going out in a crowd. She would go out, and she would become very angry because people were crowding in on her. She didn't like it.

But this time when she went out for a walk, she thought, *Well, I'm going to try my secret word and see how it works.* She sang it softly to herself as she was walking along the street.

Along came a man walking a dog. They have a lot of dogs in Sweden. As the dog and the man passed her, the man smiled at her.

Now, this didn't happen often, because she had been carrying so many negative thoughts with her that people didn't smile at her. There was nothing to smile at. They would just walk past this shield of negativity she had thrown up.

But this time Ingrid walked along, smiling, feeling very happy. She said it was interesting how her mood had lifted. And when the man smiled at her and she smiled back, there was this tingling of pure happiness in her chest.

She said, "Now I have a tool to transform my old, negative thoughts and feelings into well-being." She said she uses her secret word every day and that "It's a precious gift."

And it really is, for those of you who have your own word. There's a different word at each initiation. Each initiation then fits your vibrations to those of the Holy Spirit, the ECK. It's called the Holy Spirit, but It's more or less a current.

It's a current. It's a melody. And It's a melody of life. It's that which sustains all life and keeps it together. It's the Voice of God.

God, or the Sugmad, is in the Ocean of Love and Mercy, the home of God. But the Voice of God issues forth and takes care of the day-to-day things that need doing, or the eon-to-eon things that need doing. This is within the scope of Divine Spirit.

So coincidences are not outside Its realm of possibility. Coincidences are only outside the understanding and the imagination of man. That's why some people say the Holy Spirit couldn't arrange all these little coincidences. Well, they're not ready for Eckankar—yet.

They have a lot of experiences to go through— learning about the ways of Spirit, learning about the ways of life. How things actually work. You learn by your own experience that they do work in certain ways, that there is a certain structure. There is a hierarchy that works all the way down

*Ingrid said, "Now I have a tool to transform my old, negative thoughts and feelings into well-being." She said she uses her secret word every day and that "It's a precious gift."*

from God, through the beings on the other planes, and then down into the physical world.

Even in this physical world there are layers and layers of hierarchy. Because that is the order of things in all the worlds. Some people have a hard time with that. They think they're above that sort of thing. They're not. They're right in the middle of it, but they don't have the wit to recognize it. But they have to figure that out for themselves.

All happens in good time.

## "HOW DID YOU LIKE YOUR GIFT?"

"Ellen" has had a fear of flying ever since her husband died in a plane crash, ten or more years ago. Ever since then, she has been very afraid to go on planes. But she did because of time and expense. Planes sometimes were necessary for her to get here or there.

So Ellen flew to an ECK seminar. At the HU Chant Sunday morning, she suddenly remembered she had forgotten to print out her boarding pass for the flight home. She wasn't paying much attention to the HU Chant. She said to herself, "Oh, no. Now I'm going to have to get in that line, and there's going to be a mad rush to get to the airport." She was very upset at her lapse of memory.

The question is, Was it a lapse, or was it part of a greater play, part of a greater plan? We'll see.

When she called the airline, she found out that her flight was delayed due to mechanical problems. That was the last thing she needed to hear—mechanical problems. She told a friend, "There's no way I'm getting on that flight." And then, tearfully, because she was really upset, she said, "I have no faith. No faith."

*Ellen was very upset at her lapse of memory. The question is, Was it a lapse, or was it part of a greater play, part of a greater plan?*

Of course Ellen had faith. She had a lot of faith. She said she lived on faith every day, not knowing where her next job was coming from. She lived on faith. But at this particular moment she felt she had no faith. It happens. We drift in, we drift out sometimes for a short while.

A bit later, she called the airline again to find out the status of her flight. They said the flight was canceled, and she was booked on another flight. This meant Ellen could go to the airport with two dear friends of hers. She was feeling more buoyant now. She was feeling that everything was going to be OK. She just somehow knew it.

But at this point she said, "Somehow I'm going to have to face my fears, and I have to test my faith. How am I going to do it?"

She got on the plane and asked the Mahanta, the Inner Master, for companionship. She settled down in her seat and went into contemplation. And as she did, she saw the Inner Master. She also saw the profile of somebody else. She didn't recognize this person in profile at first, but it was the ECK Master Fubbi Quantz.

She said that until this time, she had thought the ECK Masters were just a nice story. She hadn't really ever believed in them. She figured this must be a myth of Eckankar—something that's just tossed about very lightly, nothing to take too seriously. The Mahanta, the Living ECK Master, sure; she had had experience there. But the other ECK Masters—just a myth.

*Until this time, Ellen had thought the ECK Masters were just a nice story. Through this experience, she realized these guys are real.*

Through this experience, she realized these guys are real. There really are such guys. Besides Fubbi Quantz, there are more, like the ECK Masters Rebazar Tarzs, Lai Tsi, and others. They're good friends. Good friends for you, good friends for me.

Each one of these Masters who are working in this realm has at one point been the Mahanta, the Living ECK Master. I've explained this more fully, but the ones that are known—the ones we most often talk about—have all been in this position that I am in now. And when each succeeding Master is appointed by Sugmad, the one who has been replaced becomes one of the ECK Masters who helps the Mahanta, the Living ECK Master of the times perform his mission.

This mission is helping Souls find their way back home to God. That's it. There's not much else that interests them but this. And they walk among you, usually in disguise. Once in a while, they'll let themselves be known. We have reports in the files of people who have met these Masters out here in the flesh.

Well, in contemplation, Ellen saw the Inner Master, and she also saw Fubbi Quantz. And in his hands he was holding a golden ball. It had tiny holes in it, and a brilliant golden light was pouring out. Fubbi spoke to her telepathically. With a twinkle in his telepathic voice, he asked, "How did you like your gift?" She didn't know what he was talking about. What gift?

So he asked again, "How did you like your gift?" Ellen was really puzzled. She couldn't figure it out. She sat there, scratching her head. So he gave her a clue. He said, "How did you like your experience this morning? It was just for you."

And then she got it. The whole thing with the plane—forgetting to print out her boarding pass the night before, getting upset, calling the airline, having the flight delayed with mechanical problems and then canceled, and everything else. All this

*Fubbi spoke to her telepathically. With a twinkle in his telepathic voice, he asked, "How did you like your gift?" She didn't know what he was talking about. What gift?*

was a play.

Much to her surprise, she heard herself say, as tears came to her eyes, "I loved it. It was wonderful." Again, only in Eckankar.

So Fubbi then asked her, "How do you feel about your faith?" And she said, "I do have faith. I've always lived by faith." By the time she got off the plane in Chicago, she was feeling really good. She had just been on a flight with two ECK Masters, and she knew everything was going to be fine on her connecting flight back to her hometown. She knew that the Mahanta was by her side and she would reach home safely. She realized it was an amazing lesson.

## HEALTH ON THE ROAD TO GOD

I would like to briefly mention two books. One is *The Longevity Project*, by Friedman and Martin. It's based on an eight-decade-long study of people, from when they were very young children all the way through to their passing. The authors look at those things which are said to lead to a long, happy, and healthy life, and based on the study, they point out which things appear to be true and which things are myths.

I would like to mention some of the myths here. The book is very good in this regard.

I think some of you will enjoy it, because one focus in Eckankar is health, since good health makes it easier for one to strive for God Consciousness. That's why I'm interested in things about health and why I mention items like this. Here are some of the myths:

- Take it easy and don't work so hard; you'll stay healthier. Myth.

*One focus in Eckankar is health, since good health makes it easier for one to strive for God Consciousness.*

- Thinking happy thoughts reduces stress and leads to long life. Sounds logical. Myth.
- If you have hobbies like gardening, walking, and cooking, you should take up more vigorous forms of exercise like running. Myth.
- Worrying is bad for your health; cheer up. It's a myth. I won't go so far as to say it's good, but it's not very bad for your health.
- Give your children a big head start in school, and they'll thrive for life. That's a myth.

That's why our society puts such emphasis on getting children indoctrinated early, even at the age of three or four. Get them so they all think alike, march alike, move alike, sing alike.

Well, those who are destined to be on the path of ECK are going to break out, and a big head start in school isn't going to do them a bit of good as far as society, parents, and everything conventional are concerned. Because they're going to go off and do what they feel is right within them. Not what society or everybody else says—e.g., you should be this, you should be that. No.

They're going to begin listening to the Inner Master. And what I'm speaking of here as the Inner Master is the Voice of God telling them, "This is for you to get the best spiritual experience," or that it is not. This applies to food, to mates, to whatever else you want to consider.

Here's another myth. You'll love this one: Get married, and you will live longer. That's a myth. So for all you singles, according to this study, you've got an even chance.

The other book I want to mention is *The Body Toxic*, by Nena Baker. This book mentions all the hazardous chemicals that are part of the world we live in.

*Those who are destined to be on the path of ECK are going to begin listening to the Inner Master. It's the Voice of God telling them, "This is for you to get the best spiritual experience," or that it is not.*

Even if you can get away from wrinkle-free clothing and from the flame retardants that are mixed into your computer, clothing, mattresses, furniture, drapery, and all kinds of things, you haven't even made a start, because there are a whole lot of other things out there. *The Body Toxic* talks about them, and there's no way to escape the sea of chemicals that make up our life.

But on the other hand, no matter what is going on around you, you're going to run your course of life. As sure as you were born, you're going to come to the end of your life—sooner or later. Some people do it sooner, some do it later. That's how it is. It's always been that way. This is the nature of life.

*You, Soul, are eternal. You are of the same substance as the ECK, the Voice of God. It's heartening.*

But also remember that you are Soul. You are not the body. You are the eternal thing—the eternal thing that has a body. You do not have a soul; you have a body. You, Soul, are eternal. You are of the same substance as the ECK, the Voice of God. It's heartening.

May the blessings be.

*ECK Springtime Seminar, Minneapolis, Minnesota*
*Saturday, April 23, 2011*

The man said, "I don't care what anyone says; I know the crow was thanking me for saving its life."

# 11
# A CLEAR MESSAGE

'd like to welcome all of you this evening to the 2011 ECK Worldwide Seminar. Also a welcome to the ECK youth, who have a very nice, big sign that says "Happy Anniversary—30th." It's hard to believe it's been so long. Thank you kindly, very much.

Thirty years ago you were still in the wings, waiting for your chance to come into this lifetime and have another opportunity to make a bid for the higher states of consciousness and to go through the gates of heaven. So to you, welcome. You came a little after I started this, but that's OK. We're glad you're here.

The title of tonight's talk is "A Clear Message." For each person's privacy, all the names given here will be pseudonyms. It's a lot of fun picking names. I go through and see what the person's real name is and what the story is, and then I try to match the name with the heart of the story.

## MEMORIES OF **HU**

I'd like to mention the word *HU* and how it's filtered down into some personal names. Hu is a Welsh name. It means intelligent. And for the ancient Egyptians, Hu was the nature god. I find this interesting. HU, the Voice of God, intelligent? Yes, all-intelligent. Nature god? Well, the Egyptians were framing this word, or this sound, within the reference of their times. Then the English have two names—Hugh and Huey. Again, all derivations.

Some might criticize this and say, Well, people make a lot of sounds, a lot of different names, and they could have just stumbled on these things by chance. Anything's possible. But it's not so.

These names are drawn from the memories, the ancient memories of people. As in the past, they have run into the sound of HU and then the word *HU* too.

## SOLVING THE MYSTERY OF SOUL

Many people don't realize that this lifetime is a rare opportunity. Of all the billions of people who are here, not so many will find ECK. But it's a precious lifetime for every Soul who is here. We come here, in a sense, like people walking into a dark room—into a dark hallway even—where there are a lot of sharp edges. And we stumble along, trip over things, bump into walls, get turned around, run into the corners, and things like that. Eventually we begin to look around for the light, or a voice, a sound—anything to give us a clue. How can we get out of this dark place?

This is earth. This is existence in the lower worlds. We bump around, and each bump gets us a little bit farther along in our search for truth. No, we don't like the troubles. In fact, we do everything we can to avoid them. It only makes sense. If we can't learn from the past, well then, we're bound to repeat the past. And I think we would like to go on to a higher class of trouble.

*This is earth. This is existence in the lower worlds. We bump around, and each bump gets us a little bit farther along in our search for truth.*

We've come to solve the mystery of ourself, the mystery of Soul—who we are. And it's a wonderful journey. Sometimes we get inundated. The tidal waves of life come sweeping over us. We go under again, and again, and again. And we wonder, *Will this never end?*

Well, this never-ending thing that's going on is called reincarnation, or the Wheel of the Eighty-Four. It goes round and round, and it happens again and again. At some point we've learned enough. We've gained the experience to begin searching in earnest—searching for truth, searching for the Mahanta, the Living ECK Master.

*Reincarnation, or the Wheel of the Eighty-Four, goes round and round. At some point we've learned enough.*

## PANTHER AND GROWLER AT THE FOOD DISH

My sister wrote that two feral cats had come to their home. They had been just the neighborhood cats for a while, but my sister kept putting out food, and pretty soon the cats decided this was home for them too. Panther is the black one. He's top cat. And Growler is orange and white.

The two get along fine except at feeding time. Panther has a habit of hogging the food dish. Whenever Growler comes up and wants to get a little bit of food, Panther will ease his body around in such a way that it very nicely pushes Growler away.

This happened day after day. But now, here's the point: People think animals are not so quick. And some people think so especially of cats. Then the ones who have cats say you don't tell cats anything; cats do just as they please. But cats can think. Cats are clever—very clever, once they put their mind to it. But that's work, so they don't always do that.

At one mealtime, Panther, as usual, crowded the dish. Growler sat there looking at the food dish. And then Growler's left paw moved out to the dish and pulled it out from under Panther's face. Panther just sat there shocked. He couldn't believe what he had seen. He sat on his haunches and watched as Growler ate the food.

Now Panther was going hungry because this happened again and again. So my sister said, "There's nothing for it. I've got to put out two dishes." She did, and peace has come back to mealtime. Each cat has his own dish, and they're very happy.

The point is nothing changed until Growler used his creative ability. He sat there and thought, *Yeah, this has gone on long enough. No deus ex machina is coming down from above to change anything. I'm going to take a chance and change it myself.* I think he sent a very clear message: He was hungry too.

We grew up on the farm, and as I've mentioned many times, my sister and I and our brothers all loved cats. We understood cats. We could meow like cats; we knew the different meows. You've got to be young, when your voice is still nice and flexible, to get to the high notes, the trills, and all the other little sounds that cats make when they're saying one thing or another.

We enjoyed the cats, and they became our friends, very good friends. When sometimes the troubles would get to be too much at home—the usual child-versus-parent type thing—I'd go into the woodshed, sit down, and talk to the cat. And the cat, Zsa Zsa, was very patient. Anyway, she liked the cookies I carried in my pocket for her. So I don't know if she was really listening or didn't care.

*Nothing changed until Growler used his creative ability.*

And the same for our dog too. Lady would listen very patiently. And she knew there was food about too. Animals can smell. Yet on the other hand, they did listen even when there was no food.

## ONE SOUL SAVES THE LIFE OF ANOTHER

"Holly" is a care manager in a facility in the United Kingdom. About a year ago, a very astonishing thing happened. Holly said that one of the residents has a cat, and this cat took a liking to her. At every break time, the cat would walk in the door and wait, meowing. And if Holly didn't come right away, the cat would walk up to her and kind of scratch at her leg. Finally when Holly got up, the cat would lead the way to the break room.

One day the cat came at the wrong time. Holly was at her desk, working. The cat came to the door and meowed. Holly had more work to do; she didn't move. The cat came up and scratched at her leg. Holly thought, *No, I'm going to stay here. It's not break time.* The cat went away. From her desk, Holly saw the cat walk down the hallway and go to her owner's room.

A little bit later, the cat came back. She sat in the doorway and made a very sad mewing sound. She came up again, scratched at Holly's leg, and then started down the hallway.

Holly knew this was trouble. There was something wrong. She followed the cat into the room and saw that the resident had fallen out of bed in such a way that she would have suffocated had Holly not come. Help came because the resident's cat knew how to send a clear message.

Holly marveled at this. She said, "It was wonderful how the Mahanta, the Living ECK Master

*One day the cat came at the wrong time. She sat and made a very sad mewing sound, scratched at Holly's leg, and started down the hallway.*

sent one Soul to save the life of another."

There are so many good stories that come from you that I enjoy preparing my talks. I start in plenty of time so I can go over and savor your letters. I go through many. It's always interesting to hear how the Holy Spirit, the ECK, is working in your lives.

Some feel there are no miracles left. There are always miracles left. ECKists know this because they know what to look for. They know when to go on high alert. Because there's a special blessing. It's a gift of the Master to you.

And the gift must be accepted and returned. The Master doesn't ask for worship. But for those who are his disciples, just simply that they love and cherish him as the representative of the spiritual power, with an understanding that they also have the spiritual power.

## A CROW'S THANK-YOU

The local paper, the *Star Tribune*, carried an item about a week and a half ago. It was in a question-and-answer column about animals. It was less a question than a statement. This person wanted to tell something about crow behavior. He said one day he was out by a pond and saw a crow tangled in a fishing line that was hanging down from a branch of a tree.

So the man got in a boat, paddled over, and worked at the fishing line until he was able to get the line off the crow. Then the crow flew up in the tree.

The man paddled back and got in his pickup truck. Then the crow flew down, landed on the cab of his truck, and rode it the few blocks to the man's home.

*The Master doesn't ask for worship. But for those who are his disciples, just simply that they love and cherish him as the representative of the spiritual power, with an understanding that they also have the spiritual power.*

When he got there, the crow began to call and call. Pretty soon a group of about ten other crows came, and they all flew in a circle around his home. The man said, "I don't care what anyone says; I know the crow was thanking me for saving its life."

I thought this was just a beautiful story. There are all kinds of little expressions of God's love that turn up, even in the daily newspaper. It's this link between life—between Souls. Cats are Souls, as are dogs and crows. They're Souls in certain forms.

Hearing me say this would offend some people. Because a lot of people feel they are the special creation of God, and they try to elbow out others, especially of the lower animal world—like cats and dogs and crows.

But it's a vanity that was very much alive during the Middle Ages before Columbus came to America. Columbus was very wise. He picked up some of the natives—which was unfortunate for the natives—and took them back to Europe. If he hadn't, he likely would have been accused of heresy for saying there was a land with people other than the ones in the known world. But the Native Americans were proof positive that something strange was going on out there.

You are Soul. We are Soul. And this expression of Soul extends far beyond the human form.

## JAMES AND THE VANISHED AD

"James" told how he came to know about the teachings of ECK and how he came to Eckankar. This was years ago.

As a fourth-grader, he was a member of the Catholic Church—that was his upbringing. He was an altar boy. One time, the church was going to

*You are Soul. We are Soul. And this expression of Soul extends far beyond the human form.*

have a mock mass. For some reason, James was chosen to be the priest. So he played his part through all the rehearsals. But he said he noticed a very interesting thing: He had never felt such a close connection with the Holy Spirit before. And he liked the role.

All through the rehearsals and then into the final play, this impressed him so much that he decided to keep open the idea of being a priest someday. Until then it had never occurred to him.

Years later, he had the opportunity to go hiking on a mountain. He got there near sunset. As he looked over the beautiful scene, he said he had his first conversation with God. Now, this left an imprint on his heart, because he realized that he didn't need a building to worship God. He could worship God or speak with God wherever he was.

We're going to jump ahead now. He went into the air force. While he was there, even as I did, he studied many different paths to God. He tried this, tried that, and practiced different forms of meditation. He tried out-of-body travel. He admits he didn't have a whole lot of luck with that. But he wanted to learn all sides of the Holy Spirit and verify for himself that God was real.

Next he got into psychic healing. He felt here that he was walking a very fine line. But he feels he came away unscathed.

I remember my own experience in Texas. I had come across a book about palmistry and studied it quite extensively. A couple of my very wild classmates came to me—guys whose lifestyle suggested they would have a very short life. I realized that in reading their palms, I could have a great deal of power over them and could shape their future.

A good palm reader will tell you that just be-

*Hiking on a mountain near sunset, James had his first conversation with God. Now he realized he didn't need a building to worship God.*

cause something shows on one of your hands, it does not mean that is necessarily the way things are going to turn out. There's a strong predisposition of something, but free will is supreme.

*Free will is supreme.*

I saw a very short life line in one of the hands, but I didn't say anything. I just said, "You know, you can live a very long life, and a good life, if you just take care of yourself a little bit."

Now, I doubt that Pete would have done anything as sensible as take care of himself. He loved life and all its ways. These two guys were something else. Pete was from Hawaii. He was half Hawaiian and half Irish. The other one was Slick, from New York City, off the streets. During the Vietnam War, the draft brought recruits in from off the street. That's how it was then. It's not like today. With today's voluntary enlistment, there is a higher quality of GI, or soldier.

Anyway, James realized, just as I did, that he had power over people and that he was walking a very fine line with psychic healing.

One day, when he was back in the States, James was looking through the classified ads. One said "Learn to Soul Travel." He dialed the phone number, and someone told him where to find the ECK Center. Then, very carefully, he yellow-highlighted the ad and put this classified section into his special secure place.

The following weekend he went to the ECK Center. But he went early. He sat outside in his car because, frankly, he wanted to see what the ECKists looked like. When they came, he thought they looked like normal people, so he figured it was safe to go inside.

Several different things were going on at the ECK Center. There were classes in one area, and so on. The ECKist who greeted him at the door said, "Just a minute; I'll be right back." Another person had also come in. The greeter came back and said, "OK, follow me. This way." They went into another room and sat down, and the ECKist explained very briefly what the HU was all about. Then they sang *HU*.

It was interesting because James saw a blue light all around him. Everything was blue. This meant, spiritually, that he was on the Mental Plane. Blue equals the Mental Plane. Blue also is a sign that the Mahanta, the Inner Master—that's the inner part of the Mahanta, the Living ECK Master—is here. The Blue Light means the Master is here, that the individual is in his presence.

*They sang HU. James saw a blue light all around him. The Blue Light means the Master is here, that the individual is in his presence.*

When James was about to leave, the individual who had met him at the door said, "Oh, by the way, I forgot to put down on this form how you heard about our ECK Center." James said, "Well, I saw your ad in the paper." The person said, "We didn't put an ad in the paper recently." James insisted, "Yes, you did."

It could have turned into a "did not, did too" exchange, but it didn't go there. James instead went back to the barracks, to the place where he had put this classified-ad section with the yellow highlighting on it. He looked everywhere. It was not there.

In retrospect, he decided it had been a very clear message for him to find the ECK Center and the teachings of ECK. Because he had become a seeker way back—looking, looking, looking. And now he had bumped into enough corners in a dark hallway. He had earned the right to meet the Master. And so, in time, he got to the ECK seminars and was able to be in the Master's presence.

You know, I feel a little awkward sometimes, speaking about the Master's presence. I don't want to sound like a stuffed shirt or anything, but it's the way it is. I've got to tell it the way it is. And so I try to do that.

## TOWART MANAGI CALMS ABU'S STRESS

The next story is from "Abu," a Nigerian. He was out of money and very depressed. He needed the money to pay for the education of his children and for their textbooks. He had retired a year ago and had been waiting, waiting, and waiting for money in the form of a gratuity, his pension.

It had been a year with no money, and he was at his wit's end. So at bedtime that night, he reviewed one of the ECK discourses he had read before. He had it all marked and underlined. So he looked at the underlined passages, and then he went to bed, singing *HU* silently.

He awoke in the dream state. But these money worries were so heavy upon him that he had carried them into his dreams. So he was weighed down and heavy and feeling so depressed. A friend came along and asked, "Abu, what's the matter?" Abu told him. And the friend said, "Oh, come for a walk. It's a beautiful night; let's enjoy the breeze. Let's go for a walk. Let's just go down the street here." Abu didn't want to. He didn't feel like it. His heart wasn't in it.

Finally, he gave in, and they walked down the street. They came to a school campus, and there was a group of people there. There were several buildings, and it looked like a political rally or something was going on. But his friend steered him

*Abu awoke in the dream state, feeling so depressed. A friend came along and said, "Oh, come for a walk. It's a beautiful night; let's enjoy the breeze."*

to another building off to the right. And when they came up to it, it turned out to be a lecture hall.

A young, energetic, and alert young man came out and greeted Abu very warmly. The young man took Abu inside and showed him around. They came to a certain hall where someone was giving a talk, and the young man showed Abu in. Abu seated himself and looked around. He recognized the speaker. It was Towart Managi, who many years ago had served as the Mahanta, the Living ECK Master in the ancient kingdom of Abyssinia, which is Ethiopia today.

Towart Managi was speaking from a lectern with a big book on it. Occasionally he would look down at this book, The Shariyat-Ki-Sugmad, and read from it. During the talk, Abu felt this coolness coming down, washing over him, and with it his troubles went away.

By the time Abu awoke, his depression had left. He realized that the Master had heard him and had allowed him to go to this holy place and hear this lecture.

At the time Abu wrote me, he still hadn't gotten the money. There are basically three possible outcomes to his situation. One, the check is in the mail. I think we've all heard that or used it ourselves. Two, he may have to find a new source of income. Three, since he's retired, maybe at least some of his kids will have to fend for themselves.

The point is, as long as we're here—and we are Soul, a spark of God—this creative power is within us. It lets us exercise our talents and seize the opportunities that are there. But sometimes we spend so much time looking at the closed doors that we don't look around to see if there are any open ones. There are.

> Towart Managi was speaking from a lectern with a big book on it. Abu felt this coolness coming down, washing over him, and with it his troubles went away.

For instance, today there are many people coming back from the war who have suffered severe injuries and are disabled. And it's interesting: Some people are survivors; they're going to make do no matter what. And other people aren't survivors.

But Soul, in Its pure state, is a survivor. There is always a way. But we must exercise our creative talents.

Abu realized that a clear message had come to help him out for the moment. And maybe he'll get more help in time. But he shouldn't be surprised if he has to pull the wagon himself.

*Soul, in Its pure state, is a survivor. There is always a way. But we must exercise our creative talents.*

## Rebazar's Test on Creativity

In this next story, we'll again deal with creativity. Creativity simply means going beyond conventional limits. That's all it is. But you'd be surprised how very difficult it is for some people to go beyond conventional limits. We're taught to think in certain ways in our schools. Society expects us to act in certain ways.

"Charity" is from Ghana, and she has pictures of the ECK Masters on her staircase wall. One day she looked at the picture of ECK Master Rebazar Tarzs and said, "Please give me an insight on how to earn my next initiation."

The next moment, she was in a Soul Travel experience. She found herself near the top of a mountain. It was all rocky. Rebazar said to her, "Here is a test to give the insight you asked for." Then he pointed to the rocky ground. He said, "Plant some seeds here, and make sure they grow into plants."

Charity looked but didn't see any soft soil. She was bewildered. So Rebazar Tarzs gave her a big clue. He said, "Nothing is impossible for Soul. Use your creativity."

Well, she had no idea what he was talking about or where to start. She asked, "How?" He said, "Get soil elsewhere. Bring it here and plant your seed in it. It's as simple as that." She then saw the plant, which had already sprung up, and it was in a patch of soft dirt. She admits she would never have thought of that solution.

Rebazar Tarzs went on. He said, "Life on the physical plane is like the rock. And humans are constantly faced with similar challenges of planting seeds on the rocky mountains that life presents to them. However, the solutions are simple, and creativity is the source of the solutions." A very, very clear message.

*Rebazar Tarzs said, "Humans are constantly faced with challenges that life presents to them. The solutions are simple, and creativity is the source of the solutions."*

If she wanted to learn how to get to her next initiation, Charity needed to use her creative talents. She has since become an initiate of the Fifth Circle, which means access to the Soul Plane. So it worked for her.

## Books to Help You Spiritually

I'd like to mention two books. I sometimes mention books or other sources of information that will help you spiritually. At times it's in the line of health, which I have done repeatedly in the past. This time I would like to mention something about the expansion of consciousness. In other words, push the envelope of some of you into areas that you're unwilling or uncomfortable to go. If you don't want to go, don't go. That's how it is.

I think many of you will find these books very interesting. Both have been published recently. The first is *Atlantis in the Amazon*, by Richard Wingate.

Atlantis has been the stuff of legend ever since Plato wrote of it in *Timaeus* and *Critias*, about 360 BC. Plato wrote about it, and I believe it was an ancestor of his, Solon, who had gone to Egypt. There, Solon had met an Egyptian priest-historian who told him how the Greeks had been a great nation once. He went into quite some detail.

Mainline archaeologists who accept the idea that there was an Atlantis are in the minority today. These archaeologists are pretty much the way archaeologists were at the time of Heinrich Schliemann. He was a very successful German businessman in the middle of the 1800s. Then he sold his business; he had become a very wealthy man.

For years Schliemann had read accounts of Troy and all the poetry of Homer. He looked closely at what others had considered just the stuff of legend. Schliemann put together the clues and financed an expedition. He went looking for Troy. And he was one of those lucky archaeologists. He didn't spend much time searching. He got there, and a short time later he found a site that turned out to be Troy. Troy then became the stuff of history. Maybe someday Atlantis will too.

The book *Atlantis in the Amazon* goes into a very fascinating look at signs of a colony that the Atlanteans may have established in South America. Wingate goes further and speaks of traces of Atlanteans in India. It's a very wonderful book—a fascinating one. And for those of you who are interested in this sort of thing, I think you'll enjoy it. Because once you get a handle on some of the events that took place there, I think this will help you out with your dream state—help you make sense of some of the dreams you've had where you were an actor back in a different time.

*Once you get a handle on some of the events that took place there, I think this will help you out with your dream state.*

I've mentioned other books on Atlantis in the past and said the author got a lot of the points right. This book gets a lot of the points correct too. This is another take on Atlantis, and it'll be fun, I think, for you to dig around and see how you do.

The second book is *The Phoenix Lights*. This is by a medical doctor, Lynne Kitei, and she writes about having seen UFOs, unidentified flying objects. She calls them something else, but they are UFOs.

On March 13, 1997, thousands of people across the state of Arizona saw a spectacle in the sky such as they'd never seen before. It was a mile-long, V-shaped formation of lights flying close to the ground.

Thousands of people reported this. They flooded the local police stations and the military with all kinds of calls.

The author photographed these lights over Phoenix. She makes a point that such sightings take place nearly daily around the world. And some of you have seen them, or think you've seen them. Some sightings are dismissed as merely swamp gas and the like.

But it's funny—the media did offer coverage of the Phoenix lights, but not too much. They skimped on it. The military denied, debunked, and tried to explain away the sightings, as usual. I find it interesting that in Europe there is a more open attitude about UFOs. There they say frankly that we don't know what they are.

There is a section in the book that gives a lot of statements by people. Jimmy Carter was one of the people who had seen UFOs. Statements by other important people also left open the possibility that there could very likely be people from another place.

> Thousands of people across the state of Arizona saw a spectacle in the sky such as they'd never seen before.

Reagan, when he was speaking with Gorbachev, brought up a hypothetical situation at one of their meetings. He said something like, "You know, we're sitting here squabbling about one little thing or another. How much more quickly would we draw together if we were faced by a threat from outer space?" It was just put out there as a hypothetical thing. And some people will say, Well, that's not what he meant at all.

I think you'll find this book can inform you about the great variety of consciousness all around us, because the book goes further than just UFOs. It goes into other states of consciousness, out-of-body experiences that people have, and other things. Just to stretch you a little bit.

## DELIVERING A CLEAR MESSAGE

I would like to give a rundown on some of the things we've covered so far and then mention a few things in the bookroom that you might be interested in.

We covered Panther and Growler, the two cats at the food dish. And a cat alerts Holly in the care center, with one Soul saving the life of another Soul.

Oh, I missed one story here, but I'm going to let it go because it wasn't supposed to be. The ECK does that to me sometimes. It's here, clear as a bell in my notes. Last time, I said all the names are pseudonyms, and what do I do? I give one person's real name, and this blows the cover of his parents too. But he needed it.

I'm just here. I try to be as clear a vehicle as I can for this Word that comes down. It comes as Sound and comes as Light. This is the Holy Spir-

*I think you'll find this book can inform you about the great variety of consciousness all around us, because the book goes further than just UFOs. Just to stretch you a little bit.*

it, the two aspects of God—the Sound and Light, the Voice of God, the Logos.

We also saw a crow's thank-you, James and the vanished ad from the newspaper, Towart Managi calms Abu's stress and depression, and Rebazar's test on creativity.

Then we talked about the two books, *Atlantis in the Amazon* and *The Phoenix Lights*.

One item in the bookroom I would like to mention is a very favorite of mine: the 2012 *Eckankar Journal*. In it are your stories. Excellent. Also, the *Illustrated ECK Parables*. This is for children. Beautiful, beautiful work. I'm just amazed by the things that today's technology can accomplish so quickly.

I worked in the camera department at the Eckankar International Office back in Menlo Park, California. Some of the things I was doing there are done now within minutes, whereas it used to sometimes take me a couple of days. It's wonderful. I love the technology, but I'm sensitive to EMR, and so is Joan, my wife. We have to dance around the heavy electromagnetic stuff as much as we can.

I'd also like to mention that a discourse workbook is ready. Joan put a lot of work into it, as did several others in the office. A couple of people spearhead the project, and they do the majority of the work. Then Joan comes along. She's one good editor, and she's tough. Everything's got to sing, just like the sound of HU.

*Joan's one good editor, and she's tough. Everything's got to sing, just like the sound of HU.*

She'll juggle the layout until it's just right. Sometimes I'll look at it, just take a quick look at something and see what she's working on. The staff has done a great job. They've done as much work probably as Joan will do when she gets it from

them. She does wonderfully. And I'm not just saying it because she's my wife. We get along anyway.

The last book I'd like to mention is *The Spiritual Life*, by myself.

This is wonderful—I got through the whole talk
without having to resort to the glass of water. I
don't like to come up here and make my efforts to
deliver a clear message to you such an effort for
you, the listeners. So I'm grateful to the ECK.

May the blessings be.

*Joan juggles the layout until it's just right. She does wonderfully.*

*ECK Worldwide Seminar, Minneapolis, Minnesota
Saturday, October 22, 2011*

I was dropped right into the middle of all these medical professionals, and I was very happy to be with them. We had a lot of laughs, and I think the benefits ran both ways, everywhere.

# 12
# A Mission Renewed

W⌐hen Heidi read the little notice that was put into the seminar program, she went on Facebook and said, "This is going to be something special." The program note read "Sri Harold will show in his own person a new side of spiritual unfoldment. It's more than you think." And here it is, in my own person.

## Life's Curveball

As things have been going, you just make do. If something doesn't work, you do something else.

Here's the thing. Life tosses us a curveball or something. You can sit and complain about it. You can do whatever you want, but it doesn't change one thing. *You* may change, but what happened happened. And a lot of spiritual growth can occur in the meantime.

When I got into this position in 1981, I had a choice of whether to see the future or not. I said, "Not." Why sit and worry for ten years, twenty years? If it's your destiny, you can't outrun it; you can't outwit it, outfox it, or anything. You'd just rather take it. And so I said, "No, I don't want to know the future."

When I got into this position in 1981, I had a choice of whether to see the future or not. I said, "Not." Why sit and worry for ten years, twenty years?

I was taking the trash out in the morning. We have a little overhang on the roof—very safe. And the ice looked like that crinkly sort that would melt later in the day. It looked like the sun would come out, and everything would be fine. So I said, "OK, I'll just kind of inch out the way I did when I was a kid." And then just slide along if it's a little more slippery.

## A Slip on the Ice

The next moment I was on the ground, and I knew I had broken something. Overnight there had been a light rain, and it made the crinkly ice look very harmless. Now, this is one of the mildest winters Minnesota has ever recorded. And here I go bouncing down on black ice.

*I knew I was in trouble. But I had a plan. I knew there was a broom in the corner beyond the other side rail, if I could just get there.*

I knew I was in trouble. When I went outside, Joan, my wife, had just gotten up. I heard her snap the light on upstairs. But our home is very soundproof.

The ground was cold, and I knew I had to get off it. So I tried in several different ways to pull myself up on the nearby side rail of the open garage door. I couldn't do it. But I had a plan. I knew there was a broom in the corner beyond the other side rail, if I could just get there.

And so I did, in some very painful way. I dragged myself there, and I was just able to reach the broom. I had this bright idea: turn the broom upside down, and put it under my arm like a crutch. I did. It immediately collapsed.

In the medical profession they have a pain scale so that they know how much medication you need. And the scale goes like this: 1 to 4, you'll live; 5 to 8, you think you won't; 9, you're pretty sure; and 10, you scream. They call it *shriek*, but it's scream. Number 10, they call it.

So the first time I fell against the door going into the laundry room, it was a number 10. I stood there a little bit and then said, "I'll try it again." Because I didn't know if Joan could hear anything. The next time I tried it, the door opened, banging against the cupboard in there—KA-WOOMP!

Then Joan called down. She asked, "Are you OK?" I said, "No." It was very painful because I had a broken hip.

As Joan got there, I said, "Get under my left arm, and just get me on the bench." We have a padded window bench in the laundry room. She got me there. I did some number 9s and 10s. And then I just sat there, all hunched over, and said, "Call 911."

So she ran off, called 911, and then came back. She asked, "Are you OK?" I said, "Yeah." I was all hunched up on this padded bench. But I was not moving at all.

After a little bit I heard the sirens. People from the sheriff's department were the first to come. They asked my name, and I told them. They wanted to make sure I could answer. Often, when people fall like this, it's much worse. They hit their head, break their elbow, and break their hip too. But I just broke my hip.

*After a little bit I heard the sirens.*

The next thing, the paramedics were there. They came in with a stretcher. They said, "OK, cross your arms over your chest." I said, "This is going to hurt." Number 10!

They got me on the stretcher. I don't know what they had on the soles of their shoes. They must have had special grippers. But as we went out, I said, "Be very careful. It's slippery out here." And they said, "We know."

Pretty soon we got to the emergency room, and they took X-rays. To take X-rays, they moved me off the gurney and put me on this hard metal table. I was doing number 10s all along. Then they said, "Now we're going to have to move your leg one more time to get another angle on this." It went on and on. Finally they said, "Yep, just as you thought—broken."

So they said, "Now we're going to have to pack you up again and send you off to the hospital."

When they asked, "What hospital?" I said, "We don't know. What do you recommend?" They suggested one, and I said, "OK." Next someone asked, "What surgeon?" We said, "We don't know. What do you recommend?" Somebody said, "If I had it done, I would want Dr. so-and-so." I said, "OK, Dr. so-and-so."

Finally we got to the hospital. Word had arrived that the leader of Eckankar was coming in with a broken hip. They were very respectful, professional people at this hospital. Top-notch, the whole bunch of them.

## RESTRICTION AGAINST PAIN

We got up to my room, and several nurses came in and did things. Soon another nurse came in—just a dear, dear person. Her name is Faye. She was taking information and had been talking to Joan. She found out a friend of ours was going to make the food for us—three meals a day—because we have special diets, and the hospital food just wouldn't have worked.

So Faye, the nurse, asked, "Apart from your diet, do you have any other restrictions?" And I said, "Yes, I do." She poised her pencil over the notepad, and she said, "Yes?"

I said, "I have a restriction against pain. But it's doing absolutely no good."

From that moment on, we got along well. We got talking later, because in the room they had this little computer, and every time a nurse did anything—gave me anything, moved me, looked at me, or anything—she entered it on the computer.

So over the time I was at the hospital, Faye would often be typing there, and as she typed, we would talk. Everything went fine, and we got to be very good buddies. So much so, in fact, that some of the other nurses were thinking she was being disrespectful to me. The others were trying to be very respectful to the leader of a religion that none of them really were very familiar with.

The ECK had dropped me right smack into the middle of medical professionals, into this whole new arena. For the next three weeks or so, I was going to spend my time with them—first in the hospital and then in the transitional-care unit, which is where you recover, get fixed up, and are taught how to strengthen muscles and all that.

*The ECK had dropped me right smack into the middle of medical professionals, into this whole new arena.*

So we got to know each other very well. And it was just a joy working with Faye and the other nurses there. There was another nurse, Jane, whose humor was very subtle. It's hard to put it into words, but she did one thing I thought was very special.

Jane didn't need her glasses except to type on the computer when she was the nurse on duty. The rest of the time, she carried her glasses up on her forehead. When she went to the computer, she'd stand there and wrinkle her nose, and the glasses would slide right down into place. Then she'd start typing, typing, typing. When she was done, she'd flip the glasses up to her forehead. I asked, "How long did it take you to learn to do that?" And she arched an eyebrow, which was one of her subtleties. She was just a wonderful, wonderful wit, and she had a lot of good qualities.

When you're in a hospital gown, the nurses are looking at your front and back. If you've had modesty before, you soon lose it. One time, Faye said, "You're *sunning* me"—as opposed to mooning, because she was looking at my front side, not the back side.

## JOURNEY TO SURGERY

That evening, the doctor came. A very young man, he seemed to me, and full of energy. He drew a sketch, which I couldn't make out at all, of everything he was going to be doing. He had looked at the X-rays and said it wouldn't have to be a full hip replacement, which is very tough.

Later in the rehabilitation facility, I saw a lot of the patients there. They were all really tough, but they were going through it. They were paying their dues.

Anyway, the doctor told me everything that was going to happen, and then he went away. Next morning, bright and early, they came and got me. They wouldn't let me eat. They never let you eat before these operations.

The person wheeling me along on the gurney was really going fast, even around corners. You can't see around the corners; there are no mirrors. All I could see were these fluorescent ceiling lights whizzing past. I asked, "Do you ever hit anybody at one of these corners?" She said, "Not in four years!"

> I saw a lot of the patients there. They were all really tough, but they were going through it. They were paying their dues.

Well, I hung on tight because things happen. But she hit no one. As we were whizzing along, I saw faces of people standing off to both sides, because apparently gurneys going to the operating room have the right of way. They can go as fast as they want, even around blind corners. It was funny. We went around several of these corners, and I would see people pinned against the wall.

Anyway, we got down there early. We were waiting, and pretty soon the anesthesiologist came out. Now, by this time, they knew Joan.

Joan had been staying in the room with me. Back when the ambulance left our house, she was in the front seat. And she was with me the whole time. She never left once.

They knew she wanted to muscle-test everything—kinesiology. So the doctor came out, and he had two drugs. He asked, "Would you like to test these?" She said, "Yes." Soon she said, "This one is good. I'm not sure about the other one." He said, "Well, I'll tell you what they do. This one that you said is good takes away all pain. And the other one makes you forget; if you didn't take it, you would hear and remember everything that they do during the operation." I told Joan, "I don't care how the muscle-testing comes out; I'm taking both!"

We went into the operating room, and everybody was wearing masks and green scrubs. You don't know who's who, who's going to be doing what to you.

They were about to put the needle in my arm. They were laughing, and I couldn't see. "What are you laughing at down there?" I said. "It's my veins, isn't it?" They said, "Yeah." I've got these big veins. They're as big as noodles. I've had doctors and nurses in the past who could not hit them, and as

> I told Joan, "I don't care how the muscle-testing comes out; I'm taking both drugs!"

they were sticking me I'd say, "Listen, other people can hit it. Why can't you?"

So now in the operating room they were laughing. And then they nicely put the needle in my arm. They usually say, "We're going to have you count backward from a hundred," and you start counting. Well, they said, "OK, now we're going to have you count . . ." And that's it. I remember nothing more. I didn't even get to the first number.

The next thing I knew—it could have been thirty seconds, or it could have been an eternity—I started waking up. It was kind of quiet in there. I felt relaxed. Everybody was rushing around. I opened my eyes, and I asked somebody, "Were my vitals OK?" You know, my heart and things like that. I have a lot of sensitivities. And they said, "Yeah, they're fine." I asked, "How did the operation go?" "It was fine. It was fine." I said, "Good. Good." They said, "We're going to put you back on the gurney now." I said, "OK."

It didn't hurt because they had me all filled up with these pain medications. And I thought, *This is really great.* So I thanked everybody. We went out the door, and the fluorescent lights and faces whizzed by again. I was smiling and waving as best I could. I was strapped in pretty good.

We got back up to the room. And after about eight or twelve hours, that really deep anesthetic started to wear off.

I said, "Help." They knew. Because whenever the nurses moved me, I'd do a number 10. And then they'd bring me some pain medication. I'd take the pain medication, and then I would usually be at number 8. They'd wait, and then they'd ask, "What's it like now?" After a while I got to be down around number 4. They'd say, "That's OK. He'll live."

> I thanked everybody. We went out the door, and the fluorescent lights and faces whizzed by again. I was smiling and waving as best I could.

This went on and on. And they were the nicest people. I met some fine, fine folk there, and they were curious about ECK.

It turned out Faye was a very devout member of the Assembly of God church. We talked about how she had gone to a number of Protestant churches and had not felt comfortable in many of them. She came to the Assembly of God and felt good there. I said, "Wonderful. That's exactly where you belong." And so we had a very good time. When the time came to leave, I very much missed her and Jane and all the others too.

## 1981—ON THE FAST TRACK

The title for this talk is "A Mission Renewed." The first time I was put on the fast track was in 1981 when I came into this position as the Mahanta, the Living ECK Master. It was very difficult.

*The first time I was put on the fast track was in 1981 when I came into this position as the Mahanta, the Living ECK Master. It was very difficult.*

I used to work back in production with my friends. We'd try to find the best way to get the ECK works out to you in the field. We'd run into all kinds of problems. We'd put our heads together and figure out one way or another to get past problems. One day we were buddies; the next day I was their boss.

And I've always had this hard time being anybody's boss. In the service, when I was supposed to march our troop, I didn't like it. I had to do it. I goofed up at times, and other times I did very well. But I did not like it. The guy who had more time in grade and service than me was supposed to be marching us. But he got busted, and that left me with the most time in grade. So I had to march these sixty people around, and I didn't like it. I didn't like to be in charge of anybody.

But as the ECK would have it, I was always in charge of somebody. I was always somebody's boss. But in 1981, it was very, very hard. I didn't want to go in by the front door. I would come in the back door by Production. But I knew of a shortcut where I did not have to go past the windows of the Production offices—the expediter, Purchasing, and all that. I could just skip on by and go to my office. So I did.

The first time I went to New Zealand in this position, I had just been named. My predecessor was in charge of the office. He was taking care of the physical things; I was taking care of the spiritual. He had very thoughtfully arranged to send me on this trip, which he used to do, to New Zealand, Australia, and then maybe to Hong Kong and Malaysia.

So I got to the seminar in New Zealand, and I was supposed to give a talk there. But this transition had happened so recently, they didn't know what I looked like, communication not being the same as it is today.

I saw a couple of the chelas. They were seated in the hallway, and I sat down beside them. When the meeting that was going on came to an end, we all got up to go in. We had been talking just like old friends, though I was always kind of reserved. Then one of them asked, "Are you Harold Klemp?" I said, "Yes."

Right away everybody backed off, and they were very respectful. Here it goes again. I felt awkward—just very, very awkward. Yet I went in and gave the talk, and we finished the rest of the tour.

Since then I have had to get used to it. But that was one of the times the ECK turned the page in my life very quickly.

## Minimasters

We have this phenomenon called the minimasters. There's one, a woman, waiting for the next ECK Worldwide Seminar. She's thinking the Mastership is going to her there. Then there's a guy who didn't have the forty dollars to come here now. He said he'll save his money for the Worldwide, and he'll come up and graciously accept the Mastership then.

Most of these people are so full of the ego and full of themselves. They don't realize the load that would be put on them, as it was on me a year before I finally got the Rod of ECK Power. It unbalanced me, and it was a year before I was ready. Most of the pretenders would not last a week, let alone a month.

Someone coined a term for them, and it's perfect—minimasters. They're about the size of pygmies in a grown-up world. But they don't know it. You can talk straight to them, and it's like talking to a corkscrew. You just don't reach them. But I gave it my best shot just now.

Now, there are people who are in the circle for Mastership, and they're always there. They're all male; it has to do with the spiritual currents and so on. Kata Daki is a female ECK Master, and there are others. But she wasn't the Mahanta, the Living ECK Master.

These minimasters always belittle the ECK Masters. Don't do it. There are some great ones walking out among people, even here in the audience tonight.

Sometimes people think this is fantastic when I say they're walking among you. They are. We have many reports of them. They're just top-notch.

*There are some great ECK Masters walking out among people, even here in the audience tonight.*

## The ECK Turns the Page

The next time the ECK turned the page on me was my car accident. That happened in 1991. I had severe whiplash. No cuts; nothing but severe whiplash and all kinds of internal injuries. But I carried on. A lot of people probably didn't know I had been in an accident at that time.

I made the trip all the way down to Australia in spite of it. You have to understand, the burning was so severe from the whiplash, I had to wear a neck brace. But I took it off whenever I was around ECKists. It just burned. When I lay down, it was on ice, with ice on my chest, because I had all kinds of things torn in my chest.

There had been no citation for the accident. I was standing on the brake. The brakes failed, and it was just a terrible thing. I ran into the back end of a little bitty car with two girls in it, high-school age—my daughter's age. I was trying to avoid everybody. I was trying to go over on the curb, but then a huge car pulled out right in front of me, and I knew I would hit the curb at an angle that would turn my car over. And that wouldn't have been good at all.

*The front end of my car was all pushed up, but somehow I managed to get it many miles home, going slowly on back streets.*

So I tried to hit in a way that would spread the impact out a little bit between our two cars. Unfortunately, the girls had the smallest car, and the back end of their car was all bashed in. The front end of my car was all pushed up, but somehow I managed to get it many miles home, going slowly on back streets. When I drove up, of course Joan practically went into shock. But she has a pretty cool head. She doesn't go into shock very easily.

So all that happened, and then I had to do a lot of traveling. But the important thing is that my schedule had been very, very hard for ten years.

I was making all these tours and giving all these talks, and I always had to prepare. I was writing all these discourses, thirty-five hundred words in each lesson. I worked on them for the longest time. I would write all these, and then I would have to write all the articles for the *Mystic World*, Wisdom Notes, *H.I. Letter*,* and *RESA Star,* as well as the Q&As for the youth and the Q&As for the RESAs. All this writing, writing, writing.

I would get up sometimes at four or five in the morning to do this writing. I would take maybe half an hour to clean up, and then I'd start working and stay at the typewriter until around noon. Then I would take a break—maybe go out and play video games for a while. I'd go out and be around people to catch stories. I always carried a notebook in my pocket.

Then I would go to the library and do research before coming home. And I'd do it all over again the next day. I did this day after day, seven days a week. It was just a terrible, terrible schedule.

So the ECK had decided it was time to slow me down. And It did, via the car accident. Then of course this time, it was the black ice. I didn't want to know any of these things beforehand. I had opted out. I do not want to know the future. Believe me, it's better that way, because in any of these cases my attention would have been on the future, and I never would have gotten anything done. I got a lot done in the meantime.

*It's better that way, because my attention would have been on the future, and I never would have gotten anything done.*

## JOAN ON THE SCENE

When we got to the transitional-care unit, there were some interesting people there. As soon as you

---

* Now the *Golden Leaf*. —Ed.

arrive, they take pictures of you. That way, if you ever come back again, and somebody says, "Harold Klemp is here," they can go back through their photo file and say, "Oh, yeah, now I remember him."

But the day I got there, they said, "Usually we take your picture, but we can't take it. The camera's broken." I said, "Who broke the camera?" Nobody would answer me. So I asked again. Still no answer. I had this image of somebody with such a grotesque face that when they tried to take their picture, it broke the camera. But nobody ever answered that one.

Joan always had a bed in my room at the hospital. When we got to this rehab place, they didn't have a bed for her there, but they said, "We can bring something in."

They brought in an old couch or sofa bed. A bunch of springs were loose.

So we called housekeeping and said this wasn't going to work. Joan needed something better to sleep on than that. Pretty soon they came back with a really nice bed and set it up for her. So Joan was on her bed, and I was on the hospital bed right next to her. And I was so glad for her being there.

Because you're in the hospital. You're lying there, doped out of your mind, wondering what's going on. You're full of pain. And then someone says, "All right, we're going to give you this and this and this. Is that OK?" You don't know what they're saying. So they give it to you.

You should have seen Joan. She got in their face in the real meaning of the term. She would look the person in the eye and say, "What do you mean? What's in there?" She would write down the list of ingredients, and she would muscle-test every item. Then she'd say, "That one's OK. Take all the rest away." They did, and everything worked very well.

We muscle-test for each other to get a second opinion. But when I was like this, with the pain medicine, I didn't trust my muscle-testing at all for the mundane, day-to-day things. Because you have to totally neutralize your mind. You have to go totally neutral—no opinion left that you want something or don't want something.

The medical-records clerk came into our room. I liked her right away because she said, "All right, youse guys, I need to have this information." And every time she talked about us, she'd say, "Youse guys." That's street talk. I said, "I like this gal." She was the most wonderful person.

On one of her later visits, we were trying to remember our zip code. She said, "Aw, don't worry about it. I'll find it. I used to be in repo." That's when the bank owns the car and lets you drive it. You're late on the payments, but you figure you'll get in the car in the morning and drive to work as usual. But you get up one morning, and the car's not there. The repo gal was there. She repossessed your car, and the bank has got it. This medical-records clerk was like this. She knew the streets. She was a good gal.

So we got settled into the recovery facility. They say you don't go to a hospital to rest. You don't. They've got you doing one thing or another as soon as you can wiggle a toe. You're up, you're moving, you're doing this and that.

If you see somebody in a wheelchair, that person is new to the recovery unit. When you see someone in a walker, that's really great; that's one

*Every time the medical-records clerk came in she'd say, "Youse guys." That's street talk. I said, "I like this gal." She was the most wonderful person.*

grade ahead of the wheelchair. And when you see someone with a cane, that person is two grades ahead of the wheelchair.

We were worked so hard by the therapists. Then at night the nurses came in, and it seemed like a lot of the ones with very strong voices worked the night shift. You finally get to sleep, and someone runs in and says, "Ready for your meds?" I didn't know what to say. I'd say, "Come in" to anybody—for anything. Come in. They do anyway.

So we weren't getting any rest. Finally, Joan said to the manager of the therapists, "This is all very nice, the exercise and everything. But doesn't rest matter?"

Now Ed, the manager, was a very astute man—very, very good. He just listened. He had a very nice way of working with people. I got to see him in action again later when we went down to the gym, which is where they had all the therapy equipment. Some of the staff hadn't been filling out paperwork, so he stood at the corner of the room and said, "I'm not pointing my finger at anybody, but some of you have neglected your paperwork."

The therapists respected him so much that one of them fessed up right away. She said, "You know, I haven't seen the inside of the office for a long time. I'll be right there as soon as I finish here."

That was Lorie—pure energy. I've never seen anyone with that much energy. She was a therapist. Physical therapists did everything from the belt on down; occupational therapists strengthened you from the belt on up. That's how you knew them apart. Anybody who worked on your leg, for example, was a physical therapist. Lorie was an occupational therapist, and she was one of the dear people there.

*That was Lorie—pure energy. Lorie was an occupational therapist, and she was one of the dear people there.*

They put you through a bunch of exercises and get you strengthened. I needed that, because I had been lying around for a good week and a half. They want you strong.

## LITTLE VICTORIES

I hadn't cleaned up for eight days, and I had never looked at myself in the mirror. When I went into the bathroom, I just did my business and came out. The mirror was in the wrong position, and I had to pay attention to the walker so I didn't trip or anything. So I never looked at myself.

One night I did look at myself, and I said, "Oh, my gosh!" Someone said I looked rather bohemian. I thought I looked rather Neolithic. I said, "This isn't the way a representative of ECK should look." I decided I had to get those whiskers off.

Now, I don't use an electric razor; I use a hand razor. And this was a lot of fun. First of all, I didn't know if I could stand. But I got up to the sink, and I tried to shave dry first. Ouch! No, you don't want to pull the hair out dry. So then I put all kinds of creams on my face and made it wet.

I went through the razor real fast because it got loaded up with hair and I had to clean it out. But they don't want patients to burn themselves, so the water that came out of the faucet was just on the warm side of ice cold. And it came out in about ten or twelve weak jets, just a fine spray. Trying to clean a razor with that—well, it took a while. But eventually I got through it. And then I was ready for a full cleanup.

One day, we were talking to another occupational therapist, Mary. She said, "Tomorrow you're scheduled for a shower." But we looked at our time

*I hadn't cleaned up for eight days. Someone said I looked rather bohemian. I thought I looked rather Neolithic.*

schedules with the therapists, and it didn't look like it would work. Mary said, "I'll work something out." And she ran off.

Soon after, the social-service woman, Barb, came in—a very nice woman, very meek, very good. She was asking us a whole bunch of questions. Just then, Mary ran back into the room and said, "Harold, you shower with me tomorrow at two."

I was so happy! My first shower after eight days—with Mary. I said to Joan, "Honey, did you hear that?"

So came the big day. But right away, Mary said, "I pride myself on not getting wet." And I thought, *What kind of shower is this going to be?* Well, it was a disappointment. But the occupational therapists have to tell you exactly how to get in and out of the shower and how to grab hold of things when everything's wet. Everything's slippery, and you want to wash your hair and all.

*Wearing blue scrubs, you look pretty much like you work there, except you can't walk. Other than that, you look pretty cool.*

I was wearing blue scrubs at this time. They're the cool things to wear in a hospital. You look pretty much like you work there, except you can't walk. You're in a wheelchair or pushing a walker. Other than that, you look pretty cool.

But the big thing about them is you can slide in and out of bed, which is neat, because that's one of the tests for leaving. You've got to be able to get in and out of the bed. I first tried it in my flannel pajamas, but I think the sheets were made out of Velcro. The first time I tried, I couldn't get into bed. I got my right leg in somehow, but everything hurt. Then they said, "All right, now get your surgical leg in."

I got to the bed with a walker, but for a couple of days, I couldn't get my left leg up there, even though I'd been doing exercises and all. One day

I got a bright idea: Hey, I've got two legs. I very cleverly hooked my right toe under my left heel, and I was able to lift my left leg into the bed. And was I ever happy! These are the little victories that you come to.

That also worked out fine at home, by the way. Home was great! We now had to learn how to do everything at home though.

## MAKING FRIENDS IN RECOVERY

While we were at the recovery facility, we made friends with the charge nurse. She was from Mexico, and she had been here awhile. She was a good heart. The first time we saw her, she started asking me questions. She said, "I'm going to name three things. Try to remember them, OK?" Then she said, "The sink, the counter, and the refrigerator. Have you got those?" "Yes."

*At the recovery facility, we made friends with the charge nurse. She was from Mexico. She was a good heart.*

She asked me other questions that were kind of off-the-wall too. "What county are you in?" I gave the wrong county. We had crossed the county line, and I didn't know it. I said, "Well, what city are we in?" She told me. "I don't know what county this city's in," I said. So she said, "OK, that one doesn't count."

She asked more questions like this, and then she said, "OK, tell me in order again, if you can, the three objects I named." I said, "The sink, the counter, the refrigerator."

The reason they did it was to check a person's mental condition upon arrival and before departure. They ran into all kinds of people there—people who were there for drug or alcohol rehabilitation, or most anything.

I saw some people who had been on drugs, no

question. One time I mentioned it to one of my therapists. I was just thinking out loud and said, "Is he here for drugs?" She said, "We can't talk about other patients." I said, "I understand. I apologize." Because as a professional, I can't talk about private things either.

That patient's eyes were just one-quarter full, if you can imagine such a thing. There wasn't much of him in there. At one point, it looked like he had about a third of himself inside that body. I kept looking at him and thinking, *What have you done to yourself?* You see people who want to take a shortcut on the spiritual path, and it doesn't work.

Every time the ECK has wanted me to move along into another arena, it's been to reach new people or to change my mission. So it's a mission renewed.

Now I was dropped right into the middle of all these medical professionals, and I was very happy to be with them. They got to see who I was. We had a lot of laughs, and I think the benefits ran both ways, everywhere.

The first time I came out of my room, I was using my walker to go as far as a drink dispenser, which was twenty feet or so away. It seemed about a mile. As I came out of the room, here came this tall, thin woman with a walker. She was stumbling along the same way I was. I said, "Beep, beep. Careful there, you're going too fast." And she said, "Incredible, isn't this? I'm going to be out of here sooner than later." I said, "I hear ya." She went crawling by, and I went crawling by right behind her. It takes all your strength just to do these things.

She was just one of many people I saw once I was able to come out of my room. Very heartening, these people, very good and special people.

> *Every time the ECK has wanted me to move along into another arena, it's been to reach new people or to change my mission. So it's a mission renewed.*

## A LUCKY MAN

We had an appointment with the doctor at the recovery facility. She was a kind woman, a petite woman from India. She looked through the records. She also wanted to see the incision, which was a marvel.

Every time the nurses looked at the incision, they would say, "Ooh, only three and a quarter inches long. And so neat!" They would come to see how well it was healing, and they would always marvel at it.

It became quite a thing. People would come in and ask to see it. I'd say, "OK. How do you like it?" They really liked it. I could never see it; I couldn't bend over far enough to see it. It was just a little bitty thing, and very neat. The doctor cut it really straight.

Anyway, we went to see this physician from India. She looked through the records, and she said, "Your wife has been with you all this time?" I said, "She has." She said, "You're a very lucky man." I said, "I know it." She said, "I don't know a single wife who would have stayed with her husband all this time."

I know that in many cases there are other family members who need attention, and it's not possible. But in our case, it was possible. Joan never looked back. She didn't care. She was going with me; that was it. And that's how it was.

*This physician from India said, "Your wife has been with you all this time?" She said, "You're a very lucky man." I said, "I know it."*

## JEAN TELLS EVERYONE ABOUT HU AND ECK

Here's a Vahana letter about one of our new chelas. And she's not really new.

Jamie's mom, Jean, is ninety-one. She likes the ECK books that I write, and she has been reading them for years. She told Jamie, "I really like his books." And she added, "You know, I'm an ECK chela." Jamie asked, "You're an ECK chela?" She said, "Yes. I'm an ECK chela and have been for a long time."

Over time, Jamie had shared the HU with her, so she knew the HU and had read my books. So Jamie signed her up to be a member of Eckankar.

One day, Jamie took her shopping. The brand name of something she bought to wear was Hue, and when they got back she took the label off and put it right next to her bedside clock. Jamie asked, "Why are you doing that?"

She said, "I'm a new member. I just don't want to forget HU. It's important."

Then she said, "I wish I had learned about Eckankar when I was young." Jamie asked why, and she said, "Because I would have told everybody about HU and Eckankar. I would have told them about this." She meant the whole thing. And she said, "Here I am in this apartment, and I can't get out and tell everyone."

Well, Jean, tonight you have. Thank you.

May the blessings be.

*Jean said, "I would have told everybody about HU and Eckankar." Well, Jean, tonight you have.*

*ECK Springtime Seminar, Minneapolis, Minnesota*
*Saturday, April 7, 2012*

Love moves. It flows. It is like the stream of God, the Voice of God. This is love in its purest form. We call it the ECK.

This is a living thing; It gives life to all of us.

# 13
# LOVE IN MOTION

Our talk title this evening is "Love in Motion," because divine love is not the static thing that we often just take for granted.

## LOVE IS LOVE

Love is love, we think. It's this thing that comes in a square block with nice, soft edges, and when you touch it, it's kind of velvety. That's love. And divine love—well, it's got a light inside, and maybe it hangs up a little above the floor. Who knows? That's love. It just sits there.

But love moves. It flows. In fact, it is like the stream of God. It is the stream of God, the Voice of God. The Light and the Sound. This is love in its purest form: Light and Sound, divine love, the Voice of God, the Holy Spirit. We call it the ECK. Same thing.

This is a living thing; It gives life to all of us. It's in motion, even as we are in motion. Rivers are in motion. Watch birds flying, planes flying—all these things are in motion. And when something stops being in motion here, then it's in motion there—in the higher worlds.

*When something stops being in motion here, then it's in motion there—in the higher worlds.*

So, love in motion. We are Soul. And in a way, then, we too are in motion.

We are created of the essence of God, and this is love. God loves Soul. And Soul exists because God loves It. It's very simple. All that we're about is becoming more aware—more aware of this divine love that we are, encapsulated in the human form.

*Sometimes we make the mistake that we are the body, not the light, not the love inside it.*

Sometimes we make the mistake that we are the capsule, not the light, not the love inside it. A lot of times you'll hear people say, "This is me," pointing to their body. Or, "I am . . . ," and they mean their body. If someone asks, Who are you? Well, I am Harold Klemp. Yeah, OK; you've got to use that when you're here.

But when you get to the real identity and ask, "Are you Soul?" they say, "No, no. I *have* a Soul." See, that's where they get the wrong side of the capsule. We *are* Soul; we have a body. That's the right way around. But if somebody wants to believe another way, well that's fine.

We're not a strong-arm group in that regard. And anyway, how do you strong-arm love? As soon as you do that, you're talking about an entirely different creature, and that is power. They're opposed to each other. Or rather, power is opposed to love. Love doesn't oppose. Love just is.

## THE ABRASIVE GOOD MORNING

"Flo" was the host in her ECK Center. At one point she went out front to clean the windows. She was out there cleaning away, having a good time. A man came by, and she said, "Good morning!" He asked, "Do you know me?" She said, "No," thinking, should she? Or is he important? Or is something the matter with this guy?

Then he looked at her, and in a very derogatory tone, he said, "How could anyone singing *hoo* like an owl get God to love them more?" Flo was clearly puzzled, and he could see it. So he walked up to the ECK Center window where there was a sign about HU and all its benefits. He said, "Singing a word isn't going to get God to love me more."

Smiling, Flo replied, "God already loves you. That won't change. Singing *HU* will change how you understand life." He heard that, and he stopped to consider. In all fairness, the man was aware. It wasn't going to be a monologue where he just preached and preached and put the other person to sleep. He listened.

But then he went back to his original argument. He said, "You're wrong to support a religion that isn't Christian." Flo looked him in the eye and said, "Is your spiritual path right for you?" And he said, "Well, yes it is." Flo said, "If it's right for you, then it's perfect. There's nothing wrong with that." He just stood there. He was a reasonable man—reasonable in the true sense, meaning you could reason with him even when it wasn't what he wanted to hear.

And do you know what he did? He changed the subject. This was a good sign. It meant the man was open. He was open to new ideas. He had very strong opinions, and he may have them still, but at least the seed has been planted—a divine seed in his heart.

## CELIA AND THE BROKEN-HIP STORY

So, here we go to Celia. And this is her real name. I don't usually use people's real name. Flo's name was not real; I made it up. That's to protect

*Flo replied, "God already loves you." The man listened.*

me in case she thinks I didn't tell her story cor-
rectly and wanted it some other way. I'll say, "It
wasn't yours."

Celia lives in Cape Town, South Africa. That's
way down on the Cape of Good Hope, right at the
very bottom of Africa. There's an eighty-four-year-
old Second Initiate there. She had come in from a
distant town when she'd broken her hip.

Celia went to visit her and found that this
elderly woman was in very low spirits. So Celia
wondered what to talk about. She then began to
talk about my experience, which was the same as
this woman's. She had a broken hip; I had a broken
hip. Celia began to talk about the experiences I
told at the 2012 ECK Springtime Seminar.

Pretty soon the woman was laughing and laughing. Because it turned out she had been a nurse
when she was working. When I told the stories
about the nurses and the nurses' aides and everyone else, this took her back to a time when she
was younger and stronger and could take care of
herself and take care of others.

Now others had to take care of her. This was
very, very hard for her. But she started laughing,
and by the time Celia had finished telling my stories, the woman was just laughing at everything.

Then this initiate said, "I now am beginning to
understand Eckankar more clearly."

Celia also told about a woman from Angola.
That's two countries up on the west side, on the
Atlantic side. The woman had been having strange
dreams. She went to get information from her astrologer, who said, "I don't know what it is, but I
think this can help you. It is called Eckankar."

So this woman went to the internet, looked

A woman had been having strange dreams. She went to her astrologer, who said, "I don't know what it is, but I think this can help you. It is called Eckankar."

around, and got the contact information for Celia in South Africa.

When the woman was briefly in Cape Town, she called Celia and said, "I'm leaving town tomorrow. Can we meet?" They could, and they did. The woman was so happy to have heard about the teachings of ECK. She had gone out of her way. When she had gotten the information, she just wanted a contact. Celia was able to give her ECK contacts right in Angola.

## WHEN GOD CALLS SOUL HOME

When Soul has heard the Voice of God calling It to come home, It will stop at nothing to make the connection.

I get teary on this simply because I remember how hard I had looked for something. And when I found Eckankar, I wasn't real sure yet that it was it. But my life began to settle out. Other people who come in contact with Eckankar for the first time know right away.

It may not be for you now, or it may be in maybe five years, ten years. I've heard from people who have become members of Eckankar fifteen and twenty years later, and they said, "I heard of it a long time ago, but I just didn't come until now." And that's it. It's as if no time was lost between way back when and the moment they came into Eckankar.

## SALLY'S GROCERY RECEIPT

This is love in motion again. "Sally" went grocery shopping and got her receipt, her tally. And as she was walking out in the parking lot toward her car, this wind came along and took the receipt right out

*When Soul has heard the Voice of God calling It to come home, It will stop at nothing to make the connection.*

of her hand. As she was chasing it, she was thinking, *What do I really need this receipt for?*

But beforehand, she had set a high spiritual purpose for herself—Mastership in this lifetime. This is certainly something worth aiming for.

It takes a focus of attention that is with you like your breathing, like your heartbeat. It's like your voice; it's like your vision. It's you. Your vision, that's you. Your dream, that's you.

Anyway, the wind blew this receipt out of her hand. She chased it across the parking lot. And it went flying. But she was determined to get that receipt. At this point, it was her and the wind and the receipt. She chased it all over and almost got it. The wind took it up and started blowing it toward a road where cars were, but she didn't take her eye off this grocery slip. She was thinking, *Is it worth getting run over if I keep my focus right on it?*

And then she stomped her foot at it when it came down on the ground—stomping and stomping and stomping, like a horse doing tricks. You know: the horse's owner says, "How much is one and one?" And the horse goes tap-tap with its hoof. Well, that's what she was doing out there—tap-tap. She felt like a horse doing tricks.

Finally she got the receipt. She reached down and picked it up. A woman who was gathering carts for the grocery store hollered out, "With a focus like that, you can have anything in life you want!"

Now, this is true. But the point is, you've got to keep that focus. You've got to hold the focus all the way through. Sometimes you're in extraordinary pain, great happiness, unhappiness. So many times being unaware, being caught up in some outer entertainment or something. But you still have to keep that knowingness.

*Mastership in this lifetime takes a focus of attention that is with you like your breathing, like your heartbeat.*

It's more than focus. It's a knowingness, a be-ingness. And there are going to be things coming up that say you failed. You're going to be absolutely sure you failed. The point then is to be ever more determined in what your dream was. Then you follow it out.

And if not this lifetime, what's the difference? We aim for it in this lifetime. We can make great strides in this lifetime, but if we don't make it, what's the difference? God doesn't care. Time is a construct of man. God doesn't have a watch. He doesn't have to look at a watch and say, "OK, so that's where we are now." None of that matters.

Love is mobile. So, love in motion.

*We can make great strides in this lifetime, but if we don't make it, what's the difference? God doesn't care. Time is a construct of man.*

## A PARALEGAL GETS TRACKED DOWN

This story is about an ECKist I'll call "June."

A woman had responded to a spot on TV about Eckankar, and the Eckankar Spiritual Center had sent her an info pack. She liked what she read, so she came to an ECK service. When the service was over, she chatted and had a good time with all the ECKists there. They liked her because she felt like one of their own, like a friend.

So June and another person who later became an ECKist gave their phone numbers to this woman, but they didn't take her phone number. Two weeks later was a HU Song. They were looking for this guest from the previous ECK event, but she wasn't there. So June thought about it, and she said, "Well, I'm going to track her down."

June had a clue: the woman had said she was a paralegal. The town June lives in is of fairly good size. There are lawyers all over the place. So she got to thinking. This resulted in plan number one.

She would go to each of these law offices, tell her story, and ask, "Do you have a woman by such and such a name here?" If the answer was no—which it more than likely would be, there being so many law offices in town—then she would go to the next one and the next one.

Of course you and I are thinking, *Why wouldn't you just get on the phone? Or go online and contact all of them?* But then June made up another plan. She thought, *I'm going to contact each law office and talk with the receptionist. And when I talk with her, I'm going to ask, "Do you have a paralegal by this name working there?"* She would go through the whole list. And just thinking about it made her tired.

Later that day, she had to go to the bank. And as she went in, she noticed there was a law office right outside. She thought, *When I come out, I'll go to the law office and just check.* Yes, you can see it coming here. She went in there and said to the receptionist, "I'm looking for a paralegal by such and such name." The receptionist said, "Ah, she works here. Just a minute, I'll go get her."

A few minutes later she came back with the woman. And the woman and June had a very nice reunion.

It turned out that the paralegal had taken the HU with her from the ECK service. She had been walking around the office singing *HU.* Everybody knew; there she was HUing. When her boss would get stressed out, she would be like the good nanny and remind him, "If it gets too much, remember to sing *HU.*" This is what she had been doing.

At this point June was able to tell her about the other ECK events that were going on.

Now, I wonder: if the paralegal had wanted to

> When her boss would get stressed out, she would remind him, "If it gets too much, remember to sing HU."

come, she could have done so on her own. And why
didn't she? Well, she may have been one who
needed two weeks and someone to come and ask
her again. Usually we don't do this. At least I don't
think I would. I tell people about it. I keep in touch
with them if they want to. And I suppose nowadays,
when you're online and so on, it's very easy to go
back and forth with each other.

Somebody said, "A coincidence is a miracle in
which the hand of God is not evident." I thought
this was just a wonderful definition of a coincidence:
A miracle in which the hand of God is not evident.

Mark Twain was an American humorist back
around the late 1800s, early 1900s. He used to give
talks, and he said the most dreary place to give a
talk was in a church. He said when you're in a
church, people are afraid to laugh. Well, here it's
an auditorium; you can laugh. And at our ECK
services, if anyone says something that strikes you
funny, you can laugh.

## Seeker at the Guard Shack

"Juan" is a guard at a parking lot of a federal
building in one of the large cities on the West Coast.
He was in the guard shack one night, reading an
ECK book. He didn't say how many were in the
guard shack with him, but I think there must have
been one other person.

Juan looked up from his book and saw somebody
coming. He had seen this person before. He went
outside—for security, Juan said—and I imagine it
was for the sake of whoever was left inside.

So Juan went outside, and here was this young
man with a gang of young guys standing in the
background. Usually this person would come up

*Somebody said, "A coincidence is a miracle in which the hand of God is not evident." I thought this was just a wonderful definition.*

*Usually this young man would try to mooch ciga-rettes or money from Juan. But this time he came up and said, "How do I get home?"*

and try to mooch cigarettes or some money from Juan. But this time he came up, and he was doing different things. He said, "What time is it?" Juan gave him the time. And then the young man said, "What day is it?" Juan gave him the day. "What month?" Juan gave him the month. "The year?" Now Juan was wondering if it was time to call 911. And then the guy said, "How do I get home?"

Juan thought, *Oh, I'm dealing with an amnesiac.* But then he thought, *Wait a minute. He's with his friends. They know where he lives.* And about this time they were calling to him, "Hey, man, come on. Let's go. Hurry up." But no, the young man had come for something, and he wasn't leaving until he got it.

So they began talking back and forth. At some point the young man said something that Juan didn't know how to take. Juan had been in law enforcement before, and he knew that if anybody spoke of a certain topic the way this young man seemed to be doing, then he needed help. He needed serious help. So Juan answered him with a question. He said, "You mean dying?" The youth looked at him, and his eyes said, *Hey, man, come on. You know better than that. We both know better.*

Right away Juan knew that there was something special going on here. This time the young man hadn't come just asking for money or a cigarette.

So Juan opened himself to the Mahanta, the inner side of the Outer Master. It's one composite being; it's not that each one is a sliver, the Inner Master and the Outer Master. One isn't greater or lesser than the other. They are both of the ECK. They're both of Divine Spirit. That's how it is. Some people still try to take out a chisel or something and somehow separate the two. And they say, "I like the one but not the other." Well, I say, "You can't have one without the other."

As Juan opened himself to the inner side, to the Mahanta, he asked this question of the young man: "Where is home?" And then the young man pointed to the night sky. He said, "Home is where I'm not bound by all this!" And he pointed to his body. He was about five feet, ten inches tall—average height—and three hundred pounds—seriously obese. He said, "You know, I used to be able to close my eyes and be home." He didn't say, "go home"; he said, "be home." He was able, at one point in his life, to shut his eyes and be in the here and now, in the presence of God. And hear the Sound and see the Light, which are the two manifestations of the Holy Spirit, or the ECK.

He said, "I used to be able to close my eyes and be home. Now I can't." And then Juan relaxed. He recognized the seeker, so he began to explain the HU and how to sing it. He said, "Put your attention here between the eyebrows and a little above." The young man said, "Oh, you mean the Spiritual Eye." Juan said, "Oh, so you know then." And the young man just smiled back, and the two smiled at each other. Two seekers standing on common ground. Actually two travelers.

Juan wasn't a seeker. Nor was the other, because he had found too. No longer the seeker, but a fellow traveler on the way home to God. So then Juan showed him how to do the HU song. He also wrote it all on a piece of paper and gave it to him. Then he said, "Remember this name: *Mahanta*. This is the being who can take you home—your true home."

They shook hands, and the youth left to rejoin his group. Up to the time of Juan's letter, he hadn't heard from the young man again. But sometimes when people first hear about Eckankar and the ECK teach-

*Juan asked the youth: "Where is home?" The young man pointed to the night sky. He said, "Home is where I'm not bound by all this!" And he pointed to his body.*

ings, or HU, their life speeds up. Because basically they're facing the karma that is necessary to sweep out of the way before they can fully, completely, step on the path of ECK and become a member of Eckankar. And then when this was all over, Juan observed, "Seekers definitely know who we are."

Home is the true heaven.

I referred to Mark Twain earlier. He was in Bermuda with his friend, the Reverend Twichell. They used to go for walks after church on Sunday. When they were in Bermuda, Mark Twain said, "This is like heaven." Reverend Twichell looked at him very pointedly, and then, with a rebuke in his voice, said, "Then you'd better make the most of it." He didn't hold out much hope for Mark Twain getting to heaven.

Mark Twain liked him because he could tweak him, have fun with him. They'd get into some really good discussions, and they'd walk very long distances.

There was a walking craze at that particular time. People used to go on long walks. They just liked to walk. People would try to walk from one major city to another. This was a great stunt.

Mark Twain and Reverend Twichell tried it too. They got to a city which was the halfway point, and they planned to go further to another one. But when they woke the next morning, they just went right back home. They figured that was far enough for a day's walk, and they didn't want to make the whole loop.

## THREE BOOKS OF INTEREST

I do want to mention a few books here. There's quite a buzz about the first one. I haven't read it.

Juan observed, "Seekers definitely know who we are." Home is the true heaven.

It's called *Proof of Heaven: A Neurosurgeon's Journey into the Afterlife*, by Eben Alexander. It's about out-of-body experiences. The author was out for several days, and then he came back. He had all these experiences with light, sound, and other things. Sometimes people do get to the Soul Plane without knowing how they got there. And this, of course, is still for them to find out, to see if they can go further or if they need a guide to take them to the true home.

Now, I've got two more books to mention. The first one is mostly of historical value. I think it's a very good book. It's called *Ancient Egypt 39,000 BCE*—before the Common Era, or before the Christian Era; take your choice. It's by Edward F. Malkowski. The subtitle is "The History, Technology, and Philosophy of Civilization X." This is what Malkowski calls this civilization, which he believes is prehistoric.

The only kind of information that's generally available today about our sense of time and age is archaeology, or geology perhaps. And if not that, then legends and myths fill in the spaces. A lot of times when myths and legends arise, it's because there was something to them way back when. But by the time the story gets passed down to the current time, it may be so jumbled that it's very hard to really tell what happened.

Anyway, the author gathers many of the theories about the Great Pyramids—who built them, when they built them, and all these things. He's gathered the different theories. He goes through them in a very nice way so that the narrative moves right along. But he has questions.

I've tried to reduce what's in the book to some basic questions, to kind of group them. One ques-

*The author gathers many of the theories about the Great Pyramids—who built them, when they built them, and all. But he has questions.*

tion is about who built the Great Pyramids and why. Could people in the Copper Age really have quarried the two- or three-ton granite blocks with soft copper hammers and chisels? And then how could crude copper tools square the granite blocks as accurately as they did?

*How could crude copper tools square the granite blocks as accurately as they did? Granite is one of the hardest stones there is.*

Now, granite is one of the hardest stones there is. Diorite too. Very, very hard stones. Copper makes a relatively soft tool, even in the Bronze Age. The two ages are parts of one long period. The Copper Age came first, and then people figured out how to make bronze.

The common belief today is that this Bronze Age group of people chipped out these really straight blocks, ran them up ramps, and slid them into place.

But most of the blocks weigh two to three tons each, and they are cut so squarely that it's hard to put a playing card in between them in many places. That raises one question. Yet today's geologists and archaeologists just kind of pass over this little detail.

And why are there marks on the blocks resembling those of circular saws? The book has a lot of photographs of these things. It looks like someone did a test cut first and then made the real cut. You can actually see the swirl on these stones, and it looks like the guy running the machine went too far into the stone.

They also had the ability to make a cornerstone. Apart from these disputed Great Pyramids, usually what builders did with the later structures— those that came along in 3000–2000 BC or so—was overlap the end blocks. They'd set a block at one corner and then overlap a full block on top of that for the next layer and build on up, alternating the direction of overlap as they went. So the blocks would have to overlap. But this civilization, or whoever built the Great Pyramids, had the ability to make a block with a very nice corner on it. And I think it pretty much would be beyond the art of the soft copper hammers and chisels and all. Also these marks of a circular saw are very hard to explain. You can see nice pictures in the book.

Malkowski raises another interesting question: Was there an agricultural purpose, not a burial purpose, to the original complex of pyramids? This is intriguing.

One of the people mentioned was a German-born British inventor, Sir William Siemens. He was way up on top of the Great Pyramid, and he found that when he spread his fingers, he could hear sound.

He wondered about this. Then he made a Leyden jar. This is a jar which is basically an electrical capacitor. All it means is it's able to hold electricity. He held it up, and this thing discharged and zapped one of the guides who had brought him to the pyramid. This suggests a purpose for the pyramids.

*A British inventor up on top of the Great Pyramid held up an electrical capacitor, and this thing discharged and zapped one of the guides.*

Gardeners know it's very good when a lightning storm comes because the lightning helps set nitrogen in the soil and makes it easier for grass and other green things to grow. So that's good. And it prompts Malkowski to hypothesize how and why the Great Pyramids were set up.

There was actually a fourth pyramid there; not just three, but four. It was a black pyramid. A Danish explorer had come in the early 1700s, and he looked and reported a fourth pyramid. And in the Middle Ages, somebody from the Middle East had gone there and visited the pyramids, and he too had reported this fourth, black pyramid. So what happened to it?

Well, in 1759 some Scottish investors were looking to make a quick profit. They went down there,
and they said there's got to be a treasure in this
place. So they took the capstone down from the
top. They dismantled the black pyramid, piece by
piece, and sold the blocks to finance their expedition. They took it all the way down to the square
floor. This black base of a very hard rock is still
there. Does no one ask, What's that doing there?
Maybe the guides know; I don't know. But that's
part of what this book talks about.

The Great Pyramids and the little clusters of
other pyramids were built in a line, up and down
the Nile.

Well, I'll let you find out from the book what
they were for. Let me just say the author's hypothesis is that it was for an agricultural purpose.

This next book is more immediately important.
I'll give you a few things about it, and then we'll
close. It's called *Disconnect*, by Devra Davis. It's
from 2010, rather recent. And the subtitle is "The
Truth about Cell Phone Radiation, What the In-
dustry is Doing to Hide It, and How to Protect
Your Family."

Now, first question: Why do most cell phones
come with a notice that says, Do not hold closer
than one inch from your body? Second question:
Why do insurance companies refuse to provide
coverage to cell-phone companies and operators in
case of claims of health damage from long-term
operation of their devices?

One thing that seems to correlate with cell-
phone radiation is lowered sperm count. An interesting side note here is that during World War II,
sailors were notorious for going ashore and paint-
ing the town red after having been at sea for a

*The Great Pyramids and the little clusters of other pyramids were built in a line, up and down the Nile. The author's hypothesis is that it was for an agricultural purpose.*

long time. But before they went, they'd stand in front of the radar unit. This was their sterilization machine. They had no idea what they were doing to themselves, but this is what they routinely did. They figured they were safe now, because it destroyed the sperm cells, and they were going to have a good weekend.

In the early days, microwave ovens were first called radar ranges. But that didn't sound like such a good name anymore in peacetime, so they changed it to microwave oven. I had my first experience with one before I knew I had some sort of problem.

I didn't know it was electromagnetic radiation yet. I was in our home—a small house we had rented—and I was seated at the table one morning. Right behind me was the microwave. I popped some food in, turned it on, and sat there. I was trying to write or do something.

Suddenly I became so dizzy. I almost went out of the body, and I didn't know what was going on. I think I had this feeling that it was the oven, and I got up and quickly shut it off.

We checked for radiation leakage, but there was none. And yet I was being bombarded by something. In the meantime, right behind this house, there were cable TV lines that ran right through our backyard. And just back a little ways there was a transformer.

People are more sensitive to electromagnetic radiation now, and they're coming into more awareness of it. It's just scary stuff. They've also found other correlations—a higher risk of Alzheimer's and certain kinds of cancer.

The book answers the questions What can you do to protect yourself and your family? and Is safer cell-phone technology on the way? Well, it's

*People are more sensitive to electromagnetic radiation now, and they're coming into more awareness of it.*

like this with the companies that produce cell phones the way they are today: They've got a milk cow. Just milk it until it runs dry.

Damage from cell phones doesn't happen in the near term. Whenever they look at studies, it's one, two, or three years away. And the model they use is about a six-foot-one-inch-tall man with an eleven-pound head. Most people aren't that big.

The book tells how to use a device that lets you use the cell phone without holding it to your ears. But still there's this unit hanging around your neck, and from your neck it goes to your ears. So you're still getting the radiation. There are inventors working on this problem right now, though, trying to find some solution. Because if a lot of people just decided to give up the cell phone, there would be chaos. I'll just mention this book again— *Disconnect*, by Devra Davis. You can read it. Or roll the dice and take your chances.

*These discourse workbooks are invaluable. I encourage you to use them.*

For those of you who are ECK initiates, there's now a workbook\* for *The ECK Satsang Discourses*, Third Series. These workbooks are invaluable. I encourage you to use them. They can give you advantages that have not been available before in understanding and studying the Eckankar discourses. So when they come out, and you have an opportunity to get them, please do so.

I'd like to thank you. May the blessings be.

*ECK Worldwide Seminar, Minneapolis, Minnesota*
*Saturday, October 20, 2012*

---

\* The workbook material is now integrated into the discourse books, and the separate workbooks are discontinued. —Ed.

Jill said, "Mom, that picture! That man came in my dream last night!" From that moment on, all three went to ECK classes together.

# 14
# SEEING CLEARLY

The talk for this evening is "Seeing Clearly."

All our thoughts and actions play a part in the great drama or scheme of life. But how many of us ever clearly see this interplay?

*All our thoughts and actions play a part in the great drama or scheme of life.*

## BREAKING HABITS

I was just talking to someone who has found out a whole bunch of things about health. He said he had just been hurting himself all along. And I said, "That's what most of us do." Even now we do things unless we know better. Or we do them anyway and say, "Aw, it won't affect me" or, "That can't be it" instead of doing some sort of testing or process of elimination.

We just go on ahead, trying to have our cake and eat it too. Well, that's fine, but we pay. We learn as we go.

At some point the pain becomes greater than the pleasure afforded by whatever it is that we're doing, and so we stop. For some of us, it takes a very long time because habits are such a hard thing to break. It can be a food, a drink, or anything else we're used to.

Some nutritionists have said, "Just try to separate people from their sugars." It's one of the hardest things they have to do, because it's like a narcotic. People say no, and that's it. They have a certain health condition, but they say no. And then the nutritionists say, "Well, we'll do what we can to help you, but what you really have to do is give up the sugar."

## SHERRY'S FAMILY SEES CLEARLY

Most of the names I'm going to use here are pseudonyms. I like to do that for your privacy.

Our first story is about "Sherry." She was a truth seeker. And she'd been doing this her whole life. She'd been looking and looking. Every time there was any kind of a class or lecture that promised a spiritual subject, she went to it. One day she saw a little ad in a newspaper about a dream class.

She went to the dream class, and she liked what she heard. She said to the presenter, "Give me a book. You've got to have some kind of book on this."

*Sherry read a book on Eckankar and said, "Why, this is everything that I've come to know is true."*

I don't know if it was the presenter's only copy, but it took a little bit of wheedling on Sherry's part to get it from him. She read it and said, "Why, this is everything that I've come to know is true. But this is the first time I've seen it in writing. The very first time." And, of course, it was a book on Eckankar.

Now at the time, Sherry had two teens—a son, fourteen, and a daughter, thirteen. She went home and told the kids about the dream class, and her son said, "Mom, can I go with you?" She said, "Sure." Her daughter wasn't interested; she was more interested in something else. Then one day she said to her mother, "I'd like to go to a Weight Watchers class."

When you're thirteen, you may have all kinds of notions that you are too fat. And it may or may not be so. Yet kids of this age will often go to drastic measures. I understand there is a very high rate of self-injury to young people around the early teens because they're trying to be thinner. Usually they don't know what they're in for.

Others will switch diets. They'll go on a completely different diet from what they've been on without knowing the downside. I mentioned to this one young lady. "Everything that has an upside has a downside," I said. "All you see now is the upside." What I didn't say is that someday, as your body ages and isn't as forgiving as it used to be, that's when you're going to start paying back for your ignorance.

Anyway, Sherry's daughter wanted to go to a Weight Watchers class. And as it happened, there was a major ECK seminar happening at the same time in the same building, on the same floor, but in a different room. The times were just twenty minutes or so apart from each other. So the mother told her daughter, "OK, you can go to Weight Watchers, and then come back and sit down by me, right here."

After an interval, "Jill," the daughter, came back, sat down next to her mom, and—as a teen or anybody would—she looked around the room. All of a sudden she began to nudge her mom. The mother was trying to listen to the class, and she said, "Shhh." Everything went back to normal, and the mother was listening to the class. And all of a sudden here was this annoying nudge at her elbow again. It was her daughter. Sherry said, "Shhh."

*All of a sudden the daughter began to nudge her mom.*

She was getting a little upset now. And, of course, it happened a third time. All things of this nature come in threes.

So the daughter got Sherry's attention again. She said, "What is so important that you can't wait to tell me later?" Jill said, "Mom, that picture!" She pointed to a picture of one of the ECK Masters that was hanging on the wall and said, "That man came in my dream last night." Sherry said that from that moment on, all three went to the ECK classes and ECK meetings together.

This was a moment of clarity for the daughter, who was the last one aboard. Now the whole family sees clearly.

These are such precious times, when we first find the teachings of ECK. I like to mention the cases of when and how it comes, as well as the sacrifices that many of you have made and that I've made.

These are such precious times, when we first find the teachings of ECK.

## The Powers between Heaven and Earth

"Lamar" was working in Munich, Germany. When work was done, he had a choice. He could go back to his house, but it was such a cold place that his usual haven was a bar. He'd go to this bar where he was known and where it was friendly.

So he went into the bar this one evening. He got on a bar stool and was just sitting there, when the stranger next to him struck up a conversation in the most peculiar way. He said to Lamar, "Have you ever heard about Eckankar?" Well, Lamar gave it a good run through his brain; he thought about it a little bit, and he said, "No, I don't think so." The man said, "Well, if you want, I've got something for you in the car." Lamar said, "OK."

So the guy slid off his bar stool, and he went out the door. Lamar watched him cross the parking lot. It was a cold night in Munich. The wind was blowing; it was just cold. He saw the man get in his car, and then he saw the man coming back, head bent down against the wind. He came in the door, and then he gave Lamar a book.

It was Christmastime. The bar was decorated with fir branches all around, and off in one corner there was a Christmas tree. There were ornaments—little glittery golden balls—hanging on the tree. Very beautiful, a very nice setting, very good for the customers.

The man began to hand Lamar this book. As he did, suddenly, for no apparent reason, off in the corner one of these little golden balls burst and threw little bits of glass all over the floor. The bartender was very philosophical. He said, "There are powers between heaven and earth we simply have no explanation for."

So then Lamar had the book in hand. He saw it was a book by Paul Twitchell, the modern-day founder of Eckankar. That was Lamar's introduction to Eckankar. And ever since then he's been doing his part to help people find this path home to God, the path of love. I can't necessarily say it's a path of peace, because sometimes as we go through the karma and so on, the seas become troubled, and then we just hope the storm will pass and we'll survive. But Lamar helps people see more clearly. It was a gift to him, and he now is happy to pass it along to others.

I would like to come up here with a great big sheaf of paper sometime. Then you'd be out there, sitting and looking. You'd say, "Oh, no. This is going to be a long one." Don't laugh; this will be long

*I can't necessarily say it's a path of peace, because sometimes as we go through karma, the seas become troubled, and then we just hope the storm will pass and we'll survive.*

enough. You see, I come here and talk to you only twice a year, and I've got to make up for lost time.

There was a time I gave talks all year long, at all different seminars and trainings. I'd rush home, and then I'd have to write a discourse. And then the next weekend, I'd have to write one of the articles for the *Mystic World*, Wisdom Notes, or the youth publication, *Letter of Light*. And then I'd write something for the Regional ECK Spiritual Aides—our field leaders, the RESAs. After pretty much thirteen years of that, this body was getting a little bit on the tired side, I guess. So that was as good a time as any—if you're going to have a time—for the car brakes to fail. There isn't a good time; take my word for it.

## Jason's Dream Home

*Jason was working on self-deception. He and his wife were looking for a place to live in Minneapolis.*

"Jason" was working on self-deception. He and his wife were looking for a place to live—a place away from their current home city. They were looking for a place right here in Minneapolis, in fact. His wife came with him on one of the first trips, but after that it was cost-prohibitive for both of them to travel. And he had to come on business anyway periodically. So he followed up with a real estate agent, and they checked out more houses.

When his wife had been up here, they looked at homes and would very quickly agree or disagree on the points of what made a house good or bad. Usually they would agree, and everything would be fine. But if they had a disagreement about a house, well then, sparks would fly. Because Jason's wife, "Susan," didn't take things lying down. She stood up for herself and said what needed to be said—her point of view. And she pointed out a whole bunch of things.

One house they looked at was right alongside a golf course. Susan hadn't liked it, but Jason came back to give it another look. This was in early spring, right before golf season opened.

Jason got there, and he looked. He went upstairs. He got there a half hour before the real estate agent was to show up. This way he could walk around, look around the place, and satisfy himself that everything was the way he thought it was in spite of his wife's warnings and cautions.

A nice place. He saw the rolling hills. Everything was very gentle, and the greens were nicely manicured. It was right at the point where the greens were starting to come alive. He said, "Boy, this is really a swell place. It's our dream home."

So the agent came and again showed him the rooms. Jason admitted they were too small. But you could make adjustments. Then he looked at the basement and the way the exit was down there. He said, "Well, here in Minnesota that's going to be too cold, but maybe we won't use that room as much as we thought we might. We can work around it."

Then something else caught his eye. He looked around the outside of the house, and there was this hole in the wall. That struck him as odd, but he said, "Well, a hole in the wall here or there—you just patch it. Nothing to worry about at all." So he kept daydreaming about this peaceful home they had found.

*On the outside of the house there was this hole in the wall. He said, "Well, you just patch it." He had this funny feeling, though.*

Back home, Jason gave a full report to Susan. He had this funny feeling, though. He was starting to listen to the nudges from the Inner Master saying, "Jason, this isn't a good idea. Think again." So he looked at the whole works, and he said, "Well, the least I can do is go online and just look around a little bit and see what kind of information I can find there."

He went online to a site where golf pros and course designers said the absolute worst place to have a house is off to the right of the first hole and the first tee of the golf course. It should be no closer than 150 to 200 yards from the tee. That was a good little piece of information for him.

Then he went to another site, and it said they're designing golf clubs ever better, and the better they are, the further the ball goes. Also, there's a preponderance of right-handers in golf, as in anything. When they slice the ball, it flies off to the right. And if any house happens to be along there, it's in the line of fire. But not to worry a whole lot—if you're 150 to 200 yards away.

Then he went to another site and read something from a man who owned a house right on a golf course, only 50 yards from the course. The man said it was terrible there. He said the noise was nerve-racking. The lawnmowers came out at 5:30 in the morning because they were trying to beat the 6:00 a.m. opening. And with the vibration and everything, he couldn't sleep. He said this went on several times a week.

*Jason left a message for his agent. "How many impacts has this property had on its walls in a year?"*

He mentioned nothing about the problem with golf balls. But before Jason had begun his search, he had left a message for his agent. He was just curious. He asked, "How many impacts has this property had on its walls in a year?" Of course, his agent took his sweet time getting back to him. Meanwhile Jason was learning a lot, and what he heard wasn't real good. This man had said his house was only 50 yards away from the golf course, and all these mowers came out rumbling early in the morning before the course opened. Well, Jason's prospective house was only 30 yards from the golf course. Not 50, not 150 to 200, but 30 yards.

So when he and his wife got this last bit of information, they called up the agent. They were curious about his answer to how many impacts a year there were against the wall of this house. And very, very shortly he replied, "Several." "Several indeed," they said. "No deal. No sale." And that was the end of that.

The moment of clarity had come to Jason just in time because he got more information. He had this clear vision, finally, of what his wife and the Inner Master had been trying to get across to him. Like, "Jason, open your eyes. There's something more going on here."

Jason realized that it's our biases for or against something that usually get us into trouble. We have a very strong like or dislike for something, and because we do, we overlook common sense. Everybody has common sense, but if you look around, it isn't worth a lick. Rather than call it common sense, I like to call it good sense. Some people would say, Well, there's no difference; I've got both.

*Jason realized it's our biases for or against something that usually get us into trouble.*

## DEMBE'S MOMENT OF TRUTH

Now, this is a story about "Dembe," a Nigerian who saw clearly. But even more than that, he trusted dearly. He trusted the Inner Master. On one occasion he was driving from work to some other meeting site.

As he was going along in his car, suddenly there was this awful creaking noise. He was concerned. He said to the Inner Master, "Mahanta, you know how our purse is. Please don't let anything happen to this car right now."

He got to his meeting, but as he was driving back to work, that same creaky noise was there. That evening when work was over, he went to the service-station parking lot nearby, where his car was parked.

He got his car, and just as he was ready to leave the lot, he was flagged down by a man who asked, "Are you going out to the highway?" Dembe said, "Yeah, I'm going out to the highway." The man asked, "Can I catch a ride with you?" Dembe is very easygoing. He said, "Sure, get in." So the man got in, and they went along.

Dembe was struck by the stranger's directness and audacity. It was almost like he was the owner of the car and Dembe was along for the ride. Dembe was in the fast lane. He was going along, and he was expecting to drop the man off at the first bus stop.

But when Dembe started to pull over, the man said, "No, no, not this one. The next one!" Well, this was a nuisance for Dembe because it meant he had to pull all the way out of the fast lane and get into the service lane where the second bus stop was. He thought, *It's a nuisance. It's going to slow me down.*

But he was feeling good, and he said inwardly in a good-hearted way, "I'll give this man a good ride." So they reached the bus stop, and the man got out and said, "Give my greetings to your family." It was just a nice, courteous thing to say.

Dembe started his car and began to move back onto the freeway. All of a sudden, his car dipped down on the right front side. He took the steering wheel and turned sharply over to the right. It was just in time, because then the whole car tilted down. But he was out of traffic. He had dropped

> When Dembe started to pull over, the stranger said, "No, no, not this one. The next one!"

the man off on the safe side. The other side, just off the fast lane, wasn't safe at all. But on this side it was safe.

There he was with his car hanging down on the right front side. People from the bus stop came running up, asking, "What's the matter? What happened?" Dembe had lost a wheel. One of the men said, "It's a good thing you weren't on the highway in the fast lane, or even in motion, because you would have been seriously injured or even killed."

Now, this of course was a moment of truth for Dembe because he knew it was so. And right away he looked around the bus stop. The stranger wasn't there anymore.

Dembe looked for him every day up to the time that he wrote this report, but the stranger simply was not there. Dembe hasn't seen him since.

Within an hour, a mechanic had come out and found what had happened. All the lug nuts on the wheel had worked loose. The creaking sound was caused when just one lug nut was hanging on. It was just barely keeping the wheel on, and the wheel wasn't working quite right. The mechanic was able to replace the lug nuts and put the wheel back on nicely.

Within an hour or so, Dembe was on his way home. And there he told his wife how the ECK (Holy Spirit), or the Master, had protected him.

*Dembe was on his way home. And there he told his wife how the ECK (Holy Spirit), or the Master, had protected him.*

## MAIRI GIVES A LISTENING EAR

Mairi, which is her real name, from the Sydney area, just turned ninety last year. She was one of the first ECKists in Australia in decades past. She said that some time ago, she was with the organization Meals on Wheels. This is an organization that distributes food to the needy. They drive around, and they bring meals. One day she was out with a partner she hadn't ever worked with before. They made small talk because they didn't know each other—just chitchatted and drove along.

*Out of nowhere Mairi suddenly said, "I had an out-of-body experience when I was eight years old."*

Out of nowhere Mairi suddenly said, "I had an out-of-body experience when I was eight years old." And then she clamped her teeth shut. She thought, *Ah, what in the world made me say that?* But the man said, "Odd you should mention that." He said he had once been in intensive care, in a coma, and out of his body. And here Mairi had just said she had been out of her body around age eight. So he had been out of his body too—up there looking around. Really, you're not up there, but you are up there. You're looking around.

He saw his whole family there, waiting for him to die. They were doing due diligence. But he noticed his son was not present, and he wondered about this.

Some time before this, his son and he had been planting a tree. And this man said to his son, "In no time at all it's going to grow." Then his son said a very disturbing thing. He said, "But I won't be here to see it."

This struck the father as very odd, and it came back to him now. What he didn't know was that at this very time his son had been in a motorcycle accident and had been killed.

Mairi was listening to his story. She didn't say anything but just listened. She said she was seeing how the Master was giving him a chance to talk, because he had told her, "I've never told this story to anyone in my life, not even my wife." Presumably he meant his current wife, because this was a son from a prior marriage. He had never told her about the son nor that he'd been killed, so his present wife didn't know it.

Mairi could see how this man was being healed. Maybe some feelings were lifting from him—feelings of guilt or that he hadn't done enough. After all this time, now this could go away.

It was interesting. As Mairi listened and saw everything that was going on, she realized that the doubts in the man, and even some of his pain, were being cleared away. She and her driving partner never spoke of this again.

## AJANI STAYS THE COURSE

This story is about "Ajani," a Nigerian. He and his mother had a very close relationship up until he was twenty-three. She was a very assertive mother, and whenever there was a major decision in his life, she pretty much had her way. He was an obedient son, a good son. He'd listen to her and generally would do what she said.

But this time he had done something that was unconscionable to her. He was going to leave the Catholic Church, their church, and join Eckankar. To her this was heresy. This was absolutely heretical. So she talked with him. She tried every which way to get him to change his mind, but no, no, Ajani had made up his mind. He knew the teachings of ECK were right for him. And that was where he stood.

Now, he wrote about this many years later. He said his mother enlisted the aid of older siblings, because in Nigeria age counts for something still. I wish it did here.

Some of the relatives tried to embarrass Ajani. They said everything they could think of to him. Some would come up and speak very appealingly,

*As Mairi listened, she realized the doubts in the man, and even some of his pain, were being cleared away.*

saying, "Look, you can't do this to your family." The mother had appealed not just to his older siblings, but also to the community leader, really getting up there. Everyone came and tried to get him to change his mind. But no, Ajani knew his mind. One of them even came and said, "But you have to follow others." It didn't make any sense.

Ajani thought, *Well, what about my spiritual needs? They're not thinking about me at all.* But of course the family, the close relatives, the community leader, and everyone were afraid of what was happening here. Somebody was leaving the fold. Somebody was breaking the mold, doing something completely off the wall. The safe course was to stay with the family church, because if he left, he was damned. Because that's how it was done.

At this point, Ajani was very aware. He was only in his first or second year in ECK, and he said already he was getting ideas from the Inner Master of what to say to refute these people. He called them Soul savers. And Ajani didn't have much use for Soul savers. They tried to embarrass him in public. There would be a public event, and his relatives would point him out and say, "Here is somebody who wants to leave the church!" They thought, *Oh, yeah. He's going to bend before public opinion like this.*

Very much the same thing, the same kind of pressure, happened to me, and I've written about it. When the minister came over, I dreaded the meeting, and he probably did too. Reverend Lucht was a kindly man, just a good man. And so we all did a very uncomfortable thing. We had to go through our paces. But at the bottom line I didn't go back to church, and I didn't take communion again. And that was it. Because I had made a com-

*Already Ajani was getting ideas from the Inner Master of what to say to refute these people.*

mitment to Eckankar, to the ECK teachings, and to the Inner Master. I had set a certain date, and when that date came I said, "Now I have to act." Painful as it was, I did what I had to do. And I've never regretted it.

So while all this was going on, news of the public embarrassments got back to Ajani's mother. She heard about it, and she did not like it. So she and her son got back together. Then Ajani realized that even in their past lives, his mother had been bossy and domineering and hadn't let him have his own life.

She tried that here, but after they had gone through all this, she finally looked at it and said, "Those people are wrong." In so many words, she apologized for setting the dogs on him. And they got along from then on, the same as they had before. She also came to respect the teachings of ECK, but it's understandable that she felt more comfortable with the teachings of her church which she had followed from her youth. So she continued with them.

She lived for some time and then died just a couple of months before her son finally wrote about this. At that point the Inner Master, the Mahanta, came to Ajani.

The Master is one, but he works on many levels. He works here in the physical, which is myself, and also works on the inner planes as the Dream Master, the Inner Master, or whatever you want to call it—the ECK or the Holy Spirit. The Mahanta and the ECK are one and the same—the ECK, the Holy Spirit, the Voice of God.

*Ajani was taken to the court of judgment by the Inner Master.*

Ajani was taken to the court of judgment by the Inner Master. He looked around this great hall, and he saw his mother among all these people. It was on a first-come, first-served basis. Whoever got here first was next in line, and there were lots and lots of people.

This is just like a municipal traffic court, if you will. There are many more like it scattered around the country and on the inner planes too. There's a place for this group and a place for that group. The justice at each one of these courts is called the Dharam Raya. He's the judge. He sits there, and he takes his good-natured time going through the files. This is part of the purgatory, I suppose, that the Catholic Church speaks of—sitting there until it's your turn. It can be a long time.

Ajani looked around, and he saw the court soldiers. The soldiers are there to wait for a judgment that comes from the Dharam Raya. They'll see to it that it's carried out, that the individual gets the karma due—the karma that this individual has created over the past lifetimes and the last lifetime.

*The Inner Master whispered, "Maybe it's necessary to help your mother bypass these rigors."*

But the Inner Master looked at the whole situation and whispered, "Maybe it's necessary to help your mother bypass these rigors." He then reached out and took her out of there. Neither the justice of the court nor any of the soldiers put out a hand to stop him. He took her to a quiet, restful place. It was calm, hospitable, and beautiful.

Then he told Ajani that this is where she should continue her lessons unhindered. In other words, this was a better place where she could avoid some of the rigors that the other people in the hall were going to have to endure because they were still under the Lords of Karma. This was all a part of Ajani's realization—his moment of clear vision.

## ESTELLA'S SPANISH HU CARD

This story is about "Estella." I love that name, Estella. It means star. Of course it's not her real name, but I think it's a good name for Estella. She's from Mexico, and as she was going home after an ECK Worldwide Seminar, she had a delay in Chicago. She was thinking, *I don't want to spend the night here and have to pay for a hotel room.*

So she went up to the airline desk and said, "I'd like to save the cost of a hotel room tonight. Could you get me and my family on a flight tonight?" This way she figured they'd be sleeping aboard, and they could save the cost. So the desk clerk got on her computer and checked around. Then she said, "I'm sorry. I just can't find an opening. But what I can do is give you a savings coupon for a hotel room right here in the airport."

So Estella got the coupon, went to the hotel, and checked in. She was so happy, she decided to go back to the desk clerk. She went back there and said, "I've come to thank you for your kindness, and I will also commend you to your airline. But the real thanks I can give you is this card." As she handed her a HU card, she said, "The only thing is, it's in Spanish."

The desk clerk leaned over and took it from her very eagerly because Estella had explained, "It's for when you're in need of peace and want to feel closer to God." The clerk said to her, "I need peace and God right now. I'm going to the hospital this moment to pick up my daughter. This is the fifth time this year she's been there." Estella said, "Here, I'll show you how to do it," and she very quickly described how to sing *HU,* the love song to God.

Then Estella realized—saw clearly—that the reason she had felt such a compelling urge to go up to the desk and change her flight was because the desk clerk needed to hear about HU. It worked out well for everyone involved.

## ANNA'S ESA HEALING

This last story is about "Jackie." She's the mother, and her daughter is "Anna." Jackie said they were the very best of friends. Her daughter was her confidante. Also Anna, who was not an ECKist, would help out during times when her mother needed extra help. They were perfect complements for each other. They were two of a kind.

Now, Anna had known for twenty-nine years that her mother was an ECK cleric, and she had been an ECK Spiritual Aide, an ESA, for many of those years. An ECK Spiritual Aide is someone that anyone can go to for an ESA session. At the session, the ESA is simply to listen for the most part. Just listen, not offer advice.

Well, in all this time that Anna had known that Jackie was an ESA, she had never once asked her mother for a session. But this particular time, Anna called on the phone, and she was crying. She said, "Mother, I was thinking of going to the priest." The mother knew that her daughter had been having in-law problems. Anna said, "I was going to go to the priest, but you've helped so many people over the years, maybe you can help me too. I would like an ESA session."

Jackie was taken completely by surprise, but she was also honored. Jackie wanted to make things very clear to her daughter because this was an

ESA session over the phone. She said, "I'm putting on the cloak of ESA consciousness. I'm rising above the motherhood consciousness."

Jackie said, "This is going to be a confidential session. It will be completely private. Anything that's said here will be nobody's business but ours. And you're probably going to understand some things that you'd rather not. They'll be very unpleasant. Do you understand all this?" Anna said, "I understand and agree." Then the ESA session went about a half hour or so. Then they hung up.

Twenty minutes later her daughter called up and said, "Mom, I don't know what you did, but it sure helped. I feel great. I'm going to pick up my friend, and we're going to go around to some garage sales."

When a woman feels down or feels really good—it doesn't really matter which—she says, "Let's go shopping." Of course, you women know that's just a myth. Those things don't happen really.

Then Jackie explained something to Anna very clearly. She said, "I want you to understand I didn't help you. The ECK did the healing of your emotions. It gave you the insight to understand the reason for your problems. And in that way, by understanding, you really helped yourself." That night, eight hours later, the daughter came to visit. She was back to her happy-go-lucky, carefree self. And Jackie realized how the Master had stepped in and helped her daughter heal.

## HEALTH NEWS AND RESOURCES

For those of you who are interested in health, this is a book I think you'll find very helpful. This is *The Omega-3 Effect: Everything You Need to*

*Jackie explained to Anna very clearly, "I didn't help you. The ECK did. It gave you the insight to understand the reason for your problems. And by understanding, you really helped yourself."*

*Know about the Supernutrient for Living Longer, Happier, and Healthier.* The authors are William Sears and his son James. Both are medical doctors. William has been a medical doctor for over thirty years. His son is a pediatrician, and they're both in California.

The book's copyright date is 2012. In other words, this is very fresh information. And when the author was putting together this book on the omega-3 effect, he called together first-class advisers from some of the largest research facilities in universities. He called them together, and he said, I want to tell people about the advantages of the omega-3s and that the damage the unbalanced ratio of omega-6s people have in their diet is very harmful to their health. I want it simple—so people will enjoy it. I want it funny. I also want to make it scientific.

So these advisers, who were all scientists, got together and talked this over. They argued, but they came up with what's in this book. One of the people on his board of advisers was a man who went up to Greenland back in the early seventies to study the Inuit. He found they had a very low risk of heart disease, and he wondered about it. He found that their ratio of omega-3 to omega-6 was almost one-to-one, very unlike our typical diets nowadays where omega-3 is around one and omega-6 is around twenty—way up there, completely unbalanced.

I think you'll find this book very helpful.

I'd hoped to come up here tonight able to walk very easily without a cane. But we've learned to be thankful for whatever we're given. To be grateful for it; not to regret the things we've lost. And the healing, why is it slow?

> The author said, I want to tell people about the advantages of the omega-3s and that the damage from an unbalanced ratio of omega-6s is very harmful to their health.

A very wise woman, Joan's mom, once said, "Each decade is harder. But you have to get there to understand."

May the blessings be. Baraka Bashad.

*ECK Springtime Seminar, Minneapolis, Minnesota*
*Saturday, March 30, 2013*

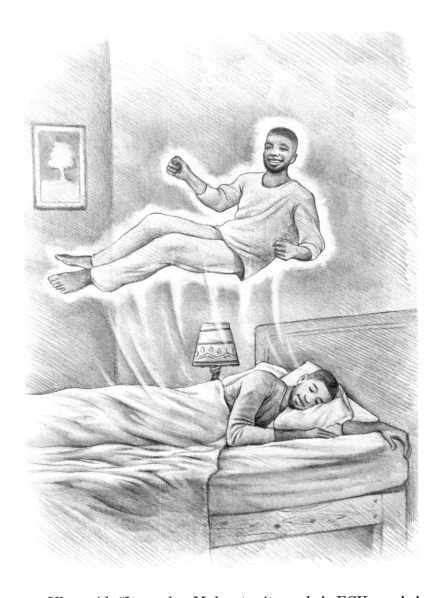

Uba said, "It works, Mahanta, it works!  ECK works!
Thank you, Mahanta."

# 15
# JUST KEEP TRYING

We have a number of guests here tonight. We hope there's something here that'll help you find your way a little bit. We try to sweep away the cobwebs from your path so that you can find the most direct way home to God. That's what we're about. Sometimes we have a good time doing it and have a lot of laughs. Sometimes we don't. And that's just the way it is.

Duke Ellington was an American bandleader and composer in the mid-twentieth century. He had it all pretty much down. He said, "Life has two rules. Number one: never quit. Number two: always remember rule number one."

Our topic for this evening is another side of "never quit." We'll say, "Just keep trying."

I know many of you had a very challenging time getting here, sometimes from many, many miles away, continents away. But we're glad you're here. It seems that life will throw things at you. If there's any chance that you're going to have some sort of spiritual unfoldment, the powers that be will do everything to keep you from getting here. Or from having any kind of spiritual unfoldment. That's how it is.

*We try to sweep away the cobwebs from your path so that you can find the most direct way home to God.*

Sometimes people wonder how powerful, really, is God? Why would God let evil have free rein, running around earth like this? What is the purpose of evil?

There is a purpose, and it's a divine purpose. It's to try men's souls, if you will. It's to put up test after test—making things difficult for people. When you're going toward the path of ECK, maybe things get a little harder. And when you're going away from the path, maybe things get real easy because you're going in the right direction as far as the powers that be here are concerned.

I know religions have tried to explain evil, but they can't come close to it unless they figure out that it's part of the divine plan. It is.

## Connie's Call for Help

Connie is a senior, but she's still able to take care of herself, to manage her own home.

Connie was working out in the garden one day, and she did a bit too much. She has a big yard.

As she was working, her back ached, the way it will when you're working in a garden or in the yard. The next thing, her heart was pounding, and then she was getting dizzy. She said, "Ah, what have I done to myself?" Very slowly and carefully she made her way back to the house, got out of the sun, and rested.

Connie said to the Mahanta, the Inner Master, "Mahanta, I need someone to help me—now." And she put a big emphasis on *now*. Just at that moment, her phone rang. It was a friend calling to chat.

Now, the friend didn't know that this was a really good time to call because Connie was having a crisis. But there she was, and this was the first help that the Master had sent—in a nice quiet way, without any kind of flamboyancy.

They talked a bit, and then Connie said, "Wait a minute. I've got an idea. I've got to call the radio station." The friend said, "What for?" Connie said she had to call a buy-and-sell show by twelve o'clock. The friend said, "Well, it's twelve now." Connie looked at her clock. It was two minutes to twelve. So she said good-bye and hung up.

This radio show was very popular, so there was a queue. Connie dialed once and couldn't get through. She dialed again, and a voice said, "Thirty-seventh caller." Next she heard the announcer's voice. He said, "What's your question?" And she said, "I need someone to help me with yard work. I guess I'm getting too old for this." The announcer said, "No, you're not!"

When you're a senior, this is what you like to hear. Some days you get down. Something's not going right, and somebody comes up and says, "Boy, you're looking good!" It helps.

The announcer took her name and address, and then Connie hung up. And just as she hung up, her phone rang. A man said, "I want to work in your yard." Connie said, "OK, what's your name, and what do you charge?"

Connie grew up in the Great Depression, when there was very little money and people did a lot by bartering. So she was very careful with money. Seniors have to watch the money because it's not flowing in the way it used to when they had jobs.

The man said, "My name is Marv, and I don't charge. Can I come over now?" A little emphasis on the word *now*. Connie had told the Mahanta, "Now." And here came Marv, saying, "Now. I want

*Some days you get down. Something's not going right, and somebody comes up and says, "Boy, you're looking good!" It helps.*

to come now." So she said, "OK, come on over."

Marv came over and did all kinds of work. He replanted shrubs, worked in the garden, and raked up the yard debris from winter. He really worked hard. And he said to Connie, "I told my wife not to expect me home for dinner."

Connie had been going around the yard with Marv, saying what needed doing and so on. When it got to be about six o'clock, she said, "I'm tired. We're going to have to quit now." Marv said, "You should have my phone number in case you need help again." Connie said, "I want your name and address." But he said, "Uh-uh. You'll just want to pay me, and I don't want to get paid."

It makes you wonder, Who is this gem? Who is this wonderful man named Marv?

Then Connie got curious. She asked, "Why are you doing this?" He said, "I don't know. When I heard your voice over the radio, I knew I had to do this." Of course Marv was the second help sent by the Mahanta, by the Inner Master.

No, it's not mind control or anything. It's a spiritual connection that exists between Souls. Marv could see, or could hear from Connie's voice on the radio, that this was a Soul that really needed help. So there he was. No charge.

Connie said, "But you know I'd like some way to show my gratitude." Because she's used to doing things herself. Marv thought, and he said, "A big hug would be great." So she gave him a great big hug. Connie reflected on it, and she said, "I'd never trust a stranger like this, and I never have before in my life." But she said, "Well, this was different. Kind of weird, but kind of nice."

It's a spiritual connection that exists between Souls. Marv could hear this was a Soul that really needed help. So there he was.

## THE TEST FOR JUJI

The next story takes us to Africa. We're going to be in Africa occasionally because we have a lot of ECKists who come from there. We're also going to go to Switzerland at some point. But for now we're in Africa with someone I call "Juji." It means "abundance in love."

I mention where she's from and what her situation was because it's so different from what many of us are used to. Juji had to go to a military hospital and see a doctor. But before she could see a doctor, she had to get a hospital card.

She had her two little kids with her. They walked down a dark corridor, and somehow it all seemed very familiar to her. She got to the room, and there were about twelve people waiting in there. She looked around. They looked awfully familiar. She just couldn't put her finger on where she had seen these people before.

Then the officer at the desk said, "New registrants, please." So she, being a new registrant, came up to the desk. The officer asked, "Name?" He took it. "Address?" He took it. "Religion?" "Eckankar." "What? Islam or Christianity? What is it?" "Eckankar."

He began shuffling and flipping through papers, looking for something. Finally he said, "I've been at this desk six years. I've never heard the name of this religion before. So, what's the name of the religion?" What's Juji going to say? She said, "Eckankar."

At this point, the twelve pairs of eyes all fixed on her, and they were glaring. These people had opinions. The clerk said, "I've never heard of this religion. Why should I issue a card to you?" And

*The military officer said, "I've never heard of this religion. Why should I issue a card to you?"*

Juji said, "Eckankar is a path of direct experience with the Holy Spirit. Eckankar is in all geographical zones of Nigeria and in every part of the world."

Now the others in the room were getting very excited about all this. In fact, they even forgot why they had come. A woman said very emphatically, "Say you're a Christian, get your card, and go!" Not very friendly folk there. The officer said, "Tell me something that I can write down here." You can see his predicament: military hospital, everything has rules. She has got to say something he can write in the empty space.

The people started in: "Who is she?" "Unbeliever!" Then Juji remembered where she had seen these people. It had been in a dream. She had seen this whole thing in a dream, and they would attack her without mercy.

So she called on the Mahanta, the Inner Master. She wondered, *Should I take my children and just get out of here?*

A latecomer had been listening to the whole conversation very calmly. Then he spoke up. Very confidently he said, "Eckankar. I heard of Eckankar when I was at the university back east. It is a religion. Their prayer is HU, which is the name of God."

He had made his statement. Now the military officer looked more kindly at Juji and said, "What is the name of this religion again?" She gave it to him so he could write it down. He then said, "Where do you worship? I want to attend a service of this Eckankar."

And, of course, with the military officer now on Juji's side, the people who were sitting and waiting for whatever they were waiting for got back to waiting for it. Because they knew he wasn't having

> The people started in: "Who is she?" "Unbeliever!" Then Juji remembered she had seen this whole thing in a dream.

any more of what they were dishing out.

Juji gave the officer *ECKANKAR—Ancient Wisdom for Today*, the ECK address, and the addresses of ECK Centers very close to the military hospital.

She realized, when all this was over, that she had been carrying an unconscious fear of expressing what her religion was. And here she was put right on the front line. She had a choice: Would she stand up and be counted, or not? She stood up because she asked the Mahanta. She asked the Mahanta for help, and she was grateful for this help. She was just about ready to quit, but then she remembered inside herself what we are talking about here. Just keep trying. Just keep trying.

*Juji had a choice: Would she stand up and be counted, or not? She stood up because she asked the Mahanta, and she was grateful for this help.*

## A New Home for Kathy and Conrad

Now this is where we go to the southern part of Switzerland, a very nice place. We're going to visit the home of "Kathy" and "Conrad." They had a lovely home. They had been there thirty-four years and had a lot of ECK friends.

Kathy had determined this was where she would stay for the rest of her life. They had a lovely garden with vegetables, flowers, and fruit. They had just about everything they wanted.

Conrad had been wanting to move up north in Switzerland, to the cold country. Kathy said, "Uh-uh, I'm not moving there." They had gone skiing up there on vacation for the last ten years. So they knew what it was like. He liked what he saw. Kathy didn't. It was too cold, much too cold. They had paradise here. Why go looking for trouble?

Then all of a sudden Kathy started getting some disquieting nudges. The first one was from the Inner Master, in a gentle way: Changes are coming. Big changes. And then, after some time, These big changes will mean a move.

Kathy said, "OK, if it's the ECK's will, so be it." The ECK is the Holy Spirit. If this was what the Holy Spirit wanted, it was all OK with Kathy. Now, when you trust in the Holy Spirit, things actually go quite easily. You just trust. Just trust.

When Kathy and Conrad knew that big changes were coming, they began doing the Spiritual Exercises of ECK more than they had before. They began to sing *HU* more than they had before. They threw themselves into ECK activities more than they had before. But it was their spiritual exercises that filled them with the divine love which would be necessary to go through the big changes.

A friend recommended a real estate agent. When the agent came over to their home, he looked around inside, and he saw all the books. Very curious, he asked, "What do you do?" Kathy said, "I translate books of spiritual content."

She saw his eyes widen, and she saw interest. Since he spoke Italian, she brought out the ECK books she had in Italian. She put them out in front of him and said, "Take whichever one you want." He took *ECKANKAR—Ancient Wisdom for Today.*

Then he said, "I'm going on vacation tomorrow, and I'll read it then. I'll be gone a week, so I'll have a lot of time to read it." The next day he called back, and he left a message: "A wonderful book. It has illuminated me. Thank you."

A month later he came back with news about how things had been going with their home. He had been out there looking to sell it. But he wanted to discuss some more important business first. He said during the past month he had been

*When Kathy and Conrad knew that big changes were coming, they began doing the Spiritual Exercises of ECK more than they had before.*

going online searching for whatever he could learn about Eckankar. Now he and his wife wanted to become members. How could they go about it?

Kathy asked, "Are you sure?" *This was kind of quick*, she thought. But he said, "Yes, we want to sign up right now." So she gave him the information. And once they had the real business—the spiritual business—done, then it was back to the real estate business.

He said, "Actually I have good news for you. There were all kinds of inquiries, and there were three parties ready to buy." He said, "The one that I have chosen—and I know you'll agree—is a young couple with a two-year-old daughter. They've got the money, and it's all set to go." And so the papers were signed.

Kathy got to speak to this couple. They said, "For a year now we've been looking for a home, but every time we'd come into a home, our daughter would start crying." But then they said, "When we came into your home, she laughed. She was happy. She ran around the room. And when she saw the piano, she just loved the piano."

*This couple said, "When we came into your home, our daughter laughed. She was happy."*

At that point Kathy said to the mother, "If you want the piano, I'll give it to you." This was a very nice gift to go along with the home. And the little girl was satisfied because a promise had been made.

In the meantime, Kathy and Conrad had found themselves a place up north—a little town in a mountain valley. They found an apartment. It was small, but it would do until they could find something better. But now that their home had sold, they started looking for a house, and they found just the perfect place. It all happened rather quickly. That meant now they had an apartment to try to get rid of. A friend said she'd rent it until they could find a buyer.

Now, these three transactions of their homes had all taken place in around two months. That was totally unheard-of just for selling one place. The apartment could be rented pretty quickly, but to find another house takes much time. The place they found had been on sale for four years with never one inquiry. But the day they signed the papers, two other people called in wanting to know about that home.

So you have to sometimes wonder. There were lots of coincidences going on. Or was there something special going on? Was there a divine hand making everything work hand in glove? There was. They just kept trying. Kathy kept trying. She knew she had to try, if changes were coming. So she made big changes, and the changes were all inside her.

> Kathy kept trying. So she made big changes, and the changes were all inside her.

## Uba Finds Success with Soul Travel

This story is about "Uba," who's currently living in the United States. In an African language, "Uba" means rich.

Way back when he was a Second Initiate, Uba wanted to Soul Travel more than anything. Because as far as he was concerned, if he could Soul Travel, this would prove that Eckankar was real, and that the ECK teachings were what they said they were.

He was so desperate to learn to Soul Travel. He tried a three-day, dry fasting technique that his Christian father had taught him before he died. Yet the deceased can also come in dreams and tell you all kinds of things.

So Uba left the quiet and calm of his village, and he went off by himself. He sat there for three days, and absolutely nothing happened. Nothing at all. So he came back.

But what kept his faith in ECK, when he got back to town, was that this complete stranger came up to him and said, "Your friend wants me to be introduced to your religion." Uba said, "What friend?" And the stranger said, "The one who goes with you everywhere in town."

Then this stranger described perfectly the ECK Master Rebazar Tarzs. A long time ago he served as the Mahanta, the Living ECK Master in Tibet.

Uba was looking at this. Here he was: he just lost his father, he had two toddlers at home, and he didn't have a job. Yet he had the company of an ECK Master.

Sometimes people wonder, *If someone else can see the Master, why can't I?* Because it isn't necessary. Sometimes it would detract you from your true goal, which is going home to God. In some way, spiritually, it's better for you that you just know that the Master—or one of the ECK Masters—is always with you.

But when Uba got the news that he had this friend, this invisible friend, going everywhere he did, he became more active in ECK activities and also the Spiritual Exercises of ECK. This is a recurring theme of those people who just keep trying in ECK. You double down.

Then one night after doing his spiritual exercises, Uba went back to bed. Before he knew it, he was out of the body, just as smooth and easy as you please. There was such ecstasy, so much ecstasy in this state.

Uba felt so good, he put his fist in the air and said, "It works, Mahanta, it works!" That was when he was still out of the body. He said, "ECK works!

*One night after his spiritual exercises, he was out of the body, smooth and easy. There was such ecstasy, so much ecstasy in this state.*

Thank you, Mahanta."

These Soul Travel experiences went on for many more nights. Then slowly, ever so slowly, they began to let up. Years later, Uba wondered, *Why can't I Soul Travel now?* Because usually when people Soul Travel, it's in one of the lower worlds, where they are spiritually. And that's where Uba had been as a Second Initiate.

But as you get into the higher areas, you no longer Soul Travel. As you move toward your goal—returning to the Kingdom of God—your expansion and your maturation take other forms.

Now, it will be different for each one of you. Some of you will have guidance through intuition, much more than before, or some other way. You'll just know. At a certain level, it's Seeing, Knowing, and Being. If you're not there yet, just keep trying.

## JAMES'S INVITATION TO THE MASTER

"James" is an ECK cleric. He was on his way to officiate at an ECK service. Before he leaves home, the first thing in the morning, he always does his spiritual exercises. He sings the HU song five times, and then he invites the Master. He says, "Mahanta, walk every step with me today." Then he leaves home with the knowing that the Master is with him.

So he set out, crossed the road, and came to a corner. A man on the other side looked at him and became very excited. The man crossed the road, came across to James, and said, "How are you people?" as if he was addressing two people. As far as James knew, he was alone. But he played along and said, "We're fine, thank you." The man kept looking just at James, and he said, "May you

> James says, "Mahanta, walk every step with me today." Then he leaves home with the knowing that the Master is with him.

people travel safely."

James said that as the man walked away, he kept glancing back, as if he had seen something truly wonderful, something very out of the ordinary.

Sometimes when the Master appears to those who have the inner vision, they can tell the difference between someone in the human form and someone in a spiritual form. So in this case, the man knew to direct all his comments and questions directly to James. And James knew—in the morning, before he left home—to just keep trying, keep on doing his spiritual exercises.

## ANGELA'S AFRICAN HELPER

Angela is a Frenchwoman. She recently broke her arm. Insurance covered the cost of a helper. This helper, a woman from Africa, came one day a week, on Friday.

One Friday when the helper came in, they started making the bed. With a broken arm, everything was very difficult for Angela. She had her whole right arm in a cast, but she tried to help make the bed. As she was struggling along, she asked this woman, "Do you believe in God?" And the woman said, "Oh, yes." Angela said, "Well, so do I."

*She asked this helper, "Do you believe in God?" And the woman said, "Oh, yes." Angela said, "Well, so do I."*

Common ground is good. And it's not very common in some of the European countries to find someone who believes in God. They kind of got over religion, to the extent that they have, because of the religious wars in Europe. There was so much bloodshed. So now it's more "Let's take it easy on each other." I think in some of the northern or Scandinavian countries, the number of atheists is in the 90th percentile. Very high.

So when Angela said she believed in God too, the woman from Africa knew that she was talking with a kindred spirit. Then the African asked, "What church?" "Eckankar." "What is that?" Angela said, "Do you know *HU*? HU-U-U-U." The woman stopped working and almost cried. She said she watched Benin TV by satellite. She had seen ECKists on a program and wondered where to find such people in France. Apparently there had been all kinds of coincidences that had brought her to Angela's home to help.

Angela gave her the information on when the ECKists were meeting, and she was invited to come to a HU Song, a HU Chant.

Of course we wonder sometimes when something untoward happens to us. We say, "Now, why did that happen?" Angela did too. She said, "Past karma, no doubt. But maybe it was also to meet all these wonderful people that I've met since I broke my arm. Especially this woman from Africa."

## TALK SUMMARY

*You don't even have to try very hard if you just trust the ECK to do your thinking for you. It's not mind control; it's not giving up your free will.*

So tonight we heard Connie's call for help with yard cleanup. Marv even carried away all the debris and took it to the dump.

Then Juji got a hospital card. Basically, it was a test to see if she would stand up for her religion, Eckankar.

And then Kathy and Conrad had this shuffling of homes which showed how easy it can be. You don't even have to try very hard if you just trust the ECK to do your thinking for you. It's not mind control; it's not giving up your free will. Some say there isn't much free will anyway, because our environment and social expectations pretty much put us in a box, so whatever free will we have has very little rein.

Next there was Uba, with the invisible Rebazar Tarzs walking beside him. Uba was supposed to pass his religion on to this stranger, and of course he did. The man even became a member of ECK, but just for a little bit. He explained later, "I can't remain a member here, because I have a church in town, and it's my livelihood."

Sometimes we have to make hard choices when we come to ECK. It can be something like, Are my neighbors and friends going to think poorly of me? Or, Am I going to lose money in the deal—lose my job or something else?

But just because you're an ECKist, it doesn't mean you have to go and shout it about. In fact, it's wise most of the time to just be quiet. Just be. Be this vehicle for the Holy Spirit.

We've come to show people the most direct way home to God. But you don't want to force people. They've got to come to it themselves. This is why we have such a low-key missionary effort. Yes, we do present ECK in the public venue, but we will not come up and strong-arm anyone.

We covered "you people" and James, and also Angela's African helper.

Sometimes as the Inner Master, the Mahanta, I meet any and all of you. This is the function of the Mahanta, the Living ECK Master. One Master, two functions. I can work with anyone at any time because, as such, it's Spirit working with Soul. No boundaries of time, space—none of that. The Master can go anywhere, to wherever you are, and help you. Just keep trying. Just try, and see if it works for you.

*The Master can go anywhere, to wherever you are, and help you. Just keep trying. Just try, and see if it works for you.*

So whenever you get disheartened, I would just say to you, just keep trying. May the blessings be.

*ECK Worldwide Seminar, Minneapolis, Minnesota*
*Saturday, October 26, 2013*

The rabbi said, "We all have our faults and failings. But, like the diamond with its scratch, it's up to us to transform them into things of beauty and value."

# 16

# THE LANGUAGE OF LOVE (2014)

Our talk tonight is "The Language of Love."

## MARY'S DIFFICULT JOB

Our first story is about Mary. She was a volunteer emergency medical technician (EMT), working out in the country where there was a long drive to the hospital.

The EMTs have a difficult job. Their task is to figure out how they can help the patient. Sometimes the patients are in great pain. The EMTs get them aboard the ambulance and check the vital signs like temperature, pulse, and blood pressure.

Mary would chat with the patients and try to cheer them up in some way, see if she could just help them feel better. Maybe they would think less about their own situation.

She noticed that if the patient smiled or laughed at some of her chatter, there was usually an improvement in the vital signs. Sometimes the pulse, the heartbeat, would go back toward normal. Sometimes even the pain would lessen.

And once in a while the patient would say, "OK, I feel pretty good now. I think we can go back

*Mary noticed that if the patient smiled or laughed at some of her chatter, there was usually an improvement in the vital signs.*

home. Let's turn around." She said, "Of course we never did." Once the wheels are set in motion, they're not turning around for anything. There are people waiting on the other end.

Mary said the whole thing that she was involved with was love. She realized that laughter, smiling, and humor show love. All these things simply show love.

## EXPERIMENT ON OSCAR'S FARM

Then she talked about her father, Oscar, who has a little farm. She shared this story as a further example of love.

In a fenced-in area there was a pond and a chicken coop. Oscar would go out and gather the duck eggs periodically. Then one day he had an idea.

He said, "I'm going to do an experiment. I'm going to take six of these duck eggs, and I'm going to put two each under three of my best sitters"—his hens. He wondered, *Are these hatchlings going to think they're chicks or ducklings?* I guess he thought, well, *Anything for a laugh.*

So he did it. And all the hatchlings made it out of the shell very nicely. In a few days, when they could walk well, it was very easy for them. The ducklings bonded to the hens, their presumed mothers, because that's all they knew.

*The hens looked the ducklings over, saw the webs on their feet, and led the way down to the pond.*

But something happened to the "mothers" too. The hens looked the ducklings over, saw the webs on their feet, and led the way down to the pond.

The little ducklings jumped in the water, paddled around, and played with their cousins. There were other little ducklings out there in the pond already, so they played in the water and had a good time.

The mother hens stood back, watching—probably with their wings folded—thinking, *Ducks. They don't make good mothers at all. They just lay their eggs in the short grass down by the water, and then they wander off. Now, we are the mothers all right.* Those are hens for you.

But after a while, when it was time to come out of the water, the hens would go to the edge of the pond and go, "Cluck, cluck, cluck." And the six ducklings would detach themselves from the rest of the flock and come paddling off to shore. Then they would go inside to have a nap, or to have a snack, or something of that nature.

Mary said strangers came to her dad's farm, and they would look at this strange combination. They would just wag their heads and laugh and say this was the oddest thing they had ever seen.

Mary believes the language the mother hens and the ducklings spoke was the language of love.

*Mary believes the language the mother hens and the ducklings spoke was the language of love.*

## SARAH'S MOM AND THE HU

Sarah was living with her mom, Miriam, and Miriam was fighting depression. For no reason at all, she would just burst into tears. A waterfall would come gushing out, and there she was, just crying and crying. Sarah felt really bad about the whole thing, and she asked the Inner Master, the Mahanta, "Mahanta, what can I do to help my mom?"

So she chanted *HU* aloud. Then she talked to her mom, and she kissed her mom. And guess what? You guessed wrong. Her mom became angry. She did not like that. Don't touch, keep away. So it didn't help.

This happened several times, and Sarah didn't

know what to do anymore. She wanted to help her mom, but she now knew not to talk or touch. So the next time, quietly, inwardly, Sarah began singing *HU*. She sang *HU* six or seven times or so. Her mom stopped crying. She just stopped.

Everything was going OK. Sarah had come into the kitchen to help her mom make lunch.

Then about half an hour after Miriam stopped crying, she looked at Sarah and said, "I wonder if my depression is due to the diabetic medicine I'm taking." Sarah went online right away and checked it out. Sure enough, this was one of the effects that this particular medicine could have.

As some of you know, when any kind of medication is prescribed, you may get sheets listing contraindications and side effects. If you've ever read some of those things, they're terrifying. And you don't want to take anything.

But sometimes it's just a question of, OK, do you want to lose your eyesight, or do you want to take the meds? Take the meds. That's how it goes. Sometimes you can go back to the doctor and say, "I'm having this reaction. Is there another med you could recommend?" This, too, is always an option. Or, "Can I cut back? Is that an option?" There are so many options. You can try this or that if you want to get past the depression or whatever your particular problem is.

But what Sarah learned from this experience was it's possible to be a pure channel for God and for the Holy Spirit and for the Inner Master without having to do anything outwardly at all—except for one thing: to sing *HU* inwardly with a pure heart. This must be with a pure heart. And by pure I mean you don't try to force the outcome by saying such things as, Make my mom not feel so

*What Sarah learned was it's possible to be a pure channel for God without having to do anything outwardly at all—except for one thing: to sing HU inwardly with a pure heart.*

depressed and so sad anymore.

Because, as her mom was feeling this way, that had left Sarah confused and hurt too. She didn't know what to do or say.

But through this experience Sarah also learned more about the three true spiritual states. I'm referring to the true states of Soul when It reaches the Soul Plane in full consciousness. These three states are Seeing, Knowing, and Being. Seeing, Knowing, and Being. Because in the high, high state there is no physical body, no material body of any sort. Therefore, the vision is not limited to peripheral vision or anything the optometrist would dally with here. None of those constrain Soul when individuals reach the Fifth Plane, or the Soul Plane, in full consciousness.

The language of love. Seeing, Knowing, and Being.

*The language of love. Seeing, Knowing, and Being.*

## A TAXI DRIVER'S ANSWERED PRAYER

Every month Sophia and a friend go from Mexico City to Guadalajara to teach a Satsang class. They're Higher Initiates. The flight takes about an hour each way. When they arrive back home, they get a taxi.

One time they found that their taxi driver was a woman. This is very unusual in Mexico, so they commented on it to their driver. They said, "Very unusual, but we're happy to have you."

They started going to their respective homes. As they were driving along, the cab driver overheard them talking in back. She said, "Do you teach a class?" They said, "Yes, we do." "A class on what?"

Right away the two ECKists, Sophia and her friend, knew the Holy Spirit, or the Inner Master, had opened the door to talk about the teachings of ECK. They said, "Well, it's a class on Eckankar, on the ECK teachings." Then they told about all the benefits they had personally received from their being in Eckankar. It can be anything. Sometimes it's healing, sometimes it's foreknowing things, and sometimes it's helping us get through periods of pain and discomfort or just loneliness. These were things they had to draw on, to talk about.

As they were going along, the driver said, "I want to tell you a terrible story, something that happened to me." She said she was home, and she went up on the roof to wash clothes. She had neglected to lock the doors downstairs, because she probably never did. She went up there, and maybe twenty or thirty minutes later she came down and looked around. Sofa cushions were thrown back or on the floor, and everything had been turned upside down. Their whole home had been turned upside down.

She didn't know what to do. She had been gone just for such a short time, and burglars had come in. It was as if they knew exactly what they wanted. They took their electronic devices, they took their savings, they took her jewelry and many other things. They cleaned them out. This is probably why she was driving a taxi, because they had to get back on their feet.

So, this terrible thing had happened. Yet she expected something worse—a scolding from her husband. She feared that when he came home and he found out she had gone upstairs and left the door unlocked, he would scold her and carry on, because he was very strict and very materialistic. She thought there was no way around this. She was going to have to face the music.

*So, this terrible thing had happened. Yet the driver expected something worse—a scolding from her husband.*

But when her husband came home, his reaction was completely different. He said, "This has taught me that no material thing is worth your life or our son's." This was the lesson he had learned.

The driver had more to say. When Sophia and her friend told her about ECK she said, "Now I understand." And she was crying. She said ever since the burglary, the family had been afraid to go in the house. They were afraid to step inside. This terrible fear has been gnawing at them, and they didn't know what to do about it.

Sophia and her friend said, "Are you a Catholic?" She said, "No." "Are you a Christian?" "Yes."

In Mexico there's a difference between Catholics and Christians. Mexico used to be predominantly Catholic and probably still is. But more and more people are going over to one of the other Christian denominations. So the driver said she was Christian.

Sophia said, "Good. Sing *HU*, and see Christ in your inner vision. Give him this worry, this fear. Give it to him. Just sing *HU*, and give your fear to Jesus." The driver liked that. She said, "I can do that."

A few days before, the driver had talked to a friend who said, "Ask your angels or your God to send someone or something to help you overcome this." So when the ECKists came, the driver looked at this and said, "Thank God, thank God. I realize now what happened. God really heard my prayer, and he sent you."

When they got to Sophia's home, before she got out of the cab to go inside, they all sang *HU* together. Then they got out and hugged. And they wished each other well.

Through this single experience, the husband learned that there is something more important

*Sophia said, "Sing HU, and see Christ in your inner vision. Give him this worry, this fear." The driver said, "I can do that."*

than material things; the driver learned that God really heard her prayer; and the ECKists had their faith renewed in the miracles of Divine Spirit.

When I speak about ECK, I'm talking about the Holy Spirit. And if I happen to mention the Sugmad, this is the way we ECKists, among ourselves, speak of God. Or we'll say "God" too. So there is Sugmad (God), the ECK (Holy Spirit), and the Mahanta.

The Mahanta is the Inner Master. The Mahanta, the Living ECK Master is the full title of one and the same being. Some people try to split them up, as if somehow I am two things or two different things. No, I'm just one. But I operate in two different arenas. Simply put, that's it, that's all—just two different arenas. On the invisible planes and when people are far away, the inner side of myself can go over there and communicate and help. Whereas out here I'm limited to the constraints of this human body. And as the birthdays pass, I become ever more mindful of how constrained I am. But all in all it's good to have a body.

The language of love.

## "Turn the Carpet" or "The Two Weavers"

This was written by Hannah More. In 1745 she was born, and she died in 1833. She lived eighty-eight years. She wrote this poem, which is rather sing-song.

We had a professor when I was in prep school who did not like anyone reading things sing-song. He had the driest course. And when he read anything, you were sure never to want to read that again. So I'll try to spare you that extreme.

The title is "Turn the Carpet" or "The Two Weavers." Now, I knew it as "The Two Weavers." I read it way back when I was a kid on the farm, maybe twelve years old or so. It stayed with me over the years, and I could recite some of the verses by memory.

Two of my friends went online, and somehow they dug it out. It was listed under "Turn the Carpet," not under "The Two Weavers" as I had known it. They dug it out, and I'm grateful.

> *I read this poem back when I was a kid on the farm. It stayed with me over the years, and I could recite some of the verses by memory.*

As at their work two Weavers sat,
Beguiling time with friendly chat;
They touched upon the price of meat,
So high, a Weaver scarce could eat.

What with my brats and sickly wife,
Quoth Dick, I'm almost tired of life;
So hard my work, so poor my fare,
'Tis more than mortal man can bear.

How glorious is the rich man's state!
His house so fine! his wealth so great
Heaven is unjust you must agree,
Why all to him, why none to me?

In spite of what the Scripture teaches,
In spite of all the Parson preaches,
This world (indeed I've thought so long)
Is ruled, methinks, extremely wrong.

Wheree'er I look, howe'er I range,
'Tis all confused, and hard, and strange;
The good are troubled and oppressed,
And all the wicked are the blessed.

Our ignorance is the cause, said John,
Why thus we blame our Maker's laws;
*Parts of his ways* alone we know,
'Tis all that man can see below.

See'st thou that Carpet, not half done,
Which thou, dear Dick, hast well begun?
Behold the wild confusion there,
So rude the mass it makes one stare!

A stranger, ignorant of the trade,
Would say, no meaning's there conveyed;
For where's the middle, where's the border
Thy Carpet now is all disorder.

Quoth Dick, my work is yet in bits,
But still in every part it fits;
Besides, you reason like a lout,
Why, man, that *Carpet's inside out.*

Says John, thou say'st the thing I mean,
And now I hope to cure thy spleen;
This world, which clouds thy soul with doubt,
*Is but a Carpet inside out.*

And when we view these shreds and ends,
We know not what the whole intends;
So when on earth things seem but odd,
They're working still some scheme of God.

*So when on
earth things
seem but odd,
They're working
still some
scheme of God.*

No plan, no pattern can we trace,
All wants proportion, truth, and grace;
The motley mixture we deride,
Nor see the beauteous upper side.

But when we reach that world of light,
And view these works of God aright;
Then shall we see the whole design,
And own the workman is divine.

What now seem random strokes, will there
All order and design appear;
Then shall we praise what here we spurned,
For then the *Carpet shall be turned.*

Thou'st right, quoth Dick, no more I'll grumble,
That this sad world's so strange a jumble;
My impious doubts are put to flight,
For my own Carpet sets me right.

I think Dick here had his love for life renewed.
The language of love.

That poem by Hannah More stuck with me all
those years. Certain parts are like old friends come
back, old friends come home. I was just so very
happy.

## THE SCRATCHED DIAMOND

This is "The Scratched Diamond" from *The
Hungry Clothes and Other Jewish Folktales* retold
by Peninnah Schram. Here it's being retold by me.

A student was walking along with his master
one day. This master was known for always answer-
ing questions with a parable. His student said,
"Rabbi, I have so many imperfections. What can I
do? How can I work with them so that I can be a
better person?" The Rabbi said, "Listen, and I'll tell
you a story.

*His student said, "Rabbi, I have so many imperfections. How can I work with them so that I can be a better person?"*

"There was once a king, and he had a beautiful
diamond without a flaw—not a single flaw anywhere.
You could turn it in the light, and it just sparkled.
The facets all sparkled in an expected way, and
when dignitaries came over, the king would show
them his priceless diamond. He was so proud of it.
Dignitaries would say, 'We're going to have to see
His Majesty's diamond again.' 'That's OK, just make

believe you enjoy it.'

"They would go in and say, 'Oh, wow! Yep, sure is good. As pretty as can be. Just the same as last time.'

"But one day the king looked at it, and he noticed there was a scratch on it. Maybe he had been tossing it around with his other jewels, and he shouldn't have done that. Anyway, it had a flaw now. But he had an ace up his sleeve.

"He called in the best diamond cutters in the kingdom. And he said, 'All right, you guys. You're the best there is. What can you do to restore this diamond?'

"Then one by one they took it, looked at it, and said, 'Your Majesty, there isn't a blessed thing we can do to restore this diamond to its original condition.'

"But standing by, looking on, was a young diamond cutter. He just finished his apprenticeship with the best diamond cutter in the kingdom, and he asked the king, 'May I look at that?' The king said, 'Sure. Why not?' The young man looked at it. He studied it very carefully, and he said, 'If you will allow me to take it with me and to work uninterrupted, never asking for updates or anything, I'm going to try to make it a thing of worth and value.'

*This young craftsman went to work on this scratched diamond with all his love, because he loved his craft.*

"Well, what's a king to do? He had a lot of other jewelry. This diamond was worth as much as all the rest of his jewelry. When you've got a lot, you don't care a lot. Unless you don't have a lot anymore, like it's all gone all of a sudden. But he wasn't faced with that kind of problem.

"So this young craftsman went to work on it with all his love, because he loved his craft. Because it takes a great deal of skill and dexterity and vision. You've got to have vision to create something unusual and something from nothing.

"When he brought the diamond back to the king, the king looked at it, and he was amazed. He was delighted. And he said, 'You did this to it?' And what did he do to it?

"Well, when the young man had looked at the diamond, he saw the scratch as the stem of a rose. Very carefully he etched roots onto the stem, and then leaves onto the stem, and then a flower onto the stem. From the scratch he had created a thing of beauty and value. In fact, it was more beautiful and more valuable to the king now than it had ever been."

When the Rabbi finished his story, he looked at his student and said, "We all have our faults and failings. But, like the diamond with its scratch, it's up to us to transform them into things of beauty and value."

And so I say that to you too. It's also a constant lesson to me. When we see the shreds and ends of our own lives, turn the carpet. Look on the other side. See what's there. See the beauty that speaks to the handiwork of the creator.

## HEALTH RESOURCES

I don't know how many of you are familiar with The Great Courses. I have no financial interest in the company other than a one-way street: I send money to them every time I want a course.

They have excellent teachers. They're the best. I wish I'd had just four or five sprinkled throughout my college years, just to make the days seem brighter. These professors are excellent. They know their stuff.

*When we see the shreds and ends of our own lives, turn the carpet. Look on the other side. See the beauty that speaks to the handiwork of the creator.*

First of all, the Great Courses people check around. They get reports in from colleges and schools about so-and-so who has won so many awards, teaches a certain subject, and is a good teacher.

But The Great Courses and The Teaching Company, which is the parent of The Great Courses, don't stop there. They ask their students, "Here is the teacher, here's a sample. Would you or would you not order this course?" Then everybody gets to have a say as to whether they would or not and why or why not. And only, I believe, something like one out of five hundred prospects finally becomes a teacher for The Great Courses.

This particular course is "The Science of Natural Healing." Those of you who are longtime members, or even members of just a short time, realize how much emphasis we put on healing in Eckankar. Because being as healthy as we can lends itself to spiritual unfoldment. It makes us more able to understand and able to participate in this life. Because this life is a gift. It's not a curse; it's a gift.

*There was a time I thought in terms of life's problems. Then I tried to dress it up: life's issues. Then I upgraded to life's challenges. And now I realize it's really life's opportunities.*

There was a time I thought in terms of life's *problems*. Then I tried to dress it up: I was starting to think in terms of life's *issues*. Then I upgraded to life's *challenges*. And now I realize it's really life's *opportunities*.

Every time we hit a wall, we've hit ourselves. Because here karma comes into play. Sometimes there are past-life things we have to go through that cannot be forestalled. Other times they are things we've created in this lifetime, not lives past. And some things can be worked out in the dream state. But when they can't, they hit here. We try to do the best we can.

So the course is "The Science of Natural Healing," and it's taught by Mimi Guarneri. Her students just call her Dr. G. I like to call her Mimi. But the course itself highlights nature-based health care.

The professor is board certified in cardiology and internal medicine. She's won all kinds of awards. Before she became a holistic practitioner—*holistic* meaning the whole body, not just its parts—she used to put stents in, left and right. Sometimes she'd even call to the operating room, "Anybody need a stent down there?" She was always up and raring to go. In the course she tells her story about how she slowly switched to realizing that something was going on that medicine couldn't answer.

In one case, a patient was given just a short time to live and told to have bypass surgery. He said, "I'm not going to do it."

Now, I'm not saying that's what you should do. By all means, if this is the best course of action, take it. Everyone's different. But this particular man said, "I ain't going to do it. I have things to do. I've got a family to feed and support. I just can't go in there and take a chance of getting laid up or possibly never coming out of the operation. No, I ain't gonna do it." And that's how it was.

They checked in on him some years later. There he was, still going. She looked at this case, and she said, "Something's going on that they didn't teach us in medical school." And from that came this course.

I'm just going to touch on some of the things covered. It's a twenty-four-lecture course. "Food Matters" is one lecture, and then "Not All Foods Are Created Equal." She also talks about natural approaches to inflammation. Inflammation can lead to all kinds of problems, as some of you know.

A patient was given just a short time to live. Some years later, there he was, still going. Dr. G. looked at this case, and said, "Something's going on that they didn't teach us in medical school."

Another lecture is "Food Sensitivity and the Elimination Diet."

She uses studies that have had many participants over many years. Or sometimes she'll refer to meta-analysis, where they study a bunch of studies and somehow shake a bottom line out of it and say, "We've done this analysis, and this is what we've come up with."

Other lectures are, "Vitamins and Supplements," "Herbal Remedies," "Lowering Cholesterol Naturally," "Treating High Blood Pressure Naturally," "Treating Diabetes Naturally," and "Stress and Mind-Body Connection." There's a good portion on this topic.

"The Power of Love" is in keeping with our theme, "The Language of Love." "The Power of Love" is a very, very powerful lecture. Then there is "Spirituality in Health"—why it matters that you go to church, or if you don't go to church that at least you have a strong belief in something. And this doesn't exclude atheists or agnostics at all. Her course also covers "Healthy People, Healthy Planet," "Ecology and Health," and "You Are Your Own Best Medicine."

You can go online, to www.thegreatcourses.com, for the prices. You may look at it and say, "Hm, this is pricey." I get the audio CDs, because both Joan and I are hypersensitive to electromagnetic radiation or the electromagnetic fields (EMR, EMF), so we can't watch DVDs. We've tried; no go. But we can listen to CDs and other things such as battery-powered radios. We keep the volume down, though, because as you turn it up, the EMR becomes greater.

I always buy these courses on sale, when they're 70 percent off, in many cases, from the full asking

> *Then there is a lecture, "Spirituality in Health." And this doesn't exclude atheists or agnostics at all.*

price. I also encourage you to just wait, if you can. I wouldn't pay the full price. They don't expect you to.

They have DVDs, video downloads, audio CDs, and audio downloads. They're all priced differently. You can also get a transcript book with a course. In this case, it's twenty-five dollars. They're very good people. These Great Courses people lay everything out for you in such a nice way.

I'd also like to mention again the Nutritional Weight & Wellness people right here in the Twin Cities. You can get in touch with them at www.weightandwellness.com. Catch their podcasts. They do the latest research, and they're good people. Their nutritionists are special.

*The Nutritional Weight & Wellness people do the latest research, and they're good people. Their nutritionists are special.*

Nutritional Weight & Wellness is the brainchild of Darlene Kvist. Joan and I had an appointment with her some years ago, and she's a good person. I have no financial interest here either. And I haven't seen her in a number of years. Very good people there.

They have a call-in show on Saturday mornings that's rebroadcast locally here on Sunday night. One caller said she went to a nutritionist thinking that all nutritionists were alike. She said, "I have this weight problem. I'd like to get it off." The first thing this nutritionist said was, "All right, we're going to have to put you on a low-fat diet." The nutritionist mentioned other things too. But right away the woman said, "Well, thank you. I'll think about it," and left.

She knew this advice was absolutely wrong. Because the brain is made up of fat cells. Predominantly fat. And to deprive the brain of all its nutrition, of much of what it needs, was wrong. There are other things it needs too, for sure. It needs ideas, folks. Ideas. And they come from the mind. And if they're inspired enough, they come from the region even beyond the mind—the Soul area.

So the Nutritional Weight & Wellness people are good. They have patients all around the world now. Because they're online, they can have all kinds of consultations via Skype and other means.

## TALK SUMMARY

I'd like to recap our talk, "The Language of Love." We had Mary talking about her experiences as an emergency medical technician; and her dad, Oscar, and his chickens and the ducklings. Then we ran into Sarah, her depressed mom, Miriam, and HU, and how that changed things. Her mom was not an ECKist, by the way, so it was a leap there for her mom.

Also Sophia and the female taxi driver. Many lessons learned there. Then "Turn the Carpet" or "The Two Weavers." My friends, the two weavers. And then we came to "The Scratched Diamond," and we finished with "The Science of Natural Healing."

I would like to thank all of you for coming. My love to you. May the blessings be.

*I would like to thank all of you for coming. My love to you. May the blessings be.*

*ECK Springtime Seminar, Minneapolis, Minnesota*
*Saturday, April 19, 2014*

# About the Author

Award-winning author, teacher, and spiritual guide Sri Harold Klemp helps seekers reach their full potential. He is the Mahanta, the Living ECK Master and spiritual leader of Eckankar, the Path of Spiritual Freedom. He is the latest in a long line of spiritual Adepts who have served throughout history in every culture of the world.

Sri Harold teaches creative spiritual practices that enable anyone to achieve life mastery and gain inner peace and contentment. His messages are relevant to today's spiritual needs and resonate with every generation. *Kirkus Reviews* comments, "The powerful optimism of these teachings should resonate with all readers, even those unacquainted with ECK."

Sri Harold's body of work includes more than one hundred books, which have been translated into eighteen languages and won multiple awards. The miraculous, true-life stories he shares lift the veil between heaven and earth.

In his groundbreaking memoir, *Autobiography of a Modern Prophet*, he reveals secrets to spiritual success gleaned from his personal journey into the heart of God. Find your own path to true happiness, wisdom, and love in Sri Harold Klemp's inspired writings.

# Next Steps in Spiritual Exploration

- **Browse our website: www.Eckankar.org.**
  Watch videos; get free books, answers to FAQs, and more info.
- **Attend an Eckankar event** in your area.
  Visit "Eckankar around the World" on our website.
- **Explore advanced spiritual study** with the Eckankar discourses that come with membership.
- **Read additional books** about the ECK teachings.
- See "Contact Eckankar," page 318.

## Advanced Spiritual Living

Go higher, further, deeper with your spiritual experiences!

Eckankar offers enrollment in advanced spiritual living courses for Self-Discovery and God-Discovery. This dynamic program of inner and outer study unlocks the divine love and wisdom within you. It offers step-by-step advances in enlightenment through initiation.

From the first day, you can have direct experience with the God Current and begin to meet life's challenges on the highest possible ground.

You will enjoy monthly discourses from the spiritual leader of Eckankar, Sri Harold Klemp, creative spiritual practices for daily life, and the quarterly *Mystic World* publication. Optional classes with like-hearted Souls are available in many areas.

Here's a sampling of titles from the first course:
- In Soul You Are Free
- Reincarnation—Why You Came to Earth Again
- The Master Principle
- The God Worlds—Where No One Has Gone Before?

# BOOKS

You may find these books by Harold Klemp to be of special interest. They are available at bookstores, from online booksellers, or directly from Eckankar.

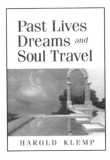

## Past Lives, Dreams, and Soul Travel

These stories and exercises help you find your true purpose, discover greater love than you've ever known, and learn that spiritual freedom is within reach.

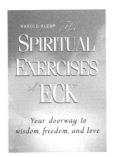

## The Spiritual Exercises of ECK

This book is a staircase with 131 steps leading to the doorway to spiritual freedom, self-mastery, wisdom, and love. A comprehensive volume of spiritual exercises for every need.

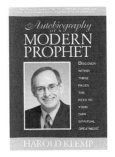

## Autobiography of a Modern Prophet

This riveting story of Harold Klemp's climb up the Mountain of God will help you discover the keys to your own spiritual greatness.

## Those Wonderful ECK Masters

Would you like to have *personal* experience with spiritual masters that people all over the world—since the beginning of time—have looked to for guidance, protection, and divine love? This book includes real-life stories and spiritual exercises to meet eleven ECK Masters.

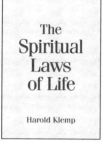

## The Spiritual Laws of Life

Learn how to keep in tune with your true spiritual nature. Spiritual laws reveal the behind-the-scenes forces at work in your daily life.

## CONTACT ECKANKAR

For more information about ECK, to order ECK books, or to enroll in ECK membership, you may

- visit www.ECKBooks.org;

- enroll online at "Membership" at www.Eckankar.org (click on "Online Membership Application");

- call Eckankar (952) 380-2222;

- write to
  ECKANKAR, Dept. BK 157
  PO Box 2000
  Chanhassen, MN 55317-2000 USA.

# GLOSSARY

Words set in SMALL CAPS are defined elsewhere in this glossary.

**Blue Light**   How the MAHANTA often appears in the inner worlds to the CHELA or seeker.

**chela**   A spiritual student, often a member of ECKANKAR.

**ECK**   The Life Force, Holy Spirit, or Audible Life Current which sustains all life.

**Eckankar** *EHK-ahn-kahr*   The Path of Spiritual Freedom. Also known as the Ancient Science of SOUL TRAVEL. A truly spiritual way of life for the individual in modern times. The teachings provide a framework for anyone to explore their own spiritual experiences. Established by PAUL TWITCHELL, the modern-day founder, in 1965. The word means Co-worker with God.

**ECK Masters**   Spiritual Masters who can assist and protect people in their spiritual studies and travels. The ECK Masters are from a long line of God-Realized SOULS who know the responsibility that goes with spiritual freedom.

**Fubbi Quantz**   The guardian of the SHARIYAT-KI-SUGMAD at the Katsupari Monastery in northern Tibet. He was the MAHANTA, the LIVING ECK MASTER during the time of Buddha, about 500 BC.

**God-Realization**   The state of God Consciousness. Complete and conscious awareness of God.

**HU** *HYOO*   The most ancient, secret name for God. It can be sung as a love song to God aloud or silently to oneself to align with God's love.

**initiation**   Earned by a member of ECKANKAR through spiritual unfoldment and service to God. The initiation is a private ceremony in which the individual is linked to the Sound and Light of God.

**Kal Niranjan**   The Kal; the negative power, also known as Satan or the devil.

**Karma, Law of**   The Law of Cause and Effect, action and reaction, justice, retribution, and reward, which applies to the lower or psychic worlds: the Physical, Astral, Causal, Mental, and Etheric PLANES.

**Kata Daki**   A female ECK MASTER, who, like all others in the Order of the Vairagi, serves the SUGMAD by helping others find the MAHANTA, the LIVING ECK MASTER. Her pet project is to help people get back on their feet during hardship.

**Klemp, Harold**   The present MAHANTA, the LIVING ECK MASTER. SRI Harold Klemp became the Mahanta, the Living ECK Master in 1981. His spiritual name is WAH Z.

**Lai Tsi**   An ancient Chinese ECK MASTER who is the guardian of the SHARIYAT-KI-SUGMAD on the Etheric PLANE. He once served as the MAHANTA, the LIVING ECK MASTER.

**Living ECK Master**   The spiritual leader of ECKANKAR. He leads SOUL back to God. He teaches in the physical world as the Outer Master, in the dream state as the Dream Master, and in the spiritual worlds as the Inner Master. SRI HAROLD KLEMP became the MAHANTA, the Living ECK Master in 1981.

**Mahanta**   An expression of the Spirit of God that is always with you. Sometimes seen as a BLUE LIGHT or Blue Star or in the form of the Mahanta, the LIVING ECK MASTER. The highest state of God Consciousness on earth, only embodied in the Living ECK Master. He is the Living Word.

**Peddar Zaskq**   The spiritual name for PAUL TWITCHELL, the modern-day founder of ECKANKAR and the MAHANTA, the LIVING ECK MASTER from 1965 to 1971.

**planes**   Levels of existence, such as the Physical, Astral, Causal, Mental, Etheric, and SOUL Planes.

**Rebazar Tarzs**   A Tibetan ECK MASTER known as the Torchbearer of ECKANKAR in the lower worlds.

**Satsang**   A class in which students of ECK discuss a monthly lesson from ECKANKAR.

**Self-Realization**   SOUL recognition. The entering of Soul into the Soul PLANE and there beholding Itself as pure Spirit. A state of seeing, knowing, and being.

**Shariyat-Ki-Sugmad**   The sacred scriptures of ECKANKAR. The scriptures are comprised of twelve volumes in the spiritual worlds. The first two were transcribed from the inner PLANES by PAUL TWITCHELL, modern-day founder of Eckankar.

**Soul** The True Self, an individual, eternal spark of God. The inner, most sacred part of each person. Soul can see, know, and perceive all things. It is the creative center of Its own world.

**Soul Travel** The expansion of consciousness. The ability of Soul to transcend the physical body and travel into the spiritual worlds of God. Soul Travel is taught only by the Living ECK Master. It helps people unfold spiritually and can provide proof of the existence of God and life after death.

**Sound and Light of ECK** The Holy Spirit. The two aspects through which God appears in the lower worlds. People can experience them by looking and listening within themselves and through Soul Travel.

**Spiritual Exercises of ECK** Daily practices for direct, personal experience with the Sound Current. Creative techniques using contemplation and the singing of sacred words to bring the higher awareness of Soul into daily life.

**Sri** A title of spiritual respect, similar to reverend or pastor, used for those who have attained the Kingdom of God. In Eckankar, it is reserved for the Mahanta, the Living ECK Master.

**Sugmad** *SOOG-mahd* A sacred name for God. It is the source of all life, neither male nor female, the Ocean of Love and Mercy.

**Temples of Golden Wisdom** Golden Wisdom Temples found on the various planes—from the Physical to the Anami Lok; chelas of Eckankar are taken to these temples in the Soul body to be educated in the divine knowledge; sections of the Shariyat-Ki-Sugmad, the sacred teachings of ECK, are kept at these temples.

**Towart Managi** The ECK Master in charge of the Shariyat-Ki-Sugmad in the Temple of Golden Wisdom on the Mental Plane. He was the Mahanta, the Living ECK Master in ancient Abyssinia (now Ethiopia).

**Twitchell, Paul** An American ECK Master who brought the modern teachings of Eckankar to the world through his writings and lectures. His spiritual name is Peddar Zaskq.

**Vahana** The ECK missionary; a carrier of ECK or the message of ECK.

**vairag** The spiritual virtue of detachment.

**Wah Z** *WAH zee* The spiritual name of Sri Harold Klemp. It means the secret doctrine. It is his name in the spiritual worlds.

For more explanations of Eckankar terms, see *A Cosmic Sea of Words: The ECKANKAR Lexicon*, by Harold Klemp.

# INDEX

actions, 255
acupuncturists, 125
Africa(n)(ns), 289, 290, 291. *See also* Nigeria(n)(ns)
  anything's possible in, 124
  gives names for, 65
  a lot of ECKists from, 281
  South, 81, 238, 239
  West, 29, 87, 162
afterlife. *See* experiences: out-of-body; heaven(s)
age (aging), 84, 85
  middle, 174
  old, 174
  past fifty, 156
aggression, 95
Alexander, Eben, 247
  *Proof of Heaven: A Neurosurgeon's Journey into the Afterlife*, 247
Alzheimer's, 251
ambulance, 217, 295
American Civil War, 86, 92
*Ancient Egypt 39,000 BCE* (Malkowski), 247
anger, 104, 178, 182. *See also* hostility
animal(s). *See also* ants; beagle; bird(s); bull(s); cat(s); cattle; chicks; cockatiel; cow; crow(s); dog(s); duck(ling) (lings); elephant; finch(es); fly; fox; hatchlings; hens; horse(s); *Kinship with All Life*; longhorn; moth; owl(s); parrot; pet(s); poodle; Prajapati; pup(py); rat; skunk; snail; snakes; Strong-

heart; turtle
  deep feelings of birds and, 141
  and divine love, 123
  have a state of consciousness, 50
  in heaven, 121
  and listening, 194, 195
Antarctic, 20
ants, 52
anxiety attacks, 71, 72
Appomattox, 92, 95
archaeologists (archaeology), 205, 247, 248
*Are You Being Served?*, 98
argument(s), 20, 167, 237
arm, broken, 289
ask(ing)
  God for a sign, 108
  for help, 67, 70, 297
  questions after a seminar, 131
  to show everything, 66
atheist(s), 23, 24, 100, 101
  friend, 129
  in Scandinavian countries, 289
Atlanteans (Atlantis), 145–48, 205, 206
*Atlantis in the Amazon* (Wingate), 204, 205
Atlas, Charles, 21
attention, 98, 223, 240
attitude, 173
attorney, 32, 33
attraction (attracting), 167
awareness, 33, 236. *See also* consciousness
  of the Mahanta's help, 64–65

Kitei, Lynne, 206
*Phoenix Lights, The*, 206, 208
Klemp, Harold, ix, 313. *See also*
    Mahanta, the Living ECK
    Master
  in the air force, 158–59
  and books, 40
  broken hip, 213, 214
  car accident (brakes failed),
    222, 223, 260
  choice to see the future, 211,
    223
  disliked being a boss, 219, 220
  *ECK Satsang Discourses, The*,
    Third Series, 252
  *ECK Wisdom on Karma and
    Reincarnation*, 145
  and electromagnetic radiation,
    84, 98, 126, 208, 251, 310
  enjoys (likes) people, 77, 78,
    161–62, 230
  expectations of, as an ECK
    Master, 115, 156
  finding Eckankar, 239
  giving talks, 130, 260
  in a grocery-store restroom,
    41–42
  in hospital, 214–19
  made a commitment to
    Eckankar, 268–69
  and a mission renewed, 219,
    230
  in New Zealand, 220
  postering in Houston, 6
  preparing a talk, 130
  in a rehab(ilitation) facility,
    223–31
  and the Rod of ECK Power,
    221
  *Slow Burning Love of God,
    The*, Mahanta Transcripts,
    Book 13, 177
  *Spiritual Life, The*, 209
  *Those Wonderful ECK Masters*,
    148
  working and writing, 83–84,
    208, 222, 223, 260
Klemp, Joan, 222

  always with Sri Harold, 213,
    214, 217, 224, 226, 231
  and electromagnetic radiation,
    84, 98, 208, 310
  in a grocery-store restroom,
    41–42
  is one good editor, 208
  presents "The Little HU Song,"
    39
  reads in the evening, 40, 58

lady, white-haired, 41, 42
Lai Tsi, 185
Larson, Gary, 57, 58
laugh(s)(ing)(ter), 230, 243, 277
  all the children were, 143
  anything for a, 296, 297
  during the spiritual exercise,
    46
  shows love, 295, 296
  and spiritual content, 99
  two former Vietnam buddies,
    44
  woman with a broken hip was,
    238
Law
  of Cause and Effect, 2
  of Karma, 2
lawyer. *See* attorney
leader(s), 80
  expectations of a spiritual, 115
  field, 260
  -ship, 136
learning, 131, 158, 255
  from (through) experience,
    174, 183, 299, 301–2
  to give love, 167
  from the past, 192
legend(s), 205, 247
lesson(s), 12, 14, 80, 117, 307
  to be ready to go, 16
  of an ecotour guide, 71, 74
  and experience, 157, 174
  about material things, 301
  for Soul, 29
*Letter of Light*, 260
Leyden jar, 249

life (lives), 61, 182, 189, 197, 308.
    *See also* lifetime(s); past life
    (lives)
  becomes more challenging, 156
  and burdens, 19
  hard (*see* hardship (hard
    time(s)))
  has two rules, 277
  a long, happy, and healthy, 187
  looking for the meaning of,
    48–49
  nudging us back on track, 97
  -saving experience, 164
  spiritual, 52, 87, 97, 128
lifetime(s), 83, 192, 241
  chance to come into this, 191
  Mastership in this, 240
  things we've created in this,
    308
light(s). *See also* Light and
    Sound
  blue(s), 45, 62, 110, 200 (*see
    also* Blue Light)
  bluish-green, 45
  golden, 186
  green, 45
  lavender, 62
  like old-time Christmas, 110
  orange, 62
  over Phoenix, 206
  pink, 45, 62
  pole, 161
  shining on a woman, 82
  ultraviolet, 110
  violet, 110
  white(s), 45, 47, 62, 110
  yellow(s), 45, 62
Light and Sound, 61, 207, 208,
    235, 245. *See also* ECK;
    light(s)
  of God, ix, 33, 62, 92, 158, 159
  saw a wave of, 72
lightning, 249
Lightning Worlds, 151
listening, 30, 226, 266, 267. *See
    also* ECK Spiritual Aide(s)
  animals, 195
  to the Inner Master, 71, 74,
    101, 188

  to the inner voice, 31
  to the nudges, 14, 261
  without opinions, 104
  for the Sound, 46, 47
"Little HU Song, The," 38–39
Living ECK Master, 109, 163.
    *See also* Mahanta; Mahanta,
    the Living ECK Master
Logos, 208
*Longevity Project, The* (Fried-
    man and Martin), 187
longhorn, 121, 122, 123
Lords of Karma, 270
love, 124, 151, 168, 182, 296. *See
    also* divine love
  comes from the Sugmad, 121
  coming from the sound of HU,
    90
  a gift of peace and, 180
  of God (*see* God: love of)
  for his craft, 306
  the language of, 297, 299, 302
  of money, 6
  in motion, 235, 236, 239
  and power, 21, 35, 236
  and relationships, 167


Mahanta, 12, 15, 163, 200, 244,
    269. *See also* Blue Light;
    Dream Master; Inner
    Master; Mahanta, the Living
    ECK Master; Master
  asking (calling) for help from
    the, 26, 66, 70, 103, 185, 282
  can make things work out, 63
  can take you home to God, 245
  checking with the, 22
  concern of the, 87
  help from the, 9–10, 13, 279,
    280 (*see also* protection: of
    the Mahanta)
  mission of the, 186
Mahanta, the Living ECK
    Master, ix, 62, 109, 302. *See
    also* Klemp, Harold; Living
    ECK Master; Mahanta;
    Master
  function(s) of the, 163, 291

Plato (*continued*)
  *Critias*, 205
  *Timaeus*, 205
poem. *See* "Turn the Carpet"
    (More)
poodle, 49
popcorn tins, 137, 138, 139
posters, 6, 16
power(s), 136, 137, 199, 259
  agents of the negative, 80
  of the church, 5
  divine, 63
  life-and-death, 5
  love and, 21, 35, 236
  and money, 21
  spiritual, 196
practitioner(s), 125
  holistic, 309
Prajapati, 119, 120, 121, 143
pressure to stay, 268
problem(s), 273
  car, 65–67
  false, 88
  in-law, 272
  looked more specifically at his,
    67
  as opportunities, 308
  with the powers that be, 7
  with sleep, 6, 7
  surrender(ing) the, 64, 66, 128
professor(s), 37, 38, 307, 309
*Proof of Heaven: A Neurosur-
    geon's Journey into the After-
    life* (Alexander), 247
protection
  from a burning stove, 163, 164
  of the ECK Masters, 105, 106
  in heavy rain, 160–61
  of the Mahanta, 13, 102, 162,
    165
  from a serious traffic accident,
    264–65
psychic wave(s), 20, 21
pup(py), 178, 179, 180
purgatory, 270
purification, ix, 21, 80
purpose, 19, 240, 278
  life without, 48

pyramid(s), 249, 250. *See also*
    Great Pyramid(s)

question(s). *See also* youth:
    questions from
  answered, 109, 130
  to quit or to continue, 60

Ramses III, 147
rat, 13
Reagan (Ronald), 207
real estate agent, 171, 172, 260,
    261
  joins Eckankar, 284, 285
Rebazar Tarzs, 87, 88, 150–52,
    185, 287, 291
  foretelling, 152
  heals a very ill daughter, 166
  saved the family in a car, 106
  teaching about creativity,
    203–4
receipt, 239, 240
reception(ist), 25, 26, 242
Regional ECK Spiritual Aides,
    260
rehab(ilitation) facility, 223–31
reincarnation, 109, 178, 193. *See
    also ECK Wisdom on Karma
    and Reincarnation*; past life
    (lives)
  in history, 27
relationship(s), 52, 167, 168
RESAs. *See* Regional ECK
    Spiritual Aides
*RESA Star*, 223
restaurant
  celebrate working off karma in
    a, 173
  telling about Eckankar in a,
    111–12
restroom(s), 41, 42
riddle of the Sphinx, 174
Roaring Twenties, 79
robbers, 101–2, 124
robe. *See* cloak
rocker (rocking), 144, 145